EDINBURGH

RIAS/Landmark Trust series of Illustrated Guides to Scotland:
(Series Editor and author of *Edinburgh, Stirling and the Trossachs,
Banff and Buchan, The District of Moray*)
Fight Blight
The Scottish Thirties
Cambridge and East Anglia since 1920
Modern Buildings in London, 1965-75
Battle of Styles

EDINBURGH

PORTRAIT OF A CITY

CHARLES McKEAN

CENTURY

LONDON   SYDNEY   AUCKLAND   JOHANNESBURG

First published in Great Britain in 1991 by
Century Ltd
20 Vauxhall Bridge Road, London SW1V 2SA

A catalogue record for this book is available from the British Library.

Cased edition: ISBN 0-7126-3867-9
Paperback edition: ISBN 0-7126-4958-1

Typeset in Goudy Old Style by
SX Composing Ltd, Rayleigh, Essex
Printed in Great Britain by Mackays of Chatham

CONTENTS

To my family

'The great city is the best organ of memory man has created.'
LEWIS MUMFORD

'But Edinburgh is a mad god's dream
Fitful and dark,
Unseizable in Leith,
And wildered by the Forth . . .'

HUGH MACDIARMID

CHAPTER ONE

THE MAD GOD'S DREAM

In the beginning was the Winged Camp. One of only three rock-girt citadels within the British Isles, it probably protected the shrine of Morgain La Fee, evil genius of Arthurian legend, after whom it was named Castle of the Maidens (Castellum Puellarum). It retained its femininity by its subsequent association with Christian St Margaret. The European trading centre that later burgeoned down its volcanic ridge rose (after some girning) to be capital of Scotland.

War and peace alike were its enemies. Edinburgh was twice the subject of vengeance: corpulent King Harry VIII instructed his armies to leave not a stick standing nor a soul alive in 1544; and in 1596 Jamie Saxt's advisers recommended the city's obliteration and replacement by a monument as an awful warning to others against accommodating religious riots. As war receded, the capital nearly fell victim to reason and baroque town planning. Only national poverty (if the Earl of Mar is to be believed) prevented the Old Town's removal, and substitution by the construction of a splendid new town on the flat plains of Leith. It remains fortunate to survive where it does.

In the face of the zeal of reformers, the ambitions of monarch and court, and the designs of improvers and planners, Edinburgh proved deeply unshakeable. Indeed, it seemed to have a life of its own. Long before a romantic overlay began to distort perceptions of the city, an unseen daemon appeared to direct the squirrellings of man on this magical spot.

Its recorded history is punctuated by a sequence of mysterious events that can best be explained by supposing the existence of a dragon under the hill (Alexander Smith compared the Old Town silhouette to that of a huge lizard), or the spirit of Morgain; in short, an unusually active genius loci which has goaded its inhabitants to efforts far beyond those that one might have expected from a small, tight town in a poor country falling off the north-west corner of Europe. The solid and unyielding nature of the site and its inhabitants exerted a powerful influence upon national politics. It was a testimony to endurance.

1

'It seems like a city built on precipices,' wrote G K Chesterton in 1905, 'a perilous city. Great roads rush down hill like rivers in spate. Great buildings rush up like rockets.' Edinburgh is indeed Castle Perilous, an embodiment of pagan myth and magic which protrudes determinedly into the landscape of serene beauty on which they built the Athens of the North. Embedded in its people's character are the contrasts of its very landscape: barely suppressed savagery beneath ordered respectability. That is how, as Sir Patrick Geddes wrote in 1918, 'architecture and town planning in such a city . . . are the expressions of local history, the civic and national changes of mood and contrasts of mind.'

The spectral quality to the city, wonderfully encapsulated in artist Benjamin Haydon's reaction: 'It is a dream of great genius,' has evoked countless volumes of romantic scribble from visitors over the last three centuries. From the south – from the Pentlands, or from the invaders' route from England through Edgehead – the tiny, saw-toothed silhouette of the fortified crag that Ptolemy christened the Winged Camp in AD 160 resembles a cub playing with something spiky, benevolently guarded by the sphinx (or crouching lioness) of Arthur's Seat. Dominating the flat-lands of the Firth of Forth, it exerts a powerful magnetism not just over its extended metropolis, but over the strange country (that land of Calvin, oatcakes and sulphur, as Sydney Smith put it) of which it assumed leadership. When the Dutch engineer Captain John Slezer sketched the city in about 1672, he depicted a formidable fortress of the sort we now associate with Bohemia or Transylvania: a vaster, secular Mont St Michel – the built incarnation of man's persistence in the face of adversity.

Any inviolate or virginal attributes of Castellum Puellarum were soon disposed of. Siege, massacre and destruction afflicted the capital with a remorselessness unusual even by pan-European standards. The most substantial Scots city within easy pillaging distance of armies surging north from England, it endured assault, bombardment or sack at least seventeen times, most cruelly the five times during the uncertain sixteenth century. It was besieged by Donald Bane in 1093, occupied by Edward I, Maleus Scotorum, in 1291 as overlord of Scotland, looted in 1296, and dismantled for the Scots by Thomas Randolph in 1314, St Margaret's Chapel the only building left intact. Edward II feebly sacked Holyrood in 1322, and Edward III wreaked havoc in 1335, capturing and rebuilding part of the castle. Six years later, William Douglas regained the castle for the Scots by the immortal subterfuge (later adapted at the Netherbow in 1573 and 1745) of jamming open the gate with a provision cart as soldiers swarmed through. Richard II demolished the Tolbooth and burnt St Giles in 1385, and that great English hero Henry V ventured north in

2

1400 for another try.

Such an upbringing scarred the Edinburgh psyche. Natives early developed habits later identified with Brer Rabbit: the custom of lying low in the catacombs and saying nothing; of refining a cautious if opaque canniness, and a discreet if remote civility and obligingness even – as William Cobbett found so praiseworthy – in persons in the lowest state in life. So long as there was a threat of war, they remained huddled for mutual defence: and it was the inescapable interaction between interests and classes of overcrowded old Edinburgh that was the impulse behind the Enlightenment.

Peace led to the geographic dispersal of the activities which had comprised the Enlightenment to different quarters of the extending suburbia during the nineteenth century. Comfort and privacy were achieved at the expense of the *idea* of the city, the notion of *civitas* expressed by the fourth-century Antioch orator Libianus (quoted in *The City in History* by Lewis Mumford):

> Well, it seems to me that the pleasantest, yes, and most profitable side of city life is society and human intercourse, and that, by Zeus, is truly a city where these are most found. It is good to talk and better to listen, and best of all to give advice, to sympathise with one's friends' experiences, sharing their joys and sorrows and getting like sympathy from them – these and countless other blessings come of a man's meeting his fellows.

Perhaps it was a perception of recessiveness that drove William Hazlitt, in the midst of a Scots divorce in 1822, to lament 'stoney hearted Edinburgh' with its cold grey walls, and the square, hard-edged unyielding faces of its inhabitants, without sympathy to impart. It resides still in the descendants of the beleaguered mediaevals, originally only too keen to quit the enforced communality of the Old Town for spacious privacy and visible social division as soon as the opportunity of the New Town presented itself. The consequence is that Edinburgh society consists of a number of co-existent groups which interlock little and mesh not.

Old Edinburgh is evidentially the result of the Scots' struggle against nature, against fellow-humans, against weather and against their combined ferociousness. What other capital city short of Lhasa stands so proudly and nakedly in defiance of the elements? Mediaeval man strove to tame the elements on this ridge by raising a city in the form of a single mass of building; stone cliffs to the outside and a deep trough, an *agora* known as the Hie Gait (or High Street), a uniquely spacious market-place sheltered by tall unbreached walls at the centre. Nippy breezes, thick clinging haars, seeping cold mists, warm azure skies and unfriendly armies were all controlled by this plan – in a curious realisation of Plato's 'the form of the city being that of a single dwelling will have an agreeable aspect and, being easily guarded, will be infinitely better for security.' It worked to the extent that when offered the occupation of a spanking new Exchange designed to the most fashionable standard in 1752, the city's merchants declined the privilege. They preferred to continue to congregate meeting *en plein air* by the Cross: for there was Edinburgh's Rialto.

Edinburgh's character has never been comfortable (were comfort a concept ever congenial to Calvinists), and what Muriel Spark identified as 'the puritanical strain of the Edinburgh ethos' was as much the consequence of climate as of Calvinism. Chill whipping winds slash at you unawares around corners, and howl up Waverley Steps, they tumbled the entire Leith Guard from Castle Hill in January 1778 to the severe hurt of some, and surprise of the rest, and lifted your Victorian bonnet on George Street to waft it to Granton. They can still hurl you willy-nilly along Princes Street at a speed to match the scudding clouds above. It was a 'vehement tempest of wind', recorded David Moyses, that brought the 'kindness sickness' (probably encephalitis) to the capital in June 1580, to kill off the aged and corpulent. Seeking virtue in necessity in 1778, Edinburgh's historian Hugo Arnott commended the 'great violence of the winds' for dissipating the noxious effluvia from the Old Town gutters.

Those accustomed to cold adapt ill to heat; and it was the latter that drove Alexander Smith, then University Secretary, away to his holiday on Skye in 1854:

> Summer has suddenly leapt upon Edinburgh like a tiger. The air is still and hot above the houses: but every now and then, a breath of east wind startles me through the warm sunshine and passes on: yet, with this exception, the atmosphere is so close, so laden with a body of heat, that a thunderstorm would be almost welcome as a relief . . . Beautiful as ever, of course – for nothing can be finer than the ridge of the Old Town etched on a hot summer azure – but close, breathless, suffocating. Great volumes of white smoke surge out of the railway station: great choking puffs of dust issue from the houses and shops that are being gutted in Princes Street.

But the converse with Burns. He wrote to his friend Cleghorn: 'From my late hours last night, and the dripping fogs and damn'd east wind of this stupid day, I have left me as little soul as an oyster.' Captain Edward Topham, in Edinburgh as the ultimate experience of his European Grand Tour in 1776, was much diverted on the North Bridge during a sharp Nor'easter: 'in walking over it this morning, I had the pleasure of adjusting a lady's petticoats, which had been blown almost entirely over her head.' James Skene of Rubislaw painted a winter in 1817 in which the sky was so penetratingly blue that it shimmered almost colourlessly upon the icicles descending many storeys from a snow-engulfed roof to the wynd below; the legacy of a frost so sharp as to make the slates snap and the very stones splinter. When viewed from Salisbury Crags on such a day, the ridge of the Old Town stands proud, static and expectant, somewhat like an army in battle array awaiting its summons.

Edinburgh's character best responds to winter. It needs its cracking frosts and its haars to give meaning to its tight closes and tall tenements. We read of carriages slithering athwart a snowbound Dundas Street, ministers permitting themselves the spare enjoyment of joining the Duddingston Skating Club, and of the town's teenagers taking on the college students in the celebrated snowball battles and ambushes in the dark streets and wynds only occasionally lit by the warmth of yellow light streaming from tenement windows. The winter sunrise over Arthur's Seat is, when viewed from the north, one of the great sights of the world: the black paganism of the castle to the west balanced against the serene classicism of Calton Hill to the east, silhouetted against a crimson sky.

Ceaselessly, Edinburgh conveys the sensation of struggle between man and nature. Even lying snug within timber dormitory cubicles, I could feel the majestic solidity of Fettes College sway as it was seized by a howling gale, listening to the wind seething up between its stone walls and timber panelling to the dirge of the Granton foghorn. It was very satisfying. There was much perverse pleasure in thus defying the elements: all part of the ethos of bracing oneself, chin out, shoulders down, determined to face it out.

No visitor to a city bestriding a ridge can remain unaware of nature: of the weather and of the landscape beyond. One of the joys of clambering up or living in citadels is the presence of the uncivilised, the untamed: the way in which the expanding view to every side reveals nature from the midst of civilisation. The unmanicured hulk of Arthur's Seat, frilled by the jagged red Salisbury Crags and suitably seasoned by climate and barometer, dominates the city and provides an antidote to the streets and squares. It proved unpleasantly natural, however, for William Gilpin, an early missionary of the picturesque, who judged Arthur's Seat 'odd, misshapen and uncouth', too raw to give him the aesthetic *frisson* he thought appropriate. It offered 'an unpleasing view from every station'. The Chinese artist and writer Chiang Yee, on the other hand, found it delightful, but quite distinctly *not* resembling a lion – a dormant elephant, perhaps; and he provided a delightful watercolour to prove it.

Nor is the wildness distant. Erupting at the heart of Edinburgh as a signal stimulator of wild fantasy, it earned even Gilpin's reluctant admiration:

> He who would see Edinburgh Castle in perfection must go to the bottom of the rock it stands on, and walk round it. In this view the whole appears a very stupendous fabric. The rock, which is in itself an amazing pile, is in many parts nobly broken, and tho', in its whole immensity, it is too large an object for a picture, unless at a proper distance; yet many of its craggy corners with their watch towers and other appendages, are very picturesque.

Ragged cliffs, hills, braes and moors can also do wonders for tedious suburbs as they punctuate the Edinburgh periphery and render the humdrum particular. Those expiring at the gallows by the Mercat Cross (as many did) were doubtless consoled by their last views of the beauties of the hills and seascape beyond. It enchanted Dorothy Wordsworth to be able to discover at the heart of the capital a pastoral hollow 'as wild and solitary as any in the heart of the Highland mountains; there, instead of roaring of torrents, we listened to the noises of the city, which were blended into one loud indistinct buzz.' Nowadays but a hum, for the city is sadly bereft of publicly echoing music, of gongs or chimes (except during the Festival) now that its churches are falling silent. There is only the strange and episodic echo of crepuscular campanology and the unsubtle bark of the one o'clock gun. Solitude and an eerie isolation may still be found today in Holyrood Park, even if the Wordsworthian buzz has been replaced by the more easily distinguishable sounds of traffic and inter-city railway horns entering tunnels, overlain in rare times of winter nights' gloom by the Granton Harbour foghorn.

In 1952, John Betjeman had addressed Edinburgh as 'that most beautiful of all the capitals of Europe'; and when he came to address the 1970 conference on the conservation of Georgian Edinburgh, his sensation of being abroad was deepened: 'When I come to Edinburgh, I am in the capital of another country.' Indeed he was. Europeanness in behaviour, dress, fodder and speech was what struck visitors most forcibly from the Union of Crowns until the early nineteenth century. English travellers could only describe the capital and its inhabitants by reference to foreign countries: women's dress according to the German and Dutch fashions, and men's comparable to the French. Even the surrounding villas were deemed 'castle-wise' (or mock-military châteaux). Although food was eaten in the French manner, its substance rarely attracted comparable praise. As late as 1776, Edinburgh conveyed a familiar continental feeling to Captain Topham:

> A man who visits this country after having been in France will find in a hundred instances the resemblance there is between those two nations. That air of mirth and vivacity, that quick and penetrating look, that spirit of gaiety which distinguish the French is equally visible in the Scotch . . . Even in Edinburgh, the same spirit [of hospitality] runs through the common people; who are infinitely more civil, humanised and hospitable than any I ever met with.

The romantic movement overwhelmed rationalism, Edinburgh's future seemed assured. It provided an incomparable stage for the impassioned. Unsuspecting nature began to be overburdened with the emotions and miseries of man. The 'pathetic fallacy' would have the rocks of the capital oozing blood, tears, sweat, misery, ghosts of headless dogs and disembodied arms, flaunting triumph and grief – in measure to what natives and visitors, poets, novelists and painters required of it. Only Naples could compare, wrote Washington Irving, and it was rambles round Arthur's Seat that prompted *Pleasures of Hope* from Thomas Campbell. Felix Mendelssohn succumbed to the roofless and overgrown Holyrood Abbey mouldering in the twilight: 'I believe I have found the beginning of my Scottish Symphony there today.' The painter David Wilkie enthused to Edinburgh magistrates in 1829:

> What the tour of Europe was necessary to see elsewhere, I now find congregated in this one city. Here are alike the beauties of Prague and of Salzburg – here are the romantic sights of Orvieto and Tivoli – and here is all the magnificence of the admired bays of Genoa and Naples – here, indeed, to the poetic fancy, may be found realised the Roman Capitol and the Grecian Acropolis.

Precipitous city, as R L Stevenson christened it, it may be; but it is far from precipitate. 'Precipitate City? Auld Reekie? Na, na, Sir! There's naething in the auld biddie as fashious nor urgent as precipitate!' There is no reason for it to be precipitate. Save for a quick blaze of mercantile glory between 1600 and 1637, when its merchants were numbered amongst the trading princes of Europe, Edinburgh has eschewed the haste and bustle of industry. Instead, its public moguls have reflected the service industries that this hive of paperwork has called into being: notably florid brewers and mild-mannered publishers. Covertly, power resided with its professionals, and professionals are measured in their movements.

My great cousin Sandy Guthrie, one of the great Dr Thomas Guthrie's fifty-two grandchildren, was the epitome of the suburban Edinburgh professional with artistic leanings. I recall him as awe-inspiring, tall, stately, and rattling in his cavernous Spylawbank 'cottage' (a discreet Edinburgh term implying more social class than dimension). A six-year-old faces an octogenarian relative with care, but the gap was made to seem less vast by his favouring an artist's beret upon the Himalayas of his head and, upon the foothills of his feet, carpet slippers. The kindest of men, Cousin Sandy was fond of going to comfort old Miss Addis (her brother being chairman of the Hong Kong & Shanghai Bank) with a pint of champagne accompanied by a whiff of his secret Edinburgh irreverence and resistance to being 'swamped by piety'. His memoirs of day-to-day life in Liberton and Colinton are less of great events than of tea and tennis parties, golf, 'the bad air and feeling very bored' in church, and the habit of Thomas Guthrie's widow of prolonging the last note in a hymn so that once the choir had stopped 'you heard a kind of long wail descending'. A gentle serenity pervaded the stone-walled privacy of late nineteenth-century Edinburgh suburbia.

That genial suburban glow concealed a slackening of momentum: for, during the early twentieth century, the city came close to losing its cultural and political leadership of Scotland.

This former European capital was being shoehorned into the role of a British provincial city and forgot that the source of Scots culture lay to the east rather than to the south. Back in 1825, Robert Chambers observed that 'common stairs are of French extraction. They still abound in Paris, from which we have recently borrowed the fashion of closing them with a door, commanded by a chain from each flat'; and he later travelled down the Rhine on a mission to seek the tenement's origins. After the Second World War, however, planners trained in the south and, unaccustomed to the traditional patterns of European urban living, persuaded us that tenements were occupied only by those who had no economic alternative. We lacked the concierges, not to say *tricoteuses*, to surge to their rescue. Given the choice, down they fell.

Inspiration departed for Glasgow, leaving Edinburgh to its whisky and shortbread. The radicals in the west were convinced that the capital had declined into provincialism: an insult the dragon under the hill was not prepared to tolerate. Almost as it were by magic, the ideal setting for a post-war cultural festival transpired to have features identical to Edinburgh, and the International Festival was born. A few decades later, the years of careful financial management bore fruit in that the capital rose to be one of the largest financial centres in Europe. Now, after almost two centuries' decline, the Old Town of Edinburgh is at the threshold of re-awakening as the heart of an ancient European capital.

History tends to be a record of winners, for those who go under usually leave little trace. The man who survives records his success; the man who is hanged tends not to. This book seeks, so far as is possible, to look beneath the great and the notable, and to so so in *their* words (although liberties have been taken to render the spelling less inaccessible). They – some famous but most obscure – record the life of a great city: whether the anonymous author of the *Diurnal of Occurrents* who witnessed history unfolding beneath his windows, the diplomat Sir James Melville, David Moyses – government official and diarist, sober John Spalding, the uneasy spymaster Daniel Defoe, Alexander Carlyle – genial if self-satisfied recorder of the Enlightenment, a sad Sir Walter Scott, the melancholy antiquarian Robert Chambers, wondrously vivid Henry Cockburn, evangelical Thomas Guthrie, magical Robert Louis Stevenson and wild Patrick Geddes. Although it could never aspire to being a victim's eye view, it attempts, however, to convey what living in Edinburgh may have been like in each of its incarnations, tearing aside the protective cloak of myth, legend, romance and outstanding topography under which natives have been accustomed to shelter from the reality of the modern world.

To warn the natives to guard against such complacency, John Ruskin paced sternly along Queen Street on his way to lecture at the Royal College of Physicians in 1854 (counting with distaste 678 tediously unadorned identical classical windows):

> That you were born under the shadow of . . . two fantastic mountains are no rightful subjects of pride. You did not raise the mountains, nor shape the shores; and the historical houses of your Canongate, and the broad battlements of your castle, reflect honour upon you only through your ancestors. Before you boast of your city, before you even venture to call it *yours*, ought you not scrupulously to weigh the exact share you have had in adding to it or adorning it?

Edinburgh has, perhaps, undergone more incarnations than most cities of similar importance: from regional city it became a reluctant capital, and then blossomed into a European emporium. After the loss of parliament, it utilised its strengths to earn itself a further European reputation in the eighteenth century: a reputation for intellectual endeavour, mirroring almost exactly that of Athens thousands of years earlier. Then followed a period of physical expansion but intellectual retrenchment until the arrival of the Festival.

Its history prompts a reflection on the nature of cities, and the values that derive from the inescapable interaction between people. The Renaissance architect Jacopo Sansovino believed that great cities did not consist of monuments, streets, squares and churches so much as people making the most of their opportunities. Yet, occasionally, a city emerges whose history is the consequence of the interaction between the people and the place itself: and one such is Edinburgh. At a time of heedless rush toward suburbia and what Martin Pawley has christened the 'private future', it is apposite to see how Edinburgh's fortunes mirror, in a miniature way, the ebb and flow of the values of civilisation itself.

CHAPTER TWO

THE WINGED CITADEL

Edinburgh was not born capital of Scotland. Its formal elevation to that honour by Charles I in 1633, took place 150 years after it had become, *de facto*, principal burgh of the Kingdom. By then, the inhabitants were only too well aware of just how sore that dignity could be.

During its formative years, Scotland was without a capital as government followed monarchs on their progress around their kingdom, from port to palace, and palace to castle. If there had to be a chief burgh, there were indeed other and better suitors for the title in the early Middle Ages. Kings were crowned customarily in Scone Abbey, whose neighbouring town of Perth, the only fully walled city of mediaeval Scotland, was well located for river transport and sufficiently inland to be safe from invasion. It was richly endowed with a Charterhouse, Greyfriars, Blackfriars, and a splendid civic kirk.

Stirling was a more likely choice. Near or around its majestic and imposing rock occurred the great battles for Scottish supremacy. As 'fair Snawdoun', it was the cultural heart of Renaissance Scotland, and the spiritual home of James IV and V. Excellent hunting, poetry, music, staged jousts and the occasional jape provided the lure. Stirling was also immensely secure, protected by the enveloping marshes, mists and floodplains of the Forth. The independence parliament in 1314 had met in the great abbey of Cambuskenneth down in the flood-plain, and the burgh was graced with a suburban Greyfriars, and a large parish church. Stirling's particular advantage, however, was that its palace, castle, and chapel royal were enfolded within the same citadel. If danger threatened, the court need venture no further than the castle's great forework. It was sufficiently far inland, perhaps a week's march for a heavily laden army, to render it just that much more immune to invasion from England. At this point, the Forth was simply too shallow for a major port or a haven for the English to land invasion fleets.

Edinburgh's rise to a vulnerable pre-eminence may largely be attributed to the success of Leith as Scotland's primary port. What drove Edinburgh burgesses was the furtherance of trade, and since there had been no land passage through the Border save for armies or embassies during almost 300 years or war between Scotland and its 'auld ynemie' of England, that trade came primarily from the east, by sea. Although other ports such as Dundee and Aberdeen had extensive trade with the Baltic, Scottish trade and Scottish communication passed primarily through Leith, its ultimate destination Edinburgh.

Leith expanded in wealth as Scotland's premier port, its prosperity reflected in its substantial merchants' houses, noble palaces, substantial tolbooth and great warehouses. Inevitably Edinburgh merchants, the principal capitalists behind Leith trade, cast covetous eyes upon it, whereas Edinburgh's military understood the danger to the city of a well-fortified citadel in the wrong hands that could be provisioned and reinforced by sea. Leithers purchased their independence as a separate burgh from their superior Logan of Restalrig and, in 1559, it was fortified by the Regent's French masons with one of the most advanced star-shaped defences to be found in Europe, as a bulwark against Edinburgh. To prevent any repetition, Edinburgh burgesses then purchased Leith's superiority from Mary Queen of Scots. They were prescient. Between 1570 and 1572, Leith was held by the King's Men whilst Edinburgh was held by the Queen's men in that savage Civil War, and when war seemed imminent in 1639, Edinburgh citizens surged to Leith to fortify it once more against seaborne invasion. It was in Leith that Cromwell built one of his great defensive citadels; and it was not until the nineteenth century that the port was finally to attain its abbreviated period of independence from the capital.

Until at least 1637, Edinburgh merchants were true Europeans, with a principal trading port in Veere in Holland, and Scots houses, chapels, colonies and colleges in most significant ports throughout the Baltic and Low Countries, many of which survive today. Custom and ceremony were frequently derived from continental models. When its masons and wrights incorporated, they petitioned the council for a place in the town's processions 'like as they have in Bruges and siclike good towns'. The High Street would have echoed to the sound of most European languages as ambassadors, travellers, traders, masons, craftsmen and books imported an internationalism from Italy, France, Spain and Denmark in decoration, clothing, eating, dress and even architecture.

Foreign travellers attracted by such an outward-looking culture and enterprising spirit must have found the city of their destination a strange if not forbidding vision, crouched and huddled as it was high upon its rock. They would have passed through Leith's walls into the cornfields beyond – a landscape dotted with lairds' châteaux and villas in their parks. By the flank of the Boar's Crag (Calton Hill), past ruins of the

Leper Hospital and site of Edinburgh's archery butts, play-acting and gibbet, they would have descended down a paved causeway into the city at Leith Wynd port (gate), overshadowed by the gracious towers of Trinity College and its gardens. Against the skyline, they would have seen tall stone eyries marching in tight formation down to the Nor' Loch. Entry to the city required passage up the narrow defile of tenements and taverns of Leith Wynd, to debouch at the mouth of the Netherbow Port.

The Netherbow was Edinburgh's principal gate – a powerful towered gateway facing eastward towards the old enemy. Once permitted to enter, visitors were astounded to find themselves, in explosive contrast to the high stone cliffs and narrow closes, in one of the largest urban spaces in Christendom, sealed against the biting wind like an enormous open-air room, in which immeasurable throngs of people met to do business before returning to lodgings in great stone caverns, seemingly extruded from the rock itself and squeezed up into the heavens. To some, it resembled Salzburg: others Prague or elsewhere in Bohemia. Wherever else, this vision of a fortified crag was certainly not British.

The burgh was not obviously walled in the manner of great European or English cities, curiously so, given its history of pillage. Time and again throughout the centuries of war, its burgesses and their descendants had observed how the court would retreat from Edinburgh to Stirling in the face of a remorseless cycle of war, invasion and sack. To its ambitious merchant burgesses, to be thus abandoned must have been profoundly depressing. Trade would be interrupted – indeed people could be killed – as were some 360 Edinburgh men (approximately ten per cent of its adult males) fighting the English at Pinkie Cleuch in 1547.

The only visible wall was the new-built and hastily thrown-up Flodden Wall constructed between 1516 and 1520 lining the High Riggs along the south side of the city. With all the majesty of *papier mâché*, it seemed hardly capable of repulsing a determined army: rather it was the sort of barrier needed to control trade and plague. Yet the appearance of defencelessness that Edinburgh cultivated was a trap, as invaders soon found out. It is the only possible explanation why the victorious English army did not invade the city after its unexpected success at the disastrous battle of Pinkie Cleuch in 1547. Instead, it camped at Meadowbank, and enjoyed casual looting and destruction in the suburbs, and then embarked on the more expensive plan of blockading throughout the Lothians to starve the city to surrender. Again, during the dreadful siege of October 1571, the anonymous diarist author of the *Diurnal of Occurrents* watched the army of the King's Men bombard and ding down the Flodden Wall but yet refuse to invade despite the paucity of defendants and the fact that they were starving. Why?

Caution. It would not take many to defend Edinburgh. Experience gained during the 1544 Rough Wooing sack revealed Edinburgh as a fly-trap. Like a carnivorous plant, it had the ability to suck soldiers into it and not let them out again despite its absence of walls. Its most vulnerable façade facing east, whence the inhabitants were accustomed to expect their 'auld enemeies' to appear, was narrowed like a stone trumpet, its mute being the great, towered Netherbow Port hemmed tightly by stone tenements. Tenements formed continuous walls down to the edge of the Nor' Loch and down St Mary's Wynd to the Cowgate Port. The western approaches were protected by the efficient and accurate cannon of the castle, and the northern by the Nor' Loch.

An army surging through a breached Flodden Wall, even on the softer south side of the city, would have been channelled into defile as soldiers wound up through steep stone canyons of the wynds and closes, many barely the width of a man with his arms outstretched. The passive resistance that Edinburgh perfected over the centuries was reflected in the density of its construction. Virtual catacombs of stone-vaulted cellars or caverns, reached only with great difficulty down terrifyingly narrow closes, tenements towering so close above that their inhabitants could shake hands across the divide, would create their own security.

A visit to the dark and sepulchral multi-storeyed caverns of Mary King's Close, now wholly preserved far beneath the basements of the City Chambers and endowed with legends of plague and headless black dogs, offers a sensation of what these stone ravines must have been like in their heyday. No army could get down a close: only individual soldiers, and only the foolish would have ventured down in the pursuit of booty (all valuable items of which would have been secreted away) at the risk of what might fall on them from above. As soon as they reappeared in the High Street – particularly if lumbered with booty – invaders would be inhibited from a more thorough sack by bombardment from the castle, if it held out as it usually did. The burgh could absorb entire armies within its catacombs: it had no need of a city wall.

In the face of periodic interruption, the capital's citizens refined a characteristic wartime mode which might best be summed up as remove what 'movabill geir' (easily movable goods) that could be carried furth of the walls, hide what can be hid, store what can be stored, dissemble what can be dissembled, and perhaps leave a few sops – token goods or token victims – lying around to assuage the invaders. This characteristic was manifest as early as the fourteenth century, when the French chronicler Froissart observed that Edinburgh could rebuild itself in three days after a sack, given sufficient quantities of thatch; and again in 1384, when the Duke of Lancaster found that he had conquered a town entirely deserted:

'nothing but empty houses, all the straw deposited for burning or taken away'. Notoriously preoccupied as they were with pursuing 'their own particular', the burgesses honed recessiveness to a fine art. Their response to war and invasion was to make themselves invisible; and in due course that habit, born of necessity, became endemic in the Edinburgh character.

The cellars and catacombs beneath the tenements provided boltholes for Edinburgh's underworld: the poor, dispossessed farmers, the 'broken men of weir', mercenaries and rogues who gravitated to the capital. Despite fearsome penalties threatened upon any sturdy beggars found to be from another parish, few are recorded as being branded or deported. For Edinburgh could assimilate and conceal. That may explain the existence of the volatile Edinburgh mob which could be summoned from the vasty depths of the closes, and surge from the wynds like sewage returning up the trap, flood the High Street, imprison councils and terrify Kings. It had the capacity to drive the court to Linlithgow and to hang Porteous; and its wrath expended, it would seep back into its trap.

The burgh's population swelled between 1516 and 1636 to flesh out a skeleton already fixed in stone, and arranged in plots twenty-five feet wide, and extending 450 feet downhill on either side of the High Street. The new occupants squirrelled into superstructures, extensions and subdivisions, grafted upon the original mediaeval houses, which had been limited to twenty feet high to suit the height of the fire ladder. Six storeys became the norm facing the High Street, whereas the steep slope behind was sometimes exploited to achieve a skyscraper – like the 14-storeyed 'great tenement' between Parliament Square and the Cowgate, burnt in 1700. As they were extended up, so also were they extended out. In 1508 burgesses were encouraged to enlarge any house facing the Hie Gait by up to seven feet if they used the timber from the recently cleared Burgh Muir to do so. Most did, and faced their buildings with timber galleries, sometimes enclosed as an extension to rooms, and sometimes open for occupiers to take the air and watch whatever gruesome scene was being enacted below. It was from such balconies that the rulers of the capital and their noble lodgers watched the history of the country unfold. Many of these timber projections were legitimised in the early seventeenth century by their rebuilding in dressed stone sitting upon arcades, as was the norm in continental cities, lending the High Street something of the character of a gigantic cloister.

Almost a hundred precipitous closes tumbled from the High Street, separating the long steep gardens behind the tenements, and as the gardens were divided into separate plots amongst successive owners' children, building intensified. In their upper reaches nearer the centre, it was to a comparable height and density, whereas further down there was space for detached houses, courtyards and gardens enjoying privileged views north or south. It was therefore space, fresh air and views that explain the secluded and rather odd location of houses of the nobility – such as Lady Stair's, Bishop Adam Bothwell's in Byer's Close, the Earl of Morton's in the Friar's Wynd, and the Marquis of Tweeddale's in Tweeddale Close – which have miraculously survived. It was the exact obverse of most other cities, in which the grander streets were fronted by the grander houses, and something that occasioned comment from several, such as John Taylor in 1618:

> Gentlemen's mansions and goodliest houses are obscurely founded in the aforesaid lanes . . . much fairer than the buildings in the High Street, for in the High Street, merchants and tradesmen do dwell.

When affairs of state required a lodging within Edinburgh, a merchant's house was rented or requisitioned: Robert Ker's house, Robinson's Land at the Salt Tron, and Nicholas Uddart's courtyard palace in Niddry Wynd. William Kirkcaldy of Grange was lodged in Robert Gourlay's great mansion prior to his execution, whereas Mary Queen of Scots stayed in a house facing the Mercat Cross as the involuntary guest of Lord Provost Sir Simon Preston on her way to captivity in 1567.

Since the burgh was already substantially complete by the time it rose to be capital, and the nobility had only been attracted to Edinburgh once it became capital, they were too late for their houses to be accommodated within the original bounds. The Stewart monarchs' selection, however, of the abbey of Holyrood in the suburb of the Canongate for transformation into their principal palace – their St James's, their Hampton Court, their Louvre, their Escorial – provided the opportunity for aristocrats to cluster in suburbs like the Canongate or south of the Cowgate. There also were to be found the European diplomatic corps (the French ambassador lived in an *hôtel* in the Cowgate).

Edinburgh had been conceived as a civic burgh. It lacked within its bounds any of those symbols we now associate with a capital city – no palace, cathedral nor abbey; not even a ceremonial square. St Giles, magnificent collegiate burgh kirk with its thirty-three craft altars as it was, was thought by visitors to be 'little stately for the building and nothing at all for the beauty or ornament'. It had all the worthiness of a civic church equipped for civic dignity, but could not satisfy the processional splendour required for national ceremonial; and when Scotland required such occasions in Edinburgh, it had borrowed Holyrood Abbey.

But once the Stewarts expropriated the abbey, the abbey's religious significance withered. Its architecture was never fully restored after its burning during the Rough Wooing, and Scotland was thereby deprived of the religious totem provided by St Paul's or by Nôtre Dame.

When Parliament met in Edinburgh, as it did increasingly during the sixteenth century, it had to be housed in the Tolbooth, until Charles I compelled his capital to pay for the construction of a new Parliament House on the site of the St Giles's collegiate buildings. Edinburgh found it difficult to adapt to being capital of Scotland, and this reluctance to becoming capital was not purely physical. Throughout the sixteenth and much of the seventeenth centuries, its burgesses found much to grieve over as they had to pay for royal gifts, marriage gifts, masques, special taxes, royal and ambassadorial banquets and, eventually, the construction of the Parliament House of Scotland. They were undoubtedly conscious of the business attracted to the capital by King and Parliament, but how they girned!

The unique feature about Old Edinburgh was its plan. Leaving aside the Cowgate and the suburbs, it was a city without streets. Just two great spaces and perhaps a hundred wynds and closes. Nestling beneath the lee of the castle lay the minor space – the Grassmarket – a smelly, busy, bustling place of workers surrounded by inns. It was generally noisome, for here were the King's stables, the meat market, and the candlemakers.

The burgh's glory, which attracted the attention of all visitors, was not the density of population, nor even the sanitation (both of which were of abiding curiosity) but the High Street: 'the fairest and goodliest street that ever mine eyes beheld,' wrote John Taylor, the London waterboatman poet. But was it a street? The Sieur de Brantôme, in Mary Queen of Scots' entourage, called it a *grande place*', and others an enormous market-place. So forget, if you will, the Royal Mile: a modern term, a tourist packaging of the Via Regis between castle and abbey. Edinburgh can be appreciated only by the realisation that the Hie Gait (it went under many names) was no street, no road, and no Royal Mile. It was a huge downhill-sloping plaza, shaped like a fat egg-timer: immensely long, a hundred feet broad, and pinched at the top end by the Butter Tron (or Weigh House), and at the bottom end by the Netherbow Port. It was constricted in the middle by the Luckenbooths, a tall island of buildings and booths separated from the north wall of St Giles only by the narrow, dank, dark and odiferous Stinking Style (or alley).

In the dog days of Edinburgh as a European capital, this 'broad and very faire' street went unpenetrated end to end save for the wynds and closes: a half-mile-long stone amphitheatre only spoilt, thought Sir William Brereton, by the timber projections and the varying gable heights. Regularise those, and it would become 'the most complete street in Christendom'. It was the best paved street he had seen, admiring the 'fair, spacious and capacious walk' at the crown of the causeway which we have now selflessly donated to motor cars save on Hogmanay and at midnight during the Festival. Once inside this cavernous stone bowl, the only emergency escape was by stumbling downhill through vennel middens. The only views were of the castle ramparts to the west, a puff of smoke hinting that shot was on its way, or of the sea, shores, and North Berwick Law to the east. From their respective gallows, the underprivileged had the former view; and the privileged the latter. The High Street of Edinburgh conveyed an overwhelming sensation either of security and protection, or of claustrophobia.

This space, this stone trough, was Edinburgh's *forum* – almost its Colosseum; it was also the womb of the Reformation, and the great college cloister of the Enlightenment. It was – and still is – Edinburgh's only civic space. The gaping wounds that have turned it into a stone colander were caused by the creation of the Bridges in the late eighteenth and early nineteenth centuries, and the subsequent widening of wynds like Blackfriars into side streets have diminished its personality. It is still recoverable.

The focus of this great street was the Mercat Cross. There was nothing of the emptiness of resurrected pageantry by picturesque town criers with large bells shouting 'Oyez oyez': shout they did, oyez also, but the Mercat Cross of Edinburgh was no picturesque location with colourful ritual. Here, almost daily, were pronounced all public decisions and all public information for the entire kingdom. Here were wars declared, nobles decreed forfeit, Kings' betrothals broadcast, dooms denounced, armies summoned, sentences of treason cried forth, and parliaments proclaimed. Here also were executions executed. Here was taken the delivery of the heads of the Lewis men slaughtered by James VI's Lowland settlers who had had them conveyed to the capital (where, after several weeks, they probably arrived less than fresh), prior to formal exhibition on the appropriate spike. The day-to-day reality of sixteenth-century Scotland was such that nowhere else in the world was the effect of the Wheel of Fortune so apparent as at the Edinburgh Mercat Cross.

Here also came soldiery to enforce factional feud, as in 1520 when the Lord Home 'caused his brother Mr William Home to pass to Edinburgh, with the number of 10,000 men' to proclaim Bishop Andrew Forman, then Bishop of Moray, to the Archbishopric of St Andrews according to a disputed papal bull. Ten thousand armed men, many presumably on horseback, would have saturated the High Street and, at that time, have augmented the population of the city by approximately seventy-five per cent.

A potent addition to the more famous smells of Edinburgh around the Mercat Cross must have been that of decomposition, from blood or burning boy, as recorded by David Moyses on 2nd December, 1584:

> A baxter's boy called Robert Henderson (no doubt by the instigation of Satan) desperately put some powder and a candle in his father's heather stack, standing in a close opposite to the Tron of Edinburgh, and burnt the same with his father's house, which lay next adjacent, to the imminent hazard of burning the whole town. For which, being apprehended most marvellously after his escaping out of the town, he was on the next day burnt quick [alive rather than previously strangled] at the Cross of Edinburgh, as an example.

Sanitation, or its lack, gained the city a fearsome reputation. 'I smell you in the dark,' growled Samuel Johnson as he first walked up into the High Street from the Canongate just after his arrival. Had it been around 10.00 p.m. and the sounding of the Tron Kirk bell, whose tolling permitted even the least of the serving wenches to throw up their casement window and tip chamberpots and slop up to a hundred feet down into the street, perhaps Johnson would have been slightly more vehement. They were supposed to cry 'Gardez l'eau' (Gardyloo) and vulnerable passers-by had the right to howl back 'Haud your hand' as they dove for the shelter of the nearest arcade, but doubtless practice on both sides was indifferently observed.

Edinburgh's method of sewage disposal (virtually identical, even to the cautionary shout of 'Gardez l'eau', to that of Antwerp) was the consequence of the city being built on rock. At its original laying out, densities were such that the drainage channels and open sewers in the streets and closes were more than adequate. Given the notoriously wet weather of Scotland, you might think it was a canny method of sewage disposal to agree that at certain times of the night, offal and faeces could be tipped into such channels which would then be sluiced by natural weather conditions downhill and along the burns that ran eastwards on either side of the city rock. When rain was scarce and the fabled winds of Edinburgh slack, matters were otherwise. Ironically, the very shape of the city, which had been determined by the need to keep the winds at bay, trapped the stench most gloriously within.

By the mid-sixteenth century, when the population had risen to about 15,000, sewage disposal was becoming difficult, and as the population virtually doubled in the next hundred years, without any increase in the land area, the problem became epidemic. The wynds of Edinburgh became so noisomely celebrated that Jonathan Swift could indulge his readers with an interesting mathematical discourse in the *Tale of the Tub* by animadverting upon the geometric properties of an Edinburgh turd he turned by toe. Natives would enjoy confusing foreigners (and indeed nineteenth-century country reel composers) by christening as 'Flowers of Edinburgh' matter of an altogether more fundamental nature. As buildings grew higher and higher, a slatternly servant girl was more likely to tip a chamberpot out of her window six floors up rather than descend six floors to tip it into a sewer if she could find it: particularly if her bad habit was hallowed in burgh regulations.

The earliest flyting of the city's slovenliness was made by the poet William Dunbar, probably anticipating the occasion of James IV's wedding to Margaret Tudor in 1503 which was to take place in Holyrood. Evidently angry at having to defend his adopted city against the charge that it was failing to live up to its newly acquired principal burgh status at a time of royal wedding, Dunbar addressed himself to the controllers of the city, the merchant burgesses of Edinburgh, possibly the most powerful non-aristocratic Scotsmen of the time:

> Why will ye, merchants of renown,
> Let Edinburgh, your noble town,
> For lack of reformation
> The common profit tyne and fame?
>   Think ye not shame
>   That any other region
> Shall with dishonour hurt your name!
>
> May none pass through your principal gaitis
> For stink of haddocks and of skates,
> For cries of carlings and debates,
> For fensum flyttings of defame:
>   Think ye not shame
> Before strangers of all estates
> That such dishonour hurt your name!

There were frequent visitations of plague. It appeared in May 1529, and in the following year the town council sentenced David Duly, tailor, to be 'hangit on ane gibbet before his own door' because he had held his wife 'sick in the contagious sickness of pestilence two days in his house and would not reveal the same to the Officers of the town while she was dead in the said sickness'; worse, he left his wife's corpse and went to attend Mass on Sunday at St Giles, risking spreading the infection to 'clean people'. Fortune duly smiled on him, because the rope broke and fell off the gibbet, and since he was 'ane poor man with small bairns', the sentence was commuted to perpetual banishment from the city 'under pain of death'.

The pest usually returned in times of war and famine, particularly during the Civil War of 1568-72 during which all infected persons and their furniture and effects were ordered to be moved to the Burgh Muir. Whenever any person fell sick 'in whatsoever kind of sickness it ever be' they were ordered to shut their doors and neither come out, nor admit any person into their house, until they were visited by the baillie of their quarter of the town, and ordered to be taken by him under pain of death'. On 7th May, 1585, it was again introduced, this time 'by a servant woman from St Johnstone [Perth] and began in the Fishmarket Close, beside the Cross'. Its most notorious visitation was in 1645 when its effect upon the capital was comparable to the Black Death.

It would be erroneous to conclude that life within the Old Town was at the level of savagery by the standards of the rest of Europe. One of the oldest interiors to survive in the city, the offices of the Old Town Conservation Committee in Advocates Close, has splendidly huge rooms with enormous carved stone fireplaces, and its plaster walls were once entirely covered with vigorously swirling, multicoloured mural paintings. Both demolitions and restorations of ancient High Street houses during the 1930s revealed encrusted plasterwork, carved timber panelling and partitions, wall painting, and well-chiselled masonry.

The interior of James Mossman's house (now known as John Knox's house) is opulently cosy, with substantial rooms lined with expensively carved panelling – two principal rooms on each floor linked by a wide, shallow turnpike staircase. It lacks the spacious grandeur that once glowed (and which could still be recreated) from the town house of Regent Morton down Blackfriars Street. Gladstone's Land, the merchant's lodging of Thomas Gledstanes in the Lawnmarket, provides an excellent picture of life in the early seventeenth century. Newly built stone arcades provide the frame for street-front trading booths, behind and above which lie a myriad of rooms and staircases linking together buildings erected at different periods. As normal, the first-floor chambers form the principal apartment, its walls framed and patterned by fine wall paintings.

Space was so scarce in central Edinburgh in the sixteenth and seventeenth centuries that private space was an immense privilege. That may explain why the most opulent houses were sometimes built in form of a courtyard; and why Baillie MacMorran's house in Riddle's Court was chosen by James VI for a banquet with his new Queen's ambassadors in 1590. The distinction of Riddle's Court was that it was one of the few wholly enclosed private courtyard houses within the burgh. That may explain, also, why James VI sheltered in the courtyard house of merchant Nicholas Uddart in Niddry Wynd, after the Earl of Bothwell's failed kidnap attempt in 1591. A continuing demand for private space may also explain why Robert Mylne, Edinburgh's first developer, should adopt the form of a courtyard or square for Milne's Court and Milne's Square: unexceptional as they may seem today, their novelty in seventeenth-century Edinburgh must have been considerable.

Southern Edinburgh, through which the King's army sought to invade in 1571, was an extension to the original burgh. The Blackfriars (Dominican), and Greyfriars both occupied the pleasant open country of the High Riggs to the south of the Cowgate, sandwiching the later Collegiate Church of St Mary in the Fields (more notoriously known as the Kirk o' Field). These lay outside the King's Wall, with which James II had instructed the magistrates to protect the soft flank of the city from 'oure enemeies of England'. Constructed of beautiful large blocks of pink stone, that wall ran halfway down the southern slope of the castle and then due east across the flank of the ridge until turning uphill north again to the original Netherbow.

The territory newly enclosed within the Flodden Wall by 1520 was a religious and educational enclave, its spacious grounds offering ample opportunity for contemplation, although the path running along the outside of the wall became so notorious that it was known as the Thief Row. The same wall thus enfolded two distinct cities: namely the high-density tenemented city to the north, and a magnificent suburb of large houses in their own gardens, and priories, to the south. These pleasant monastic and collegiate buildings offered ripe pickings once their religion was overturned, and they were sacked in 1559. Doubtless St Mary's in the Fields received due treatment whilst they were about it. The desolation that resulted is revealed in the descriptions of the murder of the King of Scotland, Henry Darnley, in 1565, whilst he lay convalescing in the Provost's Lodging of the Kirk o' Field.

In his demonology against Mary Queen of Scots, the Presbyterian historian George Buchanan attacked the decision by Mary Queen of Scots to bring her husband here from Glasgow to convalesce from his syphilis. He claimed that the building was not a fit location for a sick King, being mean and derelict and set in a remote location surrounded by ruins, deliberately chosen for its isolation where no cries could be heard. Yet those paying their respects to the sick King's lodging, including his wife who spent long hours with him in a dutiful way, would have been in no doubt about its regal nature. The principal floor had a suite of three rooms, a bedchamber, drawing room and dressing rooms, with presumably servants' rooms above, and kitchens below. These rooms were hung with sixteen pieces of tapestry, and were furnished with a velvet commode, a Turkey carpet, a leather hide chair beneath the velvet black canopy (a mark of royal distinction), and there appears to have been a purple velvet four-poster bed, and another of a similar colour.

For perhaps twenty or thirty years, this enormous monastic district remained semi-abandoned, with the faint hiss of its crumbling tombs being interrupted by the crump of a corbel crashing to the ground from the ruins of a kirk. Its gardens ran wild. The city sought the gift of these great acreages to sustain its ministers, its new schools and its poor, and was eventually partly successful when Queen Mary gifted the Blackfriars (later swapped for Trinity College) for the sustenance of the poor. Ministers and schools, however, remained dependent upon whatever revenues St Giles itself might provide.

In 1582, the Townis College was grafted upon the ghosts of the Kirk o' Field; the Blackfriars provided a home for the Grammar School; and, in later centuries, for the Surgeons' Hall and the Royal Infirmary. The Greyfriars became the burgh's second parish church (almost certainly reusing portions of the Greyfriars that had survived until that time), and over the next two centuries, this educational enclave became a virtual campus, with the arrival of George Heriot's Hospital, the Trades Hospital, and the Merchant Maiden School. When Edinburgh expanded south in the eighteenth century, the predominent inhabitants of that sector were people linked to such institutions. The social segregation that was to become such a clear and distinctive feature of Edinburgh had its origins herein: and its legacy lingers even today, as most of the university academics reside in Newington.

Between that enclave and the city lay the once-splendid Cowgate, whose attractions and relaxed suburban aspect are now impossible to fathom. Illustrations depict a dense, narrow street of tall, timber-fronted houses strangely like parts of Nürnberg. But as Alesius, an exiled Scots monk, wrote in 1550, the Cowgate was the acme of fashion. Here 'dwelt the gentry and the high municipal dignitaries, and in which are the palace of the princes of the Kingdom, where nothing is humble or rustic, but all is magnificent'. It was in the Cowgate that the French ambassador had his *hôtel*, and Sir Thomas Hamilton and Sir John Hope had their mansions. Real magnificence was reserved for the courtyard palace built by Archbishop James Beaton in the 1520s on the corner of Blackfriars Wynd: so stately indeed, with its lovely corbelled two-storey corner tower on the French model, that it was selected by Mary Queen of Scots as the setting for a banquet with the townsfolk on 9th February, 1562:

> prepared and hung most honourably; and there Her Highness
> supped and the rest with her; and after the supper, the honest
> young men in the town came with a convoy to her and thereafter
> departed to the said palace.

Edinburgh developed as Scotland's capital because the Steward Kings settled on the abbey of Holyrood, first as a convenient lodging, thereafter as a palace, and thence to being the principal royal seat in the kingdom. Holyrood had been founded as an abbey of Augustinian canons by King David I, possibly in 1128, on a site well distant from the cluster of little timber houses of embryonic Edinburgh perched on their ridge almost a mile uphill. It was graciously placed on a slightly elevated platform in the middle of a well-wooded and possibly marshy plain, in an idyllic location at the foot of Arthur's Seat. It may well have been sited against the Roman road running north-west to Cramond. The legend of King David's rescue from certain death at hunting by a mystical – but quickly evaporating – stag, magically endowed with a relic of the true Cross of the Holy Rood conveniently jammed in its antlers transformed Holyrood into a centre for pilgrimage and the fifth wealthiest abbey in Scotland after St Andrews, Arbroath, Dunfermline and Paisley. Its majesty and wealth would have been yet greater had it not, even more than Edinburgh, lain in the way of every English army. Its defenceless wealth proved irresistible for the nobles, soldiers, thugs and mercenaries for which England sometimes scoured Europe in its purpose to subjugate Scotland.

The abbey's principal misfortune was that Edinburgh Castle proved inhospitable to the Kings of Scotland. If they had to stay in it, they would stay in it; but they found it windy, and never evinced the same affection for it that they showed for their mighty seat upon the crag of Stirling rock. In 1255 Margaret, wife to Alexander III, found the castle a 'sad and solitary place without verdure and, by reason of its proximity to the sea, unwholesome'. Gavin Douglas, imprisoned there 260 years later, still considered it 'wyndy and richt unpleasant'. So a good abbey, lying sheltered in the valley floor amidst gardens, close to the hunting, would do very nicely instead. The Kings' increasingly frequent requests for hospitality from the abbots were presumably ones the latter could not refuse; and thus began the assimilation of that great abbey into Scotland's premier royal palace.

The subjection of the abbey to the 'King of Scottis palas' occurred at least sixty years before the Reformation; and the religious purposes of the abbey seem to have troubled Stewart monarchs little – particularly James IV who, as Pitscottie put it, was apparently 'devoid of hearing Mass and divine service'. James was, instead, 'gritumly given to bigging of palaces', and Holyrood's abbey functions were restricted to the church, cloister and certain supporting rooms, as the transformation of the guest house or Hospitium into a palace proceeded. James IV had completed a substantial palace with gallery and entrance wing by the time of his marriage to Mary Tudor in 1503, and save for royal ceremonial, the religious importance of Holyrood had passed. After its sacking by the Earl of Hertford in 1544 and by Somerset in 1547, it was never fully repaired: only the nave remained in use as the Canongate Parish Church.

The largely dispossessed monks provided convenient manpower to act as gaoler for any noble imprisoned within the palace for bad behaviour: as was Mark Ker for the slaughter of Scott of Buccleuch in 1552. We know this from a lawsuit against Ker over ten years later by the monk seeking recompense from his prisoner for his expenses. Only twenty-one canons were left at the Reformation in 1560 and, following the pattern of the time, these 'agit and recantit' monks probably retired gracefully upon an enviable pension and portion. Yet, whatever one assumes about the Reformation, Holyrood was not finally secularised or dissolved until fifty years later; and that it had been a religious settlement produced the curious legacy that its precincts remained sanctuary for debtors well into the Victorian period.

Like his father, James V was much given – as that other Presbyterian historian George Buchanan observed sourly – 'to unnecessary building'. He appointed as Commendator of the Abbey (effectively lay abbot who enjoyed the revenues) his infant bastard Lord John Stewart, whilst he set about the completion of an immense palace, by adding a majestic tower, not unlike Vincennes, to the north, and planning a matching one to the south (which was not realised until 1665 by Sir William Bruce). The principal façade was a shimmering array of immense, stone-mullioned flat and projecting bow windows, illuminating the gallery and chapel within. The adjacent Chancellor's Court (one of several removed by Sir William Bruce) housed a number of grandees with their own suites of chambers and their own staffs.

The pity is that Holyrood lay in the path of war: for if James V's palace had been completed and left undamaged, Scotland would have had possibly the finest expression of the northern European Renaissance, architecturally far in advance of those of the Tudor isolation to the south. But the palace was sacked by the Earl of Hertford in 1544, and again in 1547; repaired with Mary Queen of Scots' considerable wealth and then bombarded during Edinburgh's Civil War in 1572. Considerable improvements were undertaken for Charles I's coronation in 1633, but in 1650 it was burnt by Oliver Cromwell's soldiers to the extent that a virtual re-building (save for the northern wing) was required. Its current state is the result of its being rebuilt and fitted out for the Duke of Lauderdale, Scotland's viceroy, by Sir William Bruce in 1665.

Puritan retrospection has cast sixteenth-century Scotland as a land of dour barbarism. Yet, although life was not comfortable in the soft way that we might recognise, there was no question as to its magnificence.* The Holyrood household of the young James V comprised a 'Treasurer, Comptroller, Secretary, Mr Macer, Mr Household, Capper, Carver, Mr Stabler, Mr Hunter, Mr Falconer, Mr Porter, and the fool' who, in the case of James V, was called John Mackilrie, and in Mary's case was – *di immortales* – a French female. There was in addition Sir David Lyndsay of the Mount who, besides being a considerable Renaissance poet, was one-time tutor, masque organiser and personal friend of the King. A further fifty people ranging from ushers, valets, errand boys, lackeys, porters, bakers, fruiterers, and cellarers were employed under the direction of the Master of the Household who also had responsibility for chaplains, surgeons, tailors, perfumers and furriers.

James V's first Christmas in Holyrood independent of the Douglases provides a clue as to the size of the establishment. They consumed 7¾ fatted oxen; 100 sheep; 3 large calves; a boar; 42 hough fillets; 18 ox tongues; 1,340 sheeps' and 1,000 ox feet; 1 boar's head; 113 geese; 206 fowl; 302 wildfowl; 119 rabbits; 560 eggs and 40 gallons of ale for the jellies: and that was only the butcher's bill.

The Master of the Household under Mary Queen of Scots was that notable grandee George, fifth Lord Seton, one of those originally sent to France to arrange terms for Mary's childhood marriage to the French Dauphin (heir to the crown). A portrait of him depicts him in gorgeous red and gold livery with baton of office; and there is every reason to believe that rich apparel was customary amongst those who thronged this palace in the suburbs. The Queen appears to have returned to Scotland accompanied by (to judge by their names) French craftsmen, where one would have normally expected her to employ Scots: for example, her soft furnishers were Pierre Oudry and Pierre Martin, who had responsibility for repairing tapestries and hangings; her perfumer was Angell Marie, her

* The sumptuousness of the palace was enhanced, from time to time, by booty. Upon the forfeiture of the richest man in Scotland, the Earl of Huntly (after his death at the battle of Corrichie in October 1562), Mary Queen of Scots' share of the booty included nine beds, one hung with cloth of gold, one with crimson velvet with gold embroidery, the others of velvet or damask, violet, black, green, tawny or yellow in colour, and a quantity of glassware and several statuettes.

tailor Jaques de Soulis, and her chief chef Nicolas Buindrid. What the Edinburgh and Canongate craftsmen thought of being supplanted by Frenchmen, in a town already dangerously overheated against the French, is not recorded; but it may not be unconnected to the burgh's stand-offish attitude to the Queen.

But what was it like, this fortified palace in the suburbs? If you were a Canongate parishioner seeking your church, you would have passed through the Water Gate, through the gardens to the north to enter the abbey church. Those entering the palace down the Canongate faced an intimidating double towered gateway erected by King James IV as the entry into the walled outer courtyard of the palace. To your right on the west flank would have been stables and ancillary buildings. Facing you was the façade of two great courtyards; the one to the left being the royal façade adorned with painted and gilt coats of arms, shimmering and glittering with glass, towers and turrets, its roof-line enlivened by spiky and fanciful finials. A sense of the awe created by this spectacle emerges from George Buchanan's story of a little piece of dynastic revenge between supporters of the House of Lennox and those of the Hamiltons (then Regent of Scotland during the minority of James V). Lennox had been murdered by Sir James Hamilton of Finnart after he had surrendered at the battle of Linlithgow, and one of his grooms sought revenge upon the murderer, as Buchanan relates.

> He went directly to Court. There were then, in a large court which is before the palace in the suburbs, about 2000 armed men of the Douglas's and Hamilton's dependents, ready prepared for the expedition; he, seeing them, passed by all the rest and fixed his eye and mind on Hamilton only, who was then coming out of the courtyard in his cloak, without his armour; when he saw him in a pretty long gallery, and somewhat dark, which is over the gate, he flew at him and gave him six wounds; one of which almost pierced to his vitals . . . Immediately a great clamour began . . . and they were all commanded to stand in single ranks, by the walls which were around the courtyard; there the murderer was discovered, as yet holding the bloody knife in his hand.

It was bad enough being the attempted murderer of one of the leading Hamilton faction; it was much worse being low-born. His death was unenviable:

> He was tortured for a long time . . . At last he was condemned

and carried up and down the city, and every part of his naked body was nipped with iron pincers, red hot; and yet neither in his speech, nor in his countenance, did he discover the least sense of pain.

The suburb of the Canongate – a narrow, winding street fronted inter-mittently by the lodgings and town houses of those at court, intermixed with some poorer dwellings, a tolbooth, church and mercat cross – was less grand, less tall, less restricted and less homogeneous than Edin-burgh's High Street. Although the road between the principal royal palace of Scotland and its principal burgh was known as the King's Gait, the Canongate was used only rarely for ceremonial processions: and prin-cipally for the monarch riding to a state opening of the Three Estates, or parliament, when it was held in Edinburgh's Tolbooth. The following is a typical record of such an event, from 23rd October, 1579:

> The King's Majesty, his Nobility and Estates rode in state to the tolbooth of Edinburgh, the crown being borne before His Maj-esty by Archibald earl of Angus, the scepter by Colin, earl of Argyll, chancellor, and the sword of honour by Robert, earl of Lennox.

When the King rode thus to parliament, he was penetrating the burgh rather than being welcomed into it, for the Netherbow was traditionally the adversary's entry. When the burgh wished to welcome their monarch ceremonially, a different route prevailed: through the Water Gate, up the north back of Canongate (now Calton Road) beneath Boar's Hill (Calton Hill), past Trinity College (now Waverley Station) to process along the Long Gait (now George Street). Whether heralded by trumpe-ters or not, it must have been an eerily silent procession, observed by faces peering down from the cliff of stone buildings rising on the other side of the Nor' Loch, from which both reek and smoke would be spiral-ling into the sky. The procession would turn south past St Cuthbert's Kirk, down King's Stables Road, past the cattle market, and into the city through the West Port, at the head of the Grassmarket.

There, the first of the ceremonial presentations would be offered, as greeted young King James VI. A contemporary account emphasised how this ceremony on 16th October, 1579, represented the King passing in to the authority of the burgh:

> His majesty entered in at the West Port of Edinburgh, where his highness was met by a great number of the honest men of the

town, clad in fine silk gowns lined with velvet, to the number of a hundred or thereby, who used such a decent and comely behaviour as became them at the first entry of their prince.

The procession would cross the Grassmarket, to mount the steep and twisting Bow up into the Lawnmarket. Halfway up, King James VI was faced, hanging from the Upper Bow gate, by 'a large globe of polished brass, out of which a little boy, clad like Cupid, descended in a machine and presented him the keys of the city, all made of massy silver and very elaborately wrought, an excellent concert of music all over the accompanying action'. The ceremony continued down the High Street as far as the Tolbooth, where:

> Peace, Plenty and Justice met and harangued him in Greek, Latin and Scots: opposite to St Giles Church stood Religion, a grave matron who addressed him in the Hebrew tongue; upon which, he entered the Church where he heard a sermon preached by a Mr Lawson.

It was altogether a didactic ritual not likely to endear the young King to Presbyterianism. After the sermon, monarch and congregation alike repaired to the Mercat Cross where was sat 'Bacchus, on a gilded hog's head, distributing wine in large bumpers, all the while the trumpets sounding and the people crying "God Save the King!"' The pageant was guarded by 2,000 horsemen, and the windows of the buildings facing the street were hung with pictures and rich tapestry, and the Causeway was strewed with flowers.

What with the burping and barking of Bacchus, the exhortations of Presbyters, the clattering and whinnying of the horses, the cheers of the people, and the crashing of the castle cannons which continued firing until he reached Holyrood, the young King must have been relieved to pass through the Netherbow to the relative peace beyond.

CHAPTER THREE

THE RELUCTANT CAPITAL

During the sixteenth century, Edinburgh developed as a European capital city whose character survived long enough to capture the romantic imagination two centuries later. But as the reluctant epicentre of the dire dynastic turmoil tholed by the country, it was the cockpit of Scotland. No subsequent perception of Edinburgh has been able to liberate itself from what happened during these tumultuous years.

The sixteenth century was not kind to Edinburgh citizens: it offered an attenuated period of invasion, civil war, dynastic rivalry, judicial execution, dearth, crop destruction, trade embargoes and plague. There were only intermittent periods of peace, never longer than twenty years, and rarely more than five. The growth and prosperity that shone upon England for almost a full century rarely peeked north of Berwick. Scottish rents were low, commerce interrupted, buildings destroyed, and manpower depleted by slaughter or by summons to serve in the army. Periodic shortage of supply was occasionally so severe as to require rationing in the capital. War, famine and plague – the Horsemen of the Apocalypse – were consequent upon Scotland's role in the perennial struggle between England and France. Northern England was vulnerable, and French Kings were unscrupulous in asking Scots monarchs to invade whenever it suited their own dynastic interests. The Tudors were equally anxious to bind their northern wound the better to release their forces to retrieve some of their lost empire in France.

Depredations by a greedy neighbour constituted the unpalatable norm in sixteenth-century Europe; and had Scotland been vigorously and charismatically led, they might have remained just an irritating nuisance. But the country's misfortune was the curse of royal minorities. For almost half the century, it was without adult royal leadership. The regencies that attempted to direct the country for nigh on forty-four years need not, *ipso facto*, have been a total disaster: but it proved so in Scotland. Small in size and population, the country was dominated by a very small number of powerful families to whom lesser lords and lairds banded themselves. The rule (only too obvious with hindsight) was painfully simple:

the arrival of a party in power would stimulate the formation of an opposing party dedicated to its overthrow. The key players, each so close in blood to the crown as to covet it, were the Earls of Lennox, the Hamilton family (Earls of Arran and later Duke of Châtelherault), the Douglas family (Earls of Angus and Morton), and the Gordons (Earls and Marquises of Huntly and nicknamed Cocks of the North).

When James IV acceded to power in 1488, the prognostic was good. A cultivated monarch, according to the historian Pitscottie, who 'favoured all cunning and religious men well . . . he was very merciful to his subjects; great of spirit he was, and studious in the building of churches, researching of relics of Saints and gave many ornaments and chalices to the said kirks.' He neutralised the threat from the south by marrying Margaret Tudor (sister to the eventual King Henry VIII), and created a court of Renaissance poetry, music, jousting and architecture. It was during his reign that the royal lodging at Holyrood began to emerge as the nation's principal palace. His relaxations were women (sexual – occasionally bisexual – licence being a Stewart characteristic), shipbuilding and pulling teeth. That he was 'ane singular guid chirurgione', must have proved some consolation to Kinnaird the barber, who was paid eighteen shillings for 'two teeth drawn furth of his head by the King'. It was possibly an offer Kinnaird felt he could not refuse.

Shipbuilding took place in the deeper anchorage of the New Haven, west along the shore from Leith, and James's pride was the *Michael* which he began in 1511. Pitscottie was vastly impressed:

> . . . the greatest ship and most strange that had ever sailed in England or France; while this ship was of so great a stature and took so much timber that, except Falkland, she wasted all the woods in Fife . . . she was so strong and of so great a length and breadth (all the wrights of Scotland, yea and many other strangers were at her device . . .) to wit she was twelve score foot of length, thirty-six foot within the sides. She was ten foot thick in the wall, cutted jests of oak in her wall and boards on every side, so stark and so thick, that no cannon could go through her.

She required 300 mariners, 120 gunners and could carry 1,000 troops. To doubters who thought that it sounded strangely like 'Saul has his thousands, but David has his ten thousands', Pitscottie retorted: 'If any man believe that this description of the ship be not of verity as we have written, let him pass to the gate of Tullibardine and there, before the same, he will see the length and breadth of her planted with hawthorn by the wright that helped make her.' Like the world's greatest battleship of the

Second World War, the *Vanguard*, the *Michael* was never fully deployed in action.

In 1512, the French King invoked the Auld Alliance by requesting the Scots to invade England. Undoubted national gloom is what is recorded in the ghostly warnings and phantom voices which howled the nation against its purpose, first at Linlithgow. A man clad in a blue gown with a great pikestaff in his hand, came

> speiring for the King, saying he desired to speak to him: 'Sir King, my mother hath sent me to you, desiring you not to pass, at this time, where thou art purposed; for if thou does, thou will not fare well in thy journey nor none that passeth with thee.'

He then, Pitscottie relates, vanished in the presence of all, and the company dispersed grimly. It could well have been a mortal rather than supernatural event: the courtier and poet Sir David Lyndsay of the Mount was a noted organiser of courtly masques, and may well have been put up to the idea by opponents of the plan, to deviate the King from his purpose. The King, considering his honour at stake, was not for turning.

At midnight a few days later, an eerie summons echoed hollowly around the cavern of buildings at the Mercat Cross of Edinburgh. A sepulchral voice intoned the *Summons of Plotcock*. Pitscottie's informant, a young laird, heard it desire all men:

> To compear, both earl and lord, and baron and gentleman and all honest gentlemen within the town (every man specified by his own name) to compear within the space of forty days before his master, where it should happen him to appoint, and be for the time, under pain of disobedience.

He then saw an Edinburgh citizen, Mr Richard Lawson, who had been feeling ill and was taking the air in his timber gallery, call for his servant to bring his purse, take out a crown, and cast it over the balcony shouting:

> I appeal from that summons, judgment and sentence thereof, and takes me all whole in the mercy of God and Christ Jesus his Son.

No man, Pitscottie records, 'that was called in this summons, but that one man alone which made his protestation and appeals from the said summons,' escaped what was to follow. The army mustered on the Burgh Muir and marched south to Flodden. As rumours of the disaster filtered back, the town council proclaimed, on 10th September, 1513:

For as much as there is a great rumour newly arisen within the city touching our sovereign lord and his army, of which there is hitherto no certainty, we strictly command, that all manner of persons, townsmen in the city, make ready their arms of defence and weapons of war, and that they appear marshalled therewith, at the tolling of the common bell for holding out and defending the city against all who may seek to invade the same. We also charge and require that all women do repair to their work, be not seen upon the streets clamouring and crying, under pain of banishment; and that the women of better sort do repair to the church, and there offer up their prayers to God for the safety of our sovereign and his army.

The classically literate observed that a similar proclamation had been issued by the Romans after their disastrous defeat at Cannae. The city then fell subject to a severe attack of plague. It was probably more to control the pest and fix burgh controls than to offer defence against the ravening English that the council instructed the construction of the Flodden Wall to enclose the lands of the High Riggs to the south between 1516 and 1520.

The King's will named his twenty-four-year-old Queen Margaret as Regent, but to the nobility's dismay, she was 'haunted' by Archibald, Earl of Angus ('very lusty in the Queen's sight') and soon succumbed to the 'fair personage' of this 'young witless fool' (the compliment was his uncle's). She married Angus without the approbation of her nobles and thereby forfeited the regency. The Scots then looked to France for the heir to the throne if the infant King perished: James IV's cousin the Duke of Albany. Albany was not only French born and bred (needing an interpreter to speak English), but notoriously irascible, prone to casting his hat into the fire when crossed. He landed in May 1515 to be confirmed as Governor (Regent) by the parliament held in Edinburgh that July; but the next in line to the throne, should both die, was the Earl of Arran (Hamilton), around whom an opposing band of nobles duly coalesced.

Albany brought justice, relative peace, and French masons to work on Holyrood Palace and Edinburgh Castle. Leith expanded rapidly. It cannot have been with much enthusiasm therefore that burgesses of Edinburgh witnessed his departure for France in May 1517, and the inevitable dynastic mayhem that ensued over the years of his absence. Witless Angus, who enjoyed much popularity in Edinburgh where his uncle Archibald Douglas was Provost, resented the de facto regency power exercised by the Hamiltons, and still hankered after the power to which he thought he was entitled as the Queen Dowager's (now separated) husband. In April 1520, he decided to make a bid for power, and

> came pertly to the town of Edinburgh with his kin and friends in
> company, 400 spear well arrayed in jack and spear and other
> armour according to their estate.

As soon as the Hamiltons realised that their enemy Angus was trapped within their grasp 'but with a few number with him', and that by his seizure and removal they could consolidate their control over Scotland, they caused the Netherbow to be barred. All that night, Angus's friends kept 'stark watch'. Aware that 'if he passed not hastily to the gate and defend himself manfully' he would be plucked by his enemies, Angus rose at dawn, armed his troops, and took up position just within the Netherbow. Four hundred men casting to arms in the stone trough of the High Street alerted the town, inhibiting any pre-emptive strike by the Hamiltons. Angus duly dispatched the poet-bishop Gavin Douglas of Dunkeld to parley.

With all the dignity of a prelate faced with dynastic massacre, Douglas sped over the dungheaps of the Friars' Wynd to seek the prelate of the opposing party, Archbishop James Beaton in his splendid new mansion at its foot. He discovered the archbishop in the Blackfriars Church (according to the pro-Beatons) or carousing in his palace (according to the anti-Beatons). Beaton disclaimed any knowledge of the affair, and declined to intervene, emphasising his innocence by clapping himself upon the chest as he did so. Armour concealed beneath his surplice rattled, inspiring Douglas to respond: 'I perceive, my Lord, your conscience is not good, for I hear it clatter.'

Douglas then attempted to persuade Sir Patrick Hamilton, the Earl of Arran's brother, that his master, Angus, should be free to visit his wife the Queen Dowager, then in the castle, after which he would quit the capital. Sir Patrick was persuaded, but was upstaged by his illegitimate nephew, Sir James Hamilton of Finnart. The 'bloody butcher forever thirsting for blood' cried cowardice at his uncle. Flinging the oath 'bastard-smaik' at his nephew, Sir Patrick stormed from the lodging in furious disarray, up the Blackfriars Wynd, to be slain promptly by Angus's troops as he burst into the High Street: the first of some seventy-two further gentlemen and yeoman who were killed in the battle. Angus's greater preparation was more than a match for the larger number of Hamiltons.

The Earl of Arran, Sir James and his company were harried down the closes and out across the stepping stones of the Nor' Loch, while Beaton slunk back to the Blackfriars Kirk for sanctuary behind the altar. Had not Gavin Douglas threatened his own kin with hell-fire for the defilement of santuary, Beaton would have been dragged from hiding, stripped of his vestments and slaughtered where he was. The sardonic Edinburgh burghers christened the affair 'Cleanse the Causeway' a term then generally used for sewage disposal; and thus translatable as 'get that shit off the pavement'. The Provost of Edinburgh pled successfully for the appointment of four halberdiers to protect his dignity in a world 'so brokle and trublus'. Yet far from being an indication of generic lawlessness, the Cleansing of the Causeway proved the converse. The battle was one for the control of the country. The Scots had settled in a morning's brawl what other countries resolved through full-scale warfare.

The return of Regent Albany, equipped with French troops for a renewed invasion of England, proved not to be popular, particularly when in November 1522 he replaced Edinburgh's Provost and baillies with his own supporters. His troops, who failed to appreciate the Edinburgh climate, were accused of wasting 'winter fuel and were even burning their furniture'. Albany left the country again in May 1524 for another short visit to France; but almost as soon as he was waterborne, Arran (with the support of Queen and nobles) proclaimed the twelve-year-old James King, and dissolved Albany's governorship. He never returned.

In a fit of naïvety, leading nobles then agreed that they should take responsibility for the young King in turns: but the Earl of Angus declined to relinquish the youth when it came to his turn, and by purporting to act solely upon the King's instruction, he and the Douglas faction gained absolute power and most of the offices in the kingdom. Uncle Archibald returned as Provost of Edinburgh. Opposition duly coalesced and armed, leading to two fruitless rescue attempts with (if Pitscottie is to be believed) the active support of the beleaguered boy King. Pitscottie has left a vivid account of how the second appeared from a burgh perspective:

> the Earl of Angus . . . caused his friend Archibald Douglas, provost of Edinburgh to ring the common bell and put the town in order, and commanded them to rise and come with the King in all haste, to defend him against his enemies . . . then the King caused to blow his trumpets, and lap on horse and gart ring the common bell of Edinburgh, commanding all manner of men to follow him. So he rushed out of the west port, and all the town of Edinburgh and Leith with him, to the number of 3,000 men, and rode forward; but, ere they came to Corstorphine, they heard the artillery shoot on both sides like as it had been thunder.

James V slipped the Douglas leash in 1528, rode to Stirling Castle, declared them forfeit and entered Edinburgh on 6th July in full fig, accompanied by a belt of earls, some of whom – Eglinton, Montrose and Maxwell – had rarely taken part in politics at the centre, indicating the importance they attached to rallying around the young King. James V strove to be a true Renaissance prince, encouraging, like his father, music, ceremony and architecture. Like father and daughter, he was an accomplished poet, well trained by his childhood tutor and friend Sir David Lyndsay of the Mount, whose attacks on the abuses of the Catholic Church he tolerated (if not actually encouraged) by virtue of their clothing in fine poetry. Intending to confound the opinion of the Papal Legate in 1529 that Scotland was the 'arse of Europe', James embarked upon magnificent construction at Holyrood, Stirling, Linlithgow and Falkland Palaces, but money was short. Crown revenues had been drained during the regency, and it was an era of soaring inflation. James trebled the royal revenues by exercising a capriciously vindictive and greedy streak (a characteristic passed to his bastard son James, and to his legitimate grandson James VI) in the forfeiture of nobles.

The Church was also a lucrative source of revenue, as clerics sought to purchase royal influence to stem the pressure for reform. The foundation of the College of Justice in 1532, an institution otherwise of great note in constitutional history, seems not unconnected with the profit the King earned by its establishment.

> On the 24th day of April, it is statute and ordained by the King's grace and lords, that the seat of the College of Justice should be seven of the wysest, most cunning of spiritual men, and seven of the wysest most cunning temporal men, with a spiritual President.

In return for a tenth penny of all ecclesiastical revenue over the next three years, James was persuaded to stage 'a great abjuration of the favourers of Martin Luther in the Abbey of Holyroodhouse': in short, bribed away from Protestantism.

Young, cultured, determined and eligible, James was good prospective son-in-law material; and the rulers of Hungary and Spain duly played for him. His heart, however, lay in France; and on a trip to France to vet Marie de Vendôme for marriage, he spotted and then promptly carried off the probably consumptive daughter of the King of France, Madeleine, whom he married on New Year's Day 1537. She died in Scotland barely six months later. The grieving royal widower was back in France within the year, and swooped on the widowed Mary of Guise, Duchess of Longueville (two royal dowries in the same year must have proved attractive).

In revenge for perpetual Border incursions and the impounding of Scottish ships, James determined to invade England in 1542. He allowed the army a divided command and (following that fatal Stewart weakness) appointed an incompetent favourite, Oliver Sinclair, to be one of the generals. The resultant skirmish of Solway Moss was a humiliation: a few unfortunates killed, but 1,200 captured including a cast of lords removed to London for suborning towards an English marriage by Henry VIII. James visited his mistress in Tantallon, popped in to Linlithgow where his wife was in childbirth, and retreated to Falkland where, on 14th December, 1542, he expired of misery. Pitscottie records his last despairing comment at being told that his two dead sons had been replaced by a baby girl: 'Adieu, farewell, it came with a lass, and it will pass with a lass.'

He was thirty years old. In his declining years, James resembled his grandfather Henry VII in cupidity, and his uncle Henry VIII in vindictiveness. If only this noble prince, grieved Pitscottie,

> would have received the counsel of his wife and goodly lords, would have kept his body from harlotry, and had left the evil counsel of his papists, bishops and greedy courtiers, he had been the most noble Prince that ever rang in the realm of Scotland: For he was full of policy and honesty at his beginning, did so many good acts in his realms as building of palaces and castles and furnishing the realm with good artillery . . .

In January 1543, an Edinburgh parliament appointed the Earl of Arran (heir to the throne if infant Queen Mary died) as Regent. Another in March rescinded most of James's forfeitures and – under pressure from the nobles released by Henry VIII after Solway Moss, adorned with English gold chains, vehement in their support for an English marriage for baby Mary – agreed to negotiate for a ten-year truce. They had also brought with them a taste for Bibles in the vernacular, which were soon to be seen 'almost upon every gentleman's table'. Protestantism began to penetrate 'a small but influential coterie of wealthy merchants and professional men', particularly in Edinburgh. The battle lines for the next twenty years were thus delineated: French had become equated with Catholic and English with Protestant.

James's widow, tall, proud, handsome Mary of Guise (second time widow), only twenty-one years old, was as destined to be wooed as had been Margaret Tudor by lusty Angus. There followed a curious courtship pavane between the Earl of Bothwell and the Earl of Lennox, both seeking her hand and her power:

> These two earls daily frequented the court, striving in magnificence of apparel, and all courtly games, the one to exceed the other especially in the Queen's sight. The earl of Lennox . . . was of a strong body, well proportionate, of a sweet and manly visage, straight in stature and pleasant in behaviour. Bothwell was fair and whitely, something hanging-shouldered and going forward; but of a gentle and humane countenance.

They were self-deluded. Mary of Guise's affections were unwaveringly dynastic in intent: herself for Regent, and for her daughter's safe succession as Queen. It is a measure of her success that after eighteen further years of strife, George Buchanan could still praise Mary for her 'singular wit, and . . . mind very propense to equity'.

The English plans, with their overtones of Protestantism and loss of sovereignty, were welcome neither to Mary of Guise nor to Cardinal David Beaton, Scotland's leading churchman, who rallied the nationalist, Catholic interest to overturn them. The Regent, propense to wavering, wavered. But it was Henry VIII himself who sank the marriage negotiations by his haste and greed in demanding immediate custody of the baby Queen, and the ruling of Scotland by yet another Governor. As the Scots prevaricated, and Henry failed to ratify the treaty, the Regent was persuaded away from a heretical English marriage to a nationalist, Francophile policy. His former supporters duly moved into opposition. Once the infant Mary Queen of Scots had been crowned in Stirling on 9th September, 1543, King Henry decided to gain by bullying what he had lost by stealth. Tongues spoke of war. 'Upon the 16th day of December, there came a herald out of England called Harry Raa, and gave up peace between Scotland and England.' It was a sentence of execution *sine die*. The Regent and nobles vacillated: Edinburgh citizens spent an uneasy winter.

There were probably St George's Cross pennants on the 300 sails that appeared unexpectedly in the Forth on 1st May, 1544, landed near Granton and disgorged an army that marched to Leith to establish camp. Consternation seized the burgh. A small defence force manned the Netherbow: castle cannon were primed. The wealthier citizens fled the town with their 'movabill geir' (movable goods): everybody else hid. They were luckily unaware that Henry had instructed total war:

> His Majesty's pleasure is that you shall . . . put all to fire and sword, burn Edinburgh town, so razed and defaced when you have sacked and gotten what ye can of it, as there may remain forever a perpetual memory of the vengeance of God . . . Do

what you can out of hand and without long tarrying, to beat down and overthrow the Castle, sack Holyrood House, and burn and subvert it and all the rest, putting man, woman, and child to fire and sword without exception, where any resistance shall be made against you.

One of the invaders left this record:

it was determined utterly to ruinate and destroy the said town with fire; which, for the night drew fast on, we omitted thoroughly to execute on that day, but setting fire in three or four parts of the town we repaired for the night into our camp. And the next morning very early, we began where we left, and continued burning all that day and the next two days ensuing, continually, so that neither within the walls nor in the suburbs was left any one house unbrent.

It proved simple to arson some accessible thatched roofs and timber floors; much more dangerous and difficult for soldiers to venture down the hundred closes, lanes and alleyways. From the record of 'wailing of lamentation of poor women', it was clear that universal slaughter had not been achieved. After lingering sixteen days, the army sailed back down the coast, harrying as it went. From a population of about 15,000, perhaps 200 had been killed; and the town was soon busy as repairs provided healthy work for carpenters, timbermen, masons and painters. The Scottish earls, having failed to prevent the invasion, held council in the safety of Stirling to plan retaliation. Half being pensioners of Henry VIII, and the rest following a spineless Governor, no decisive plan of campaign emerged. As the chronicler noted: 'There was no credit amongst the nobility at this present.'

In 1547, the English tried again. On Saturday, 10th September, 1547, an army which had surged north along the coast met a strong Scots army on what became known as 'Black Saturday' across the Esk River at Pinkie Cleuch, by Musselburgh. To the invaders' surprise, the Scots were virtually annihilated through mis-leadership, and some 360 Edinburgh citizens (a proportion equivalent to approximately 20,000 today) were amongst those killed. The victorious English army knew better than to invade Edinburgh, fearing its tight narrow closes, plague-trapping wynds, and the powerful castle cannon. Without a fifth column, the burgh was well nigh impregnable. The army camped in the countryside near Meadowbank, and established a ring of forts throughout the Lothians centred at Haddington, to starve the city into surrender. For diversion, they trooped to Holyrood and, finding the monks all gone, 'plucked the lead from its roofs'; as lesser sport, removed the abbey's two bells, and 'did somewhat disgrace the house'.

The suburbs of Edinburgh, so patently periculous, Mary of Guise removed from twice-sacked and looted Holyrood to begin the construction of a palace within the safe masonry cocoon of Castle Hill. Under the direction of her French master mason, a splendid stone palace with large, opulent, plaster-decorated rooms, with beautifully carved stonework and timber, rose on the site of the Assembly Hall; thus confirming the north-western section of the city as the fashionable place to stay.

Six-year-old Mary Queen of Scots was spirited away, first to Inchma-home and thence to France for safety and eventual marriage with the Dauphin: for which the Regent was rewarded with the Duchy of Cha-telherault. English malice increased commensurately, illuminated by a curious progaganda pamphlet to persuade the Scots of their folly:

> What can be more for your universal commodity, profit and weal? Whereby, even at once, of foreign foes ye shall be accepted as familiar friends; of weak, ye shall be made strong: of poor rich, of bond free . . . Seek we not the mastership of you, but the fel-lowship.

Should that prove inadequately enticing, it went on:

> We have . . . a way of persuasion of the rigorous rhetoric so ven-geable, vehement (as I think ye have felt by a action or two) that if we were to use the extremity of argument, we were able to beat reason into your heads.

It is enriched by an explicit relation of how the Scots were trounced at the Battle of Pinkie Cleugh, and what outrages were planned for Scottish women if the country did not submit.

On 16th June, 1548, Mary of Guise whistled some 10,000 French troops from France; and for the next two years, the Lothians were har-ried, Scots hanged and crops destroyed as French and English invading armies trampled the land. Broken men abounded, and many drifted to the cellars of Edinburgh. The capital's role as the sump of the Scottish dispossessed grew to such grim proportions by 1554 that those moving about by night were required to take lanterns lest they became victims of the 'frequent robberies and disorders'. England and France finally signed a peace treaty in April 1550, which, as an afterthought, brought the 'Rough Wooing' to an end. Peace descended upon the capital as Mary of

Guise left on a state visit to France with her jangling nobility. Relative peace, that is: 'In this year of God 1551, all was at good rest excepting that the Laird of Cessford and Ferniehirst with their complices slew Sir Walter Scott, Laird of Buccleuch, in Edinburgh, who was a good and valiant knight.'

Edinburgh's status as the 'Paris of Scotland' was confirmed by the elevation of its chief magistrate to the majesty of Lord Provost. Such dignity demanded greater self-respect, and ordinances were duly issued (and duly ignored) for the removal of dunghills and rooting swine from the High Street and closes. When parliament addressed itself to the causes of the 'great and exorbitant dearth', it concluded that the cause was over-indulgence: the 'superfluous cheer used commonly in this realm, as well amongst small as great men'. Sumptuary laws were enacted to ration future meals: those of archbishops and earls to eight dishes of meat; of abbots, lord priors and deans six dishes of meat; of barons and freeholders four dishes of meat; and of burgess 'or other substantial man, spiritual or temporal', three dishes: 'and that one kind of meat in each dish'. An exemption was made for 'Yule and Easter, Patron Days, marriages, nor banquets to be made to strangers of other realms'.

The vacillating Duke of Chatelherault had forfeited the support of his peers by April 1554 when Mary of Guise finally managed to seize the governorship (regency). Unfortunately, she no longer trusted her bribed, suborned and divided nobles: the only salvation for her and her daughter lay with her own family and her own county – a weakness reviewed sadly by George Buchanan:

> The misery was, though the name of governess resided in her, neither did she want the virtues worthy of so great a dignity, yet she did, as it were, rule precariously: because, in all matters of moment, she was to receive answers, like so many oracles, from France.

She failed to appreciate that whilst the French might be welcomed to repel English colonialism, the English would be welcomed if the reverse applied. Few native Scots advisers were still retained by 1557, with the inevitable consequence that those used to power grouped together in opposition against the French invader. She had turned friend to enemy; and the extent of the dislike may be interpreted from Sir Richard Maitland's satire on the puffed hose, needlework, ruffled shirts, high hats and perfumed gloves of Edinburgh fashion which he ascribed to *la mode de France*.

The demise of the Catholic Church in Scotland was by no means a foregone conclusion, even after the coronation of the Protestant Queen

Elizabeth in England. Scotland's religious houses were for the most part decaying (the noble exception being the Dominican Convent of St Catherine of Siena just outside Edinburgh), largely because control of so many had been passed to powerful families or to royal bastards. Provincial councils of the Catholic church met in the Blackfriars Kirk of Edinburgh to discuss how it might be reformed from within, and introduced greater religious instruction at local level, Bibles in the vernacular and purer lives for priests.

Reforming demands were presented to Mary in November 1558 and, seen with hindsight, appear moderate: first, that all public prayers and the administration of the sacraments should be celebrated by ministers in their mother tongue that people might understand them. Second, that the election of ministers should be made by the people. Third, that those who presided over that election should enquire diligently into the lives and doctrines of all those to be admitted. Fourth, if by the negligence of former times, unlearned persons crept into ecclesiastical dignities, they might be removed out of the ministry. Of these, the Regent was disposed to agree only with the first.

A new group of nobles created the fatal confusion between politics and religion by adopting the crusading title of the Lords of the Congregation for a pro-English and anti-French party under the banner of Protestantism. The haughty and autocratic Guise princess perceived only the political aspects – the challenge to her authority – and used whatever duplicity or force was necessary to overcome it. The Reformers could not credit that the Regent was unable to distinguish between her authority and her religion. There was no meeting of intellects.

St Giles's Day, 1st September, 1558, proved to be the pivot, described here by George Buchanan:

> The inhabitants of Edinburgh look on their tutelar saint, carousing to him in great goblets, and making high entertainments for their neighbours and guests. The regent, fearing lest in such a confused rabble, some tumult should arise, was willing to be present herself . . . The papists were very glad of her coming, and easily persuaded her to see the shew and pageant, wherein St Giles was to be carried about the city: but St Giles alas! did not appear, for he was stolen out of the shrine.

The procession was not going to be halted for a missing saint. The Provost and council were directed by the archbishops either to find the old St Giles, or to replace it at their own expense. Despite its Protestant casuistry that the making of idols was against the Bible, the council had to borrow a new statue from the Greyfriars, which was nailed to a barrow. Knox relates how 'Priests, Friars, Canons and rotten Papists' assembled with tambourines and trumpets, banners and bagpipes: 'and who was there to lead the ring but the Queen Regent herself.'

Once the Regent had accompanied the procession through the greatest part of town, and spotted no danger of insurrection, Buchanan reports that she retired wearily to dine in Sandy Carpenter's house, the idol being parked in the High Street outside. Then, according to Knox, the conspirators pounced:

> and so began one to cry 'down with idol, down with it'; and so, without delay, it was pulled down . . . One took him by the heels and dadding his head to the causeway, left Dagon without head or hands and said 'Fie upon thee, thou young St Giles, thy father would have tarried four such'. This considered, we say, the Priests and Friars fled faster than they did at Pinkie Cleuch . . . Down go the crosses, off go the surplices, round capes, cornets with the crowns. The Greyfriars gaped, the Blackfriars blew and the Priests panted and fled . . . for such a sudden fray came never amongst the generation of AntiChrist within this realm before.

The Regent's marriage of her daughter to the French Dauphin had included the 'crown matrimonial' by which the Scottish crown would pass by marriage to the eventual King of France. Scotland was thereby likely to become a provincial appendage of a staunchly Catholic country. That, the Lords of the Congregation set out to forestall. On 1st January, 1559, solitary and bleary-eyed revellers would have been able to see a mysterious 'Beggars' Summons' affixed to the doors of the Blackfriars and Greyfriars, in Edinburgh as elsewhere throughout the country. It recalled not just Martin Luther's celebrated declaration of defiance but revived that mystical element used in the attempt to warn James IV against invading England in 1513. Issued on behalf of the dispossessed of Scotland, the Beggars' Summons warned all friars to vacate their properties in favour of the poor and infirm by Whitsun next.

Anticipating trouble, Mary of Guise 'caused cast the fort of Leith to an great strength and victual the same . . .' on 19th February; John Knox re-entered Scotland on 2nd May, and nine days later inflamed the citizens of Perth to the sacking of religious houses in that city, in an affray now regarded as the overture to the Reformation. Protestants and Catholics growled at each other through Fife before the Regent retreated first to Edinburgh and thence to Dunbar to await reinforcement from France. On 28th June, God's thugs (otherwise the Earls of Glencairn and Argyll supported by Lord Ruthven) put Edinburgh's religious houses to the sack: and the country slid towards civil war. The Regent's suspicion about the nature of the rebellion was confirmed when the Lords of the Congregation seized the Royal Mint, that symbol of regal authority. She occupied Leith and, from a position of military strength, negotiated a truce to the effect that 'no man should be compelled in matters of religion'. The Congregation quit Edinburgh three days later, but returned in mid-October with 17,000 men, to lay siege to Leith.

The Queen left the safety of her palace on Castle Hill and marched down to defend Leith with D'Oysel, the French army, a bibleful of bishops and Lord Seton. The Congregation occupied the citadel and demanded the departure of all Frenchmen from Scotland. They purified the churches of idolatry and images and, six days later, suspended Mary's regency, without the strength to enforce it. In the evening ten days later, the Congregation slipped out again, leaving 'their artillery void upon the causeway lying, and the town desolate'. Frenchmen reoccupied the town 'and lodged in the same to the great hurt of the inhabitants thereof'. Intent on restoring the altars and images in the kirks, they discovered that the Reformers had hoped to communicate with their new congregations by having the Lord's Prayer, the Belief, and Commandments 'patent upon the Kirk walls'. They were promptly 'blotted out', and St Giles was returned to its original state of white walls with green pillars (so much more vivid than the sepulchral gloom of today).

Although nominally the stronger, the strain proved too much for the Regent. Already ill, her condition was exacerbated by the sight of the first eight English ships which sailed up the Forth in late January, to be followed two months later by an English army of 5,000 footmen and 1,800 light horsemen. She retired to the castle, where she expired on 11th June, leaving an unhappy, war-ravaged and demoralised country, with some of the most elaborate and advanced fortifications in Europe surrounding Leith. A month later, the Treaty of Edinburgh provided for the retiral of all armies; and as soon as they had begun to move out, work began upon the demolition of the fortifications of Leith.

> How hurtful the fortification of Leith has been . . . and how prejudicial this same shall be to the liberty of this whole country, in case strangers shall at any time hereafter intrude themselves therein.

Never again were they going to let it be used as a counter against Edinburgh.
burgh.

CHAPTER FOUR

COCKPIT OF SCOTLAND

Mary Queen of Scots had been crowned Queen of France in September 1559. She had not yet resolved the question of a new Regent to replace her mother in Scotland when the Lords of the Congregation summoned a parliament to Edinburgh in 1560. It was thus with doubtful legality that the Three Estates proceeded to reform the Scottish state religion. They authorised the Protestant Confession of the Faith, banned the hearing of Mass, and abolished the jurisdiction of the Pope. They introduced an innovative and positive programme of education and local religion with parish ministers in schools.

In the baggage of the new religion was a new moral code: one more preoccupied with the externals of harlotry, adultery, fornication and swearing (with which it was pleased to identify Catholic priests) than with a more rounded philosophy. Not only were murder and infanticide soon to be shown as perfectly acceptable, but the code bore more heavily upon lesser men. That an influential reformer like Mark Ker, Commendator of Newbattle, had kept a concubine for fifteen years before he married her, fathering an illegitimate child as well, posed little difficulty. But the Deacon of Edinburgh Fleshers, John Sanderson, however, was condemned to banishment for adultery on the specious ground that his divorce had been granted by the old (thereby Catholic) courts. Sanderson was supported by his fellow Deacons of the Hammermen and the Tailors and some sixty craftsmen in the riot that followed: and yet the poor man remained deprived of office and goods.

Edinburgh merchants desired an orderly change from one religion to the other with minimum disruption to authority and trade; and when the Reformers overthrew the craft chapels in St Giles, they took great pains to safeguard the treasures with which they had been endowed. Yet a new strict Sabbatarianism disrupted the rhythm of Edinburgh life: the flesh market, customarily held on Sunday, had to be rescheduled to a weekday and now clashed with the food market. The town remained unsettled: stability had been disturbed by the recent Civil War, the absence of a Regent created a vacuum, and there was deep unease at the fundamental shifts in religion and established practices. The monasteries in the south side lay sacked, gaping and ruined. The town's cliffs, crannies and rookeries were filled with the 'broken men of weir' only too keen for a brawl: cattle who, for example, were prepared to support Logan of Restalrig in his threat to be 'evin with you' after the council had instructed that his mistress be carted through the town for adultery; and assisted the parson of Penicuik in his escape from the Tolbooth. The situation was explosive.

An unnecessarily harsh execution sentence passed upon a cordiner, James Killone, for re-enacting the old Catholic masque of Robin Hood, proved the catalyst. His fellow-craftsmen appealed to the town's minister John Knox, to the Provost and to the bailies for clemency; but they, stern men, 'would do nothing but have him hanged'. Even 'the craftsmen's children and servants passed to armour; and first they howled Alexander Guthrie, Provost and Baillies in the said Alexander's writing booth, and then came down again to the Cross, danged down the gibbet and brake it in pieces.' They stormed the Tolbooth, released Killone (and all other prisoners) and tried to leave through the Netherbow, which they found barred. As they surged back uphill to the Upper Bow, a town official opened fire from the Tolbooth with a hagbutt. This incautious act turned what had been a jolly rescue mission into a major bloody riot, guns used on both sides. Provost and baillies were trapped within the Tolbooth. Armed intervention by the Constable of the Castle was needed to rescue them, and a proclamation of a full amnesty at the Cross to quiet the tumult.

The interregnum was solved by the tragic early death of Queen Mary's husband, King Francis; and the widowed Mary Queen of Scots landed at Leith on 19th August, 1561. Perhaps because her ships could not be seen from the capital through an unusually thick haar, she was earlier than had been expected, and waited to be received for an hour in one of the many substantial merchants' houses in Leith (the only one to survive), that belonging to Andrew Lamb. Knox read dreadful omens into the haar: there 'was never seen a more dolourous face of the heaven than was at her arrival which two days after did so continue . . . That forewarning gave God unto us; but alas the most part were blind.' Those involved in the bitter fight against the late Regent's Catholicism, and her obedience to the Guise family were scarcely comforted by the sight of the new Queen's Guise uncles accompanying her down the gangplank into Scotland.

She was granted only five days of mirth, melody and quietness before a near-murderous attack on her Catholic priest disclosed the extent of her country's disorder. The Lords of the Congregation were 'gritumly annoyit' that he prepared to say Mass at Holyrood so openly, and might have slaughtered him but for the regal shoulders of Mary's half-brother Lord James Stewart. Knox opened war the following Sunday, with the first salvo of attacks on the Queen and her Mass over the next month.

Mary's entry to her capital on 2nd September was joyous, escorted by a convoy of fifty young men,

> their bodies and thighs covered with yellow taffeta, their arms and legs from the knee down bare, coloured with black in the manner of Moors, upon their heads black hats, and on their faces black vizors, in their mouths rings garnished with precious stones, about their necks, legs and arms infinite of chains of gold; together with sixteen of the most honest men of the town clad in velvet gowns and velvet bonnets, bearing and going about the canopy under which her Highness rode – which canopy was fine purple velvet lined with red taffeta, fringed with gold and silk.

At the Butter Tron, she passed through a timber gate painted with fine colours and hung with sundry arms, upon which

> were singing certain bairns in the most heavenly ways: under the which gate there was a cloud opening with 4 leaves into which there was put a bonny bairn. And when the Queen's Highness was coming through the said port, the said cloud opened and the bairn descended down as it had been an angel.

The heavenly cherub offered the Queen the keys of the town, a Bible, Psalm book, and 'three writings, the tenor thereof uncertain'. More speeches at the Tolbooth attended by virgins clad in precious attire adorning a scaffold. The hullabaloo at the Mercat Cross – whose spouts ran with wine in great abundance – was heightened by the tinkling crashes of 'people casting their glasses'. More speeches and more erections at the Salt Tron, and yet more again (and another scaffold) at the Netherbow where a dragon, having made a speech, was duly burned.

Knox left no record of his model Presbyterian matron; but it cannot have been a sophisticated, handsome, lusty, half-French widow whose depth of learning, and fondness for dance, poetry, cards, gaming, dancing, jokes and prancing with her familiars in men's clothes – a quartet of Maries in breeches – were the result of her fourteen years of French education. Fate had so arranged it that the two opposites in the Scots psyche should have occupied critical positions at the same time in Scotland. She believed in mutual toleration: he did not understand the concept.

Two days after her triumphal entrance, Mary summoned Knox to a private audience at Holyrood, attended only by her half-brother Lord James. Knox's status was that of the town's minister. He was no Archbishop of Canterbury nor Cardinal of Lorraine, and his audience with the Queen confirms Edinburgh's standing not so much as the capital of Scotland (its town minister speaking for the nation) as its place as the pith of the Reformed Church. The Queen accused him of having 'raised the great part of her subjects against her mother and against herself'. Knox riposted: 'So long as that ye defile not your hands with the blood of the Saints of God, neither I nor that Book shall hurt you or your Authority.' He added, more ominously, that if 'princes exceed their bounds, Madam, and do against wherefor they should be obeyed, it is no doubt that they may be resisted, even by power.' Knox's assessment at the end of the interview was that 'if there not be in her a proud mind, a crafty wit and an enduring heart against God and his truth, my judgment faileth me.' Accommodation formed no part of his strategy.

When the town council reissued the standard proclamation at the Cross of Edinburgh commanding 'all and sundry monks, friars, priests and other Papists and profane persons . . . to pass forth of Edinburgh within the next 24 hours after Halloween, under pain of burning upon the cheek and the hurling of them through the town', the Queen suspected conspiracy and mockery. Livid at those who, she thought deliberately, had insulted her by lumping her priests together with fornicators and whoremongers, she dismissed Provost and baillies and appointed the stolid Thomas MacKalzean as Provost instead.

Mary's Edinburgh was a wealthy community of some 300 merchants, 401 craftsmen, and a total population of around 12,500 within the walls. The leading craft guilds were horsemen, skinners, furriers, tailors and goldsmiths. Its suburb, the Canongate, with only 2,000 inhabitants, was smaller, more select, and utterly dependent upon the palace. Trade had been prospering, new houses were being built, money was being made: the time had come to buy control of Leith. On 6th October, 1565, Edinburgh offered to lend the Queen 10,000 merks in return for the superiority of Leith, for which they taxed 381 Edinburgh burghers, the preponderance being lent by twenty-five lawyers. Four days later, the Provost, baillies, deacons and the community marched proprietorially down to Leith 'and there, in the Tolbooth thereof, received estate and seized the Superiority'.

The Queen's dealings with the town were usually subtle: she exerted influence by the preferment of good, sound, moderate (and wealthier) Protestant burgesses, to the exclusion of the zealot (and generally poorer) hardliners; and they responded favourably. The two things dearest to the

Edinburgh burgess were his inherited privileges and their consequent financial benefit. He was far more concerned with ensuring a stable transition from the old order and status than with hell-fire; and that the transformation was achieved with so little civic disorder and only minor petty revenge is a matter for admiration. This self-interested inertia may explain why Knox ranted and fulminated to the degree he did: it was frustration.

In response to the plea 'our town contains a large number of inhabitants, and many of them are poor,' the Queen was prevailed to grant the lands of the Blackfriars to the council for a new poor hospital. The religious situation remained tense: a riot was sparked off simply by an unusually large attendance at the celebration of Mass at Holyrood, but, in April 1565, was followed by the potentially much more volatile one when fanatics dragged a respected former St Giles priest, James Tarbot, from saying Mass in private, humiliated him at the Cross, and pelted him with, so it was said, 10,000 eggs. Yet the city always pulled back from major religious conflict. Disorder was not in the interests of the burgesses.

Scots politicians were preoccupied with the matter of the Queen's marriage, she being young and presumably like her mother, grandmother, and most of her male ancestors: very lusty. An heir was needed for the nation's stability. Disastrously, Mary Queen of Scots fell for the eighteen-year-old, long-shanked but vacuous Henry, Lord Darnley, son of the Earl of Lennox, distantly related to the thrones of both Scotland and England, persisting against stern advice. The marriage was duly celebrated according to Catholic rites in the Old Chapel at Holyrood, with some magnificence but little noble support, on 29th July, 1565.

By her marriage, the Queen was thought to have abandoned her factional neutrality and taken sides with the Lennoxes. Many nobles, including her half-brother Lord James Stewart (now Earl of Moray) who had advised her objectively for over three years, refused to attend the wedding. They were forfeited, harried by the Queen furth of the realm and formed a new opposition. The diarist recorded revelry and Renaissance splendour back in Holyrood.

> On 10th February 1565 . . . in the evening, our Sovereign made a banquet to the Ambassador in the old chapel of Holyrood House, which was re-apparelled with fine tapestry and hung magnificently, and the said Lords made masquery after supper in an honourable manner. And upon the eleventh day . . . the King and Queen, in like manner, banqueted the same Ambassador; and at even, our Sovereign made the masquery and mumchance,

in which the Queen's Grace, and all her Maries and ladies were clad in men's apparel.

The new King was soon to prove himself worse than vacuous. 'Crabbit' after a sermon he attended in St Giles on 19th August, Darnley inflamed Edinburgh merchants by trying to 'cause discharge the said John [Knox] of his preaching'. The merchants would tolerate no interference with the town's minister, and after they complained to the Queen, Knox was restored to his pulpit: and Darnley became the resentful focus of conspiracy.

The decisive attempt was a ploy by various lords to cause the death of the pregnant Queen, through miscarriage, by subjecting her to a peculiarly Gothic extravaganza. Had they succeeded, the lords (particularly the deviously appalling Earl of Morton) would have been able to rule the country under a weak and pliable twenty-year-old long-shanked fop. The victim was a misshapen Savoyard called David Riccio, 'a merry fellow and a good musician' who, by virtue of his suitability as the fourth voice in the Queen's madrigal group, had come to be appointed her French Secretary. He interpolated himself between the nobles and the Queen, and the resentment it caused was recorded by Buchanan:

> The sudden advancement of this man from a low and almost beggarly estate to so much power, wealth and dignity, afforded a matter of discourse to the people. His fortune was above his virtue; his arrogance, contempt of his equals and contention with his superiors were above his fortune. The vanity and madness of the man was much increased and nourished by the flattery of the nobility; who sought his friendship, courted him, admired his judgment, walked before his lodgings, and observed his levee.

When Sir William Douglas approached him to offer £1,000 to persuade the Queen to lay aside the Earl of Moray's forfeiture, 'hes answer wes 20 thowsand'. It was quite insupportable: Riccio had to go, and the manner of his going might achieve several objectives at a stroke.

'This vile act' was done upon a Saturday at six o'clock at night, when the Queen was at supper in her closet. A number of armed men seized the keys of the outer palace court and the Lord Ruthven and George Douglas led a party upstairs through the King's chamber, whilst the rest remained without with drawn swords in their hands crying, 'A Douglas, a Douglas'. Ruthven, who had been very ill, is recorded as appearing white as a sheet in full armour, as though to enhance the spectral horror of the occasion. Sir James Melville recorded:

The King was before gone up to the Queen, and was leaning upon her chair, when the Lord Ruthven entered with his helmet upon his head, and George Douglas and divers others with them so rudely and irreverently that the table, candles, meat and dishes were overthrown. Riccio took the Queen about the waist, crying for mercy, but George Douglas plucked out the King's dagger, and stroked Riccio first with it, leaving it sticking in him. He making great shrieks and cries was rudely snatched from the Queen, who could not prevail either with threats or entreaties to save him. But he was forcibly drawn out forth the closet and slain in the outer hall and Her Majesty kept as a captive.

The Earls of Atholl, Bothwell and Huntly, of the Queen's faction, escaped only by leaping through a window in the Earl of Lennox's lodgings and out through the garden where the lions were lodged. The town beat to arms, but upon entering the outer courtyard the Provost was reassured by the King, Darnley, appearing at a window to say that there was no cause for alarm. The Queen failed to miscarry and escaped about midnight the following night, bent on revenge. The conspiring lords were duly banished, and the Earl of Moray and his faction were restored to favour. All was at an end between Mary and Darnley.

Riccio was murdered on 9th March, 1566. Most of the noble murderers, including the Earl of Morton, retreated across the Border: Knox, who could condemn harlotry but connive at bloodshed, fled to Ayr. There was a vacuum at court: and as the Queen became distant from Darnley, she showed a growing attachment to the powerful Earl of Bothwell, hereditary High Admiral of Scotland, and sheriff of both Edinburgh and Haddington. She visited him in Hermitage Castle, Liddesdale, as he lay badly wounded after a skirmish, bringing upon herself a near-fatal illness at Jedburgh. She recovered unexpectedly and attended James VI's baptism in Stirling, whilst his father, ill with syphilis (Darnley's record as King was scarcely noble) retreated to the safety of his family's domain in Glasgow. The Queen (it being said by some that, already pregnant by Bothwell, she sought to resume relations with Darnley to legitimise her child) induced Darnley to return to Edinburgh to convalesce in the Provost's Lodging, one of the large stone houses with timber galleries, which acted as a cloister around the well of the Kirk o' Field.

On Sunday evening, 9th February, 1567, whilst she was down in Holyrood mirthfully celebrating the wedding of Bastien, one of her pages (on a Sabbath no less), Darnley and his valet Taylor were murdered. Their corpses were found virtually unmarked, as though they had been smothered, carefully laid out in a walled orchard on the far side of the Thief

Row. An enormous explosion, which utterly destroyed the north side of the cloister buildings, acted as advertisement for the deed.

The accepted verdict is that the Earl of Bothwell had planned to blow up the sick King pretending it was an accident; but the victims woke, escaped, were captured in the orchard and were strangled there. It makes no sense. The explosion was intended to conceal the bodies rather than lay them to public view. Why leave the bodies so clearly laid out if not as further advertisement for the deed? Nor was there any sign of strangulation. It would have been scarcely easy for a syphilitic bedridden for months to clamber through or over two defensive walls. Lastly, if they had been strangled in the orchard, why then bother to blow up the buildings at all without taking back their bodies to be concealed in the ruins?

The only conclusion is that Bothwell was encouraged to pursue his naïve plan of staging an 'accident' by deeper conspirators who planned to exploit the useful murder of Darnley by ensuring that the blame stuck hard to Bothwell and the Queen herself. In that way, they would be relieved of all three. So who might they have been? The prime suspect is the Earl of Morton, head of the Douglas faction, revealed by his portrait as a powerful and dangerous Renaissance prince, wealthy but driven by cupidity, powerful but tempted to govern the kingdom itself. Morton admitted on his scaffold many years later prior knowledge that Bothwell planned the explosion by placing the gunpowder in the vaulted kitchens of Darnley's house. Perhaps, before the fuses were lit, Darnley and Taylor were smothered (which might explain the lack of mark upon the bodies) by Morton's men (which might explain the cry heard by Edinburgh natives of 'Mercy, kinsmen' – since Darnley was related to the Douglases). The corpses were then spirited over the walls to be laid out for public display in the orchard, whilst Bothwell's simple souls then unwittingly ignited the gunpowder, without realising what they were going to conceal had softly and silently vanished away.

The plan worked. Edinburgh citizens rushed to the scene to find ruins and two virtually unblemished corpses as they were meant to do. Bothwell was accused, acquitted in a palpably fixed trial, and then retreated to his lands. The outrage in Europe was universal: for Darnley was considered King, and his murder parricide.

> All Scotland cried out upon the foul murder of the King, but few
> of them were careful how to revenge it, till they were driven
> thereto by the crying out of all other nations against all Scots-
> men wherever they travelled, either by sea or by land.

Events thereafter moved speedily to a conclusion. Bothwell intercepted the Queen near Linlithgow on her return from Stirling, and took her to Borthwick, then to Dunbar. A rumour reached the capital that the Queen had been kidnapped:

> Incontinent, the common bell rang and the inhabitants thereof ran to armour and weapons, the ports were barred and the artillery of the castle shot; but the matter, as is reported, was devised by Her Highness' own consent, to cause the rumour pass that he had ravished her; but it was rather done for the staunch of the mouths of the people that alleged that the said earl was more familiar with Her Grace of long before than modesty required.

When the couple returned to Edinburgh a fortnight later, onlookers noted gloomily that the Earl Bothwell led the Queen's Majesty by the bridle as captive. The atmosphere in the palace was thunderous. For all his courtesy, his charm, and his fluent French, Bothwell was a dangerous boor: and Holyrood acquired evil and dangerous Renaissance overtones. Sir James Melville sought to show the Queen a letter from England, which warned of the damage to her reputation if she married Bothwell. Mary's secretary Lethington

> took me by the hand and drew me aside to see the said letter; which, when he had read, he asked what had been in my mind; for, says he, so soon as the Earl Bothwell gets notice hereof, as I fear he will very shortly, he will caused you to be killed . . . He said, I had done more honestly than wisely, and therefore I pray you, says he, retire diligently before the Earl of Bothwell comes up from his dinner.

There next followed the small matter of Bothwell's divorce. He had been married at the Queen's instigation to one of her confidantes, Lady Jean Gordon, sister of all-powerful Huntly. Lady Jean, with her knowing eyes, sensual lips and Mona Lisa smile, had been in love with Ogilvy of Boyne, who was then building himself a splendid palace near Portsoy, but the Queen being the Queen, she had submitted. Now, not least as the consequence of distaste she had for her husband's ploughing of her maids (Lady Jean finally obtained Ogilvy as her third husband in a post-prandial stage of life), she concurred equally easily with the Queen's suggestion of a divorce. Mary, having created Bothwell Duke of Orkney, married him in the Old Chapel in Holyrood, 'not with a mass but with preaching'. Ominously, 'there was not many of the nobility of this realm thereat'; and the atmosphere was foreboding, most unlike a normal royal wedding:

'There was neither pleasure nor pastime as use was wont to be used when Princes were married.'

Melville returned for the marriage, 'to find my Lord Duke of Orkney sitting at his supper'. Bothwell welcomed him with all the gracious hospitality of a lion to a mouse, and invited him to join the throng supping at the table with him. Sensing danger, Melville declined:

> I said I had already supped. Then he called for a cup of wine and drank to me saying, 'You need to grow fatter for, says he, the zeal of the Commonwealth has eaten you up and made you lean' . . . Then he fell in discoursing with the gentlewomen, speaking such filthy language that they and I left him, and went up to the Queen who expressed much satisfaction at my coming.

Mary had poor taste in men and her disillusionment with Bothwell was speedier than it had been with Darnley. Within days, he had become

> so beastly and suspicious, that he suffered her not to pass one day in patience without making her shed an abundance of tears. Thus part of his own company detested him, other part of them believed that Her Majesty would fain have been quit of him, but thought shame to be the doer thereof directly herself.

The marriage was unacceptable to the large body of the senior Scots lords who, led by the Earls of Morton and Moray, now proposed to remove the infant Prince James from the Queen's influence. They occupied Edinburgh with an army, making the council frantic lest the Queen thought it had done anything to welcome such an invasion. Bothwell's adherents gathered in East Lothian, and the two armies came to face each other at Carberry Hill, near Dalkeith, on 15th June, one month after the wedding. Many of those who supported the lords had the sole, short-term objective of removing the Queen from Bothwell's malign influence. It was a cutting out exercise. Perhaps naïvely, Kirkcaldy of Grange therefore persuaded the Queen to abandon the engagement without bloodshed, and to accompany the lords back into Edinburgh, permitting Bothwell to return to his own fortress unmolested. Willy-nilly, she did so as a prisoner:

> At last, a little before night, she entered Edinburgh, her face being covered with dust and tears, as if dirt had been thrown upon it; all the people running out to see the spectacle, she passed through a great part of the city in great silence, the multi-

54

tude leaving her so narrow a passage that scarce one could go abreast; when she was going up to her lodging, one woman of the company prayed for her.

She was lodged opposite the Mercat Cross, guest of the man that she herself had appointed Lord Provost of Edinburgh, Sir Simon Preston of Craigmillar (a 'right Epicurean' according to John Knox). The Queen felt an affinity with the Prestons, and had enjoyed several visits to their château at Craigmillar. But there was little enjoyment that night.

> Her Majesty again cried out to all the gentlemen and others who passed up and down the streets, declaring how that she was their native princess, and she doubted not but all honest subjects would respect her as they ought to do, and not suffer her to be abused.

But abused she was: even Secretary Maitland of Lethington refused to respond when she shouted his name from the window. There is a whiff of Morton-paid rentacrowd about Mary's harassment and the waving of Darnley's banners before her balcony, to counteract a growing sympathy from Edinburgh natives. To preclude rescue, she was swiftly removed form within Edinburgh to the relative safety of Holyrood and thence to the fortified island of Loch Leven. She was marooned in the castle of Sir William Douglas, the Early of Moray's half-brother, and Morton's heir.

Those who had supported the cutting out exercise now began to perceive its secret agenda. Soon after the Queen had endured a miscarriage of twins (almost certainly conceived before her marriage to Bothwell), she was visited by her half-brother, the Earl of Moray. He had come not to seek an accommodation but to justify his invitation to accept the regency from his fellow-lords. The Queen, as Sir James Melville recorded, was clearly expecting something else.

> Instead of comforting her and following the good counsel he had gotten, he entered instantly with Her Majesty in reproaches, giving her such injurious language as was like to break her heart. We who found fault with that manner of procedure, lost his favour. The injuries were such that they cut the thread of love and credit betwixt the Queen and him forever.

The Queen signed a deed of resignation under duress, claiming correctly that it had no legal validity. Yet it was used as the means of the appointment of Moray as Regent.

Since it is improbable that the move to dispossess the Queen would have been successful without a credible, quasi-royal alternative, Moray was pivotal in sixteenth-century Scots history. He had been a strong supporter of his half-sister to begin with, acting as her principal counsellor until the Darnley marriage. Thereafter, he was either uncertain or in outright opposition. By temperament something of a Puritan ('when he had any spare time from war, he would sit all day long in the College of Judges, so that his presence struck such reverence into them that the poor were not oppressed . . . after dinner and supper, he always caused a Chapter of the Holy Bible to be read'), he began to reveal the characteristics of his father James V in behaviour (as he had already done facially) once he assumed power. To Melville's distress,

> he would credit nothing but what came from his own familiars, who told him nothing but of fair weather . . . It was a grievous thing to see that good Regent . . . so led after other men's vain pretences and affections.

Like all Stewarts, Moray listened to favourites and flatterers, and was not exempt from cupidity. Almost immediately upon becoming Regent, he possessed himself of his sister's royal estate, even to the extent of purloining her famous black pearls and offering them for sale throughout Europe.

Mary, escaping from Loch Leven, fled to her supporters in the west of Scotland; but her infatuation with Bothwell was still bruited abroad, and generated substantial support for Moray and the 'King's Men' (as they were known, for the baby prince had by now been crowned.) The Queen was defeated at Langside, near Glasgow, fled south-west to Dundrennan, and thence inadvisedly to England.

The worst years in Edinburgh's history began with a reaffirmation by the stern leaders of the King's Men of the basic antipathy that Scots Protestantism professed for fornication. The Mercat Cross of Edinburgh redounded with this:

> that if any person or persons within his realm . . . shall commit the filthy vice of fornication and be convict thereof, that the committers thereof shall be punished in the manner following. That is to say for the first fault, both the man and woman shall pay a sum of £14: or then both he and she shall be imprisoned for the space of 8 days, their food to be bread and small drink, and thereafter presented to the mercat place of the town or parish, bareheaded, and there stand fastened, that they may not remove for the space of 2 hours; as from 10 hours to 12 hours at noon.

Further offences would bring greater fines and imprisonment; the persistent would be taken to the deepest and foulest water of the town (and Edinburgh's waters were indeed deep and foul) to be thrice ducked and thereafter banished. The income from adultery (that is to say the fines thus raised) was to be kept in a closed box, and disposed towards pious use.

When plague infested Edinburgh in 1568, the town council ordered all affected persons to remove with their furniture to the Burgh Muir. Whenever anybody fell sick, 'in whatsoever kind of sickness it ever should be', they had to shut their doors and neither come out nor admit any person into their house until visited by the baillies of their quarter. The plague persisted the following year, the consequence whereof was famine. Yet parliament still found it necessary to control indulgence and consumption of 'drugs, confectionaries and spices brought from foreign countries and sold at dear prices' and reintroduced rationing and control of imports according to rank. Gorgeous dress was anathema. Unless you were titled, landed, or had substantial yearly rent, you were forbidden to use 'any cloth of gold, or silver, velvet, satin, damask, taffeta . . . or embroidery of gold, silver or of silk, nor yet linen, camisole or woollen cloth, made and brought from any foreign countries'. Fines were substantial.

The Regent Moray coalition, purporting to act in the name of the infant King James VI, maintained a precarious order by virtue of Moray's own semi-royal status and personal authority. It duly generated an opposition rooting for the Queen, known as the Queen's Men or Marians, whose support was far wider than Knox or Buchanan would have us believe, led by Sir William Kirkcaldy of Grange, Huntly, the Earl of Argyll and the Hamiltons. Both sides claimed to act on behalf of a crowned head of state. Discord was fomented by the 'double dealer and sower in discord', the evil English ambassador, Thomas Randolph. The Marians had by no means lost hope of getting their Queen back, whereas the King's Men were determined to prevent it.

The tentative stability of the country was terminated by the murder of the Regent Moray on 23rd January, 1570 at Linlithgow by Hamilton of Bothwellhaugh. To the Earl of Morton's clear surprise and displeasure, the Mercat Cross of Edinburgh on 17th July, 1570 redounded with the election of the frail, elderly and very weak Earl of Lennox as 'chosen Tutor and Governor and Regent of James King of Scots until the time he may be able to govern his realm himself.' Lennox was Darnley's father, inclined 'to peace' but 'ignorantly driven on by the Earl of Morton', and but putty in Randolph's fingers. Two months later, the Mercat Cross echoed to declarations of civil war – namely, the forfeiture of the princi-

pal Queen's Men: Maitland of Lethington, the commendators Colding-
ham and Kilwinning, the Archbishop of Glasgow, James, Duke of Cha-
telherault, the Earl of Arran and Lord Hamilton.

In retaliation, the Queen managed to arrange for her French relatives
to issue 'a proclamation . . . through all the ports and havens [of France],
that no ship or merchant goods of Scotland within the bounds or havens
of the same with their merchants and goods should leave unless they had
the Queen's authority'. Edinburgh merchants, those burgeoning European traders, watched their hard-won stability and enterprise yet again
withering. It would have been little consolation to watch the early suc-
cesses of the theocratic sex police or 'seizers' who provided entertainment
on 1st September, 1570: the burning of John Swan and the blacksmith
John Litstar on the Castle Hill of Edinburgh 'for committing the horrible
sin of sodomy'. The *Diurnal*'s author observed: 'In no time heretofore was
it heard that any persons in this country were found guilty of this crime.'
Vigilance, however, had improved. Next followed – upon the Castle Hill
of Edinburgh – the burning together of the Bonar brother and sister
'because they had carnal copulation together'.

Regent Lennox was accidentally killed on 3rd September, 1571, in
Stirling, during an abortive coup at which William Kirkcaldy of Grange,
Captain of Edinburgh Castle, hoped to seize the entire council. Morton,
to his deep displeasure, still failed to be appointed Regent, which fell to
John Erskine, Earl of Mar. So, fourteen months later, Morton invited
Mar to supper in Dalkeith, whereafter he expired rapidly to widespread
speculation of poisoning. Morton's time had now come. Reckoned to be
the greediest man in Scotland, second in wealth only to the Earl of
Huntly, his arrogance and ambition were reflected in his châteaux
and palaces at Dalkeith (now transmogrified), Drochil (now ruined),
and Aberdour. Accommodation with the Queen's Men formed no part
of his strategy.

Kirkcaldy of Grange transformed Edinburgh back into a fortified citadel holding out for his Queen. The King's Men occupied Leith, where
they could be sure of reinforcements and victualling from England. On
28th March, 1571, Kirkcaldy fortified the St Giles steeple and ran up
defences of both town and castle against likely invasion two months
later, appointing officers to watch various stretches of the town walls. In
May, hostilities erupted. The King's Men set up three cannon on Calton
Hill, 'to ding and siege the north eastern corner of the said burgh', and
on the night of the 13th attempted unsuccessfully to force the Netherbow. The following morning, Kirkcaldy had it walled up with stone, and
set up two cannon in the Blackfriars Yards to bombard houses of the
King's Men in the Canongate.

With the removal of all timberwork fronting the houses in Leith Wynd, and St Mary's Wynd in early June, hopes of reconciliation vanished. It was time for the 'movabill geir' to go: 'the inhabitants of Edinburgh left nothing in the same, and transported that might be transported therefrom'. Two days later, all doors and windows of tenements and lands on the west side of the Wynd were built up to present a huge, unbroken wall. The nerve of some 200 burgesses broke, and they snuck out from the city, passed to Leith and the King's Men. Threats of confiscation and 'punishing of their persons to the utmost rigour' were of no avail. In July, cannon and culverin from Edinburgh Castle were added to those in the Blackfriars Yard 'to ding the Abbey of Holyrood House therewith . . . but the same did little or no hurt'.

Lest the King's party in Leith, strengthened by 300 additional men of war, assault the capital, Kirkcaldy's men made such great labour in casting of gun platforms and 'the building of the ruinous walls of same, that the said burgh was never so strong since it got its first name'. When the assault came on 22nd August, however, it was not a frontal attack. Under darkness, their soldiers crept up in the 'sundry closes, houses and barns' of the Canongate next to Jason's at the Netherbow, to wait for horses from Leith laden with meal for the beleaguered city, convoyed by six soldiers in armour concealed by 'millers' weeds'. Once the Netherbow opened to let in the food convoy, the disguised soldiers would have killed the guards, blocked the gate open, and allowed the waiting troops to pour in. Unfortunately, the town's macer Thomas Barry strolled out of the Netherbow to visit his own house down the Canongate that night, and espying fully armed men skulking in its wynds, he sped back to warn the 'watchmen and the keepers of the Netherbow Port, which caused them to bar the same quickly'. The soldiers slunk away disappointed, 'avowing to slay the said Thomas Barry if ever thereafter they could apprehend him for the revealing thereof'.

Five days later, Kirkcaldy instructed the strengthening and part-rebuilding of the Netherbow using a convenient pile of the stones of the Collegiate Church of Restalrig, which Alexander Clerk had plundered to build a new house in the town.

Continuous and bloody tit-for-tat marked the dreadful year of 1571. The Leith parliament forbade anyone, on pain of forfeiture and death, from taking provisions or coal into the city; removing, at a stroke, the principal market and means of sustenance for Lothians and Borders farmers. Those who, in desperation, ignored the blockade were duly hanged. King's – or putative King's – supporters were hanged in the town, and Queen's in Leith. The vehemence reached the demolition of houses: the victim on 15th February was the house of Nicol Uddart, a burgess 'who has eschewit forth of Edinburgh', which joined some 'thirty-two large and sundrie small' properties which were rendered to rubble. Conditions within the town worsened, the weather 'vehement cold and the coals were very scant'. The King's party compelled all the inhabitants of the Canongate to flit to Leith, and all people living within two miles of the capital were required to quit their houses and lands 'that Edinburgh should have no furnishing'.

Cannonballs landed in the great fish market, held between the head of Blackfriars Wynd and Niddry's Wynd (exactly where the Scandic Crown Hotel now is):

> but, as God would, there was none slain but one and many hurt; but through the air of the said bullets, the fishes were blawin athort the gait [blowing about the street] and slates in such abundance as was marvellous to see.

The town was in its last extremity. The Queen's Men elsewhere were reaching an accommodation with the King's, and there was starvation in empty ruined streets. In a last fling, the besieged threw off the shackles of theocracy using 'all pleasures which were wont to be used in the said month of May in the old times, Robin Hood and Little John'. How the ghost of John Killone, the cordiner executed for his Robin Hood indulgences, must have smirked.

Another invasion from England induced the town to surrender on 12th May, leaving the castle isolated. Heavy artillery – cannon, gross cannons and gross culverins – surrounded the rock and submitted it to an eleven-day bombardment: the walls collapsed, King David's Tower was ruined and the well blocked. An honourable surrender was negotiated with the English, promptly repudiated by Scots avid to see the only Scots soldier of European renown – Kirkcaldy of Grange – dead: and on 3rd August, 1573, they were satisfied. Grange and goldsmith James Mossman (constructor of 'John Knox's' house) were dragged backwards in a cart and hanged at the Mercat Cross.

The next five years of the Earl of Morton's regency was a period of relative tranquillity for Edinburgh, and the citizens began the slow task of rebuilding. Yet it was uneasy. It was said openly that those with gear should not remain within the country, for unless Morton had one part of it, they would suffer for it. There were none in Scotland who eluded his attempts at extortion.

A great curiosity was the public come-uppance of one of the 'seizers', Robert Drummond, nicknamed Dr Handie. This 'great seeker and apprehender of all priests and Papists' was discovered with another man's wife.

They were both put in the stocks at the Cross after preaching, at three o'clock in the afternoon amid popular jubilation at seeing the biter bit. One of the few times that the *Diurnal*'s author uses direct quotation implies that he witnessed the gay event.

> He should have remained until six o'clock in the evening and after branded on the cheek: [but] . . . being in a great fury he said 'What wonder ye? I shall give you more occasion to wonder'. So, suddenly he took his own knife, and struck himself three or four times foranent the heart, with the which he departed. This done, the magistrates caused hurl him in a cart through the town, and the bloody knife borne behind in his hand.

Famine in early March led to a proclamation against counterfeit money, and beggars proliferated, worrying and embarrassing the lords whenever they passed and re-passed from the abbey, 'heavy and lamentable to hear'. The General Assembly the following year cast a disapproving eye on ministers seeking to be too fashionable:

> First, we think all kinds of embroidery unseemly, all facing of velvet on gowns, hose or coats, and all superfluous and vain cutting out, stitching with silks, all kinds of costly sewing of passements, or sumptuous and large stitchings with silks, all kinds of costly sewing or variant hues in shirts, and kinds of light and variant hues in clothing as red, yellow, blue and such like, which declare the lightness of mind.

It required instead 'comely and decent apparel' in a limited range of hue: 'grave colours, black, russet, grey, sad brown, or serge, winceyette camel hair'. Sad brown indeed: how well they encapsulated their dreich ambitions.

When James VI was approaching twelve, in spring 1578, he was persuaded to retrieve his authority from the Regent Morton. When the latter sought power to punish those who had suggested it under threat of resignation, they persuaded the King to accept his resignation. On 16th October, 1579, the King entered Edinburgh in state to be greeted by a large number of the honest men of the town in fine silk gowns lined with velvet, and on the 23rd, there was a formal procession from Holyrood to the Tolbooth for the state opening of parliament: 'the Crown being borne before His Majesty by Archibald of Angus, the sceptre by Colin Earl of Argyle, Chancellor, and the Sword of Honour by Robert Earl of Lennox.'

Morton, who had outlived his usefulness, fell the following year. The English were 'angry at him for the time, because of his slowness to answer their turns'. Friends had been won only 'by his great wealth' and 'he was loved by none, and envied and hated by many.' He was executed in June 1581 on the charge of prior knowledge of the murder of Darnley. Morton had introduced his execution toy the 'Maiden' (an early form of guillotine) only to become one of its first victims. As the contemporary proverb had it: 'A swine that is fat is the cause of its own death.'

The King had a new French favourite – Esmé Stewart, Lord D'Aubigny, whose cosmopolitan influence alarmed old-guard Protestant lords. Once he became elevated to the ill-fated title of Earl of Lennox, there followed another cutting out operation. Just as his mother had been parted from Bothwell, James was seized by the Earl of Gowrie and his colleagues in August 1582. Lennox was forced into exile, and orthodoxy was reasserted. Ill pleased and humiliated, the King forgave neither the people nor their purpose. He complained bitterly to Sir James Melville, who visited him at Falkland, 'that he thought that he was but a beast by all neighbour princes for suffering so many indignities'. He escaped from Gowrie in 1583, had him executed and appointed as Chancellor the wise and learned Earl of Arran. Maitland of Thirlestane became Secretary.

James sought to retrieve authority over the Kirk which, during his minority, had been usurped by extreme Presbyterians convinced of their direct line from God. (James Melville innocently recorded his wonder at how 'God glorified himself notably with that Ministry of Edinburgh in those days'). The Black Acts of May 1584 confirmed the power of the King over all persons and estate, and reintroduced the authority of bishops. It summoned down upon the royal pate the wrath and denunciations of Andrew Melville, a fiery Presbyterian demagogue nicknamed 'The Blast' who had picked up the mantle of John Knox. Just as Knox had had a private interview with Mary, so did Melville with James: 'Mr Andrew bore down [the King] and uttered the commission as from the mighty God, calling the King but God's sillie vassal, and taking him to be the slave.' In due course, 'The Blast' would learn from imprisonment and exile that where it came to an insult to his dignity, the young James had the memory of an elephant.

As the King approached his twenty-first birthday, he displayed unusual showmanship in striving to unite the country behind him as supreme monarch. He staged a peace banquet for his aristocracy, straining to persuade them 'to like one another so well, and to enter into such familiarity, carousing and merriment'. After supper, he persuaded the Earls of Angus, Montrose, Crawford, Mar and Glencairn, and the Master of Glamis, to walk in pairs, hand in hand with other noblemen and gentlemen, from Holyrood up the Canongate to the Mercat Cross where the Provost and baillies had a table groaning with desserts which 'occasioned very great joy and mirth, and such a number of people convened thereat as the like was never seen in Edinburgh'.

Two years later, he felt secure enough to travel to Norway and Denmark to fetch his bride, whose voyage had been diverted by bad weather, and stayed away for seven months. Sir James Melville had recommended he should be accompanied by a lawyer, Mr John Skene. When the King riposted that there were many better lawyers, Melville pointed out Skene's true advantage: he was not only best acquainted with German customs, but 'could make them long harangues in Latin'.

Queen Anne of Denmark's public entrance into the town of Edinburgh had the novelty of her arriving at the West Port in a very finely ornamented coach, from which she had to alight since it would never have got up the West Bow. She was then escorted through the town to the abbey by forty-two young men of the town, clothed in white taffeta and cloth of silver, with chains of gold and black wasroms in form of Moors, dancing all the way. She was crowned, with oil, crown and a Latin harangue from Andrew Melville, in Holyrood on 17th May, 1590.

That all was not yet fully quiet was the fault of Francis, Earl of Bothwell, first cousin of the King, extreme Presbyterian and alleged warlock. Properly authenticated witches claimed he had set them upon the task of striking the King on his marriage voyage. He made four attempts upon the King: in January 1591 in Holyrood House; then when he tried to kidnap the King at Falkland Palace in June 1592; when he invaded Holyrood, allegedly to seek the King's pardon in July 1593; and lastly in April 1594 when he appears to have chased the King all the way from Leith to Edinburgh. The most characteristically menacing flavour of the time is conveyed by the 1591 episode.

The King and his court were then in residence at Holyrood, the palace probably at its peak of magnificence. Bothwell and his crew entered Holyrood precincts by a secret passage and wasted the element of surprise by their howling 'Justice, Justice, a Bothwell, a Bothwell', and fighting the porters. The porters resisted nobly, and the clashes echoed around the Outer Court. The racket alerted King, Chancellor and others who promptly barred their chamber doors to resist until relief arrived. Bothwell's own party made directly for the Queen's chamber door, where the King was supposed to be; but whilst the King was spirited upstairs, it was stoutly defended by the Master of the Queen's Household, before it was splintered, broken by hammers, and a 'great fire' was started to burn the rest.

The Chancellor, elsewhere in the palace, was defending his own door and causing his men to shoot continually, both out of the windows and through the door itself. Sir James Melville, who also happened to be supping in Holyrood, was a spectator 'of that strange hurly burly for the space of an hour, withholding by torch light forth of the Duke's Gallery their reeling, their rumbling with halberts, the clacking of their culverins and pistols, the dunting of bells and hammers, and their crying justice! justice!' Only once reinforcements arrived in the Outer Court did the Duke of Lennox venture to leave his chamber and give chase to Bothwell, who fled. Some of his companions were caught and executed forthwith.

The next disturbance was less idiosyncratic. Extreme Presbyterians had remained convinced that the Catholic lords of the north-east represented Satan at his most poisonous, and their continued toleration threatened the precariously established state religion. They criticised the King and his consort for their toleration of them, to say nothing of regal backsliding and frivolity. But in 1596, by forcing a trial of strength, they overreached themselves.

To judge by the pullulating fulminations from the pulpit, it had been clear for some months that something was afoot. James requested the magistrates to provide him with a guard to protect Holyrood. Since an extraordinary number of people seemed to be flocking into Edinburgh from all parts, householders were required to submit the names of all lodgers or strangers to the baillies, nightly. Ministers waxed large: Bruce decried the return of the Popish lords, and Balcanquhall warned that their religion was in peril extreme. Their adherents became frenzied, and 'spewed out most contentious and uncouth speeches from the pulpit'.

As the King sat in the Court of Session in late December, he was presented with a petition by representatives of a religious mob without. He was persuaded that he was more likely to defuse the riot if he gave countenance to the matter and returned a conciliatory answer. In a whipstitch, the Presbyterian petitioners returned with additional demands that heedlessly invaded the realms of the King's prerogative. His patience snapped. He withdrew the court to Linlithgow, the Court of Session to Perth, and the justices to Leith. A proclamation anent 'the late treasonable uproar' condemned the seditious speeches from the pulpit which had referred to the King 'in a most irreverent manner with speeches illseeming any subject'.

Ten days later, the King re-entered the capital from Leith, handed the keys of the city gates to his officers, confined all citizens to their houses, and instructed all streets to be guarded. In dread that the King might loose the feared wild Highlanders upon them, the merchants had removed all their 'movabill geir' the night before to the house of John

McMorran in Riddle's Close, which they thought most defensible. The town council virtually dissolved in its terror. The Lord Provost, in abject misery, denied that 'thay, or nane of them had any manner of foreknowledge of that unworthy and unhappy tumult that suddenly fell out.' The King professed not to believe them. Some of his wilder courtiers advised James to annihilate the city, and erect a column on the site thereof, as a dreadful warning for all time. In terror for their wallets, the burgesses even appealed to Queen Elizabeth to intercede on their behalf.

In truth, the tumult was but small: sufficient nonetheless to allow James to milk it for his own ends. The eventual settlement agreed with the King in March 1597 reprieved the city. Instead, it provided for the dispersal of irreverent preachers, the gift to the King of the minister's houses in St Giles Kirkyard and a fine of £20,000 to be used for the furnishing of 'His Highness' House' at Holyrood. James had done very well out of the affray: rid of the preachers, Edinburgh under his very thumb, his bishops secure, and he himself considerably richer in both land and cash.

He had every reason to be smug: although ministers continued to thunder, their day was done. Edinburgh merchants may have felt equally smug. Prosperity was now running high. The damage caused by the Civil War had been repaired, the port of Leith was booming, and the European character of Scotland was emphasised by the import of foodstuffs, fine cloth, craft materials and luxury materials, including books from European printing presses. Sweetmeat shops in the fashionable Lawnmarket were well supplied with continental wares. Even the sternest Reformers must have realised how the reimposition of strong central royal authority would be good for trade: and for the next forty years, that is what mattered most.

CHAPTER FIVE

BURSTING OF THE BUBBLE

It might not, after all, have been the crabbit Janet (Jonet or Jenny) Geddes, the herb dealer from the Tron herb market, who propelled her stool at the head of the Dean of Edinburgh on 23rd July, 1637 (she figures in history two decades later). But, as the unfortunate dean prepared to declaim from the new Service Book within the dim majesty of the now Cathedral Kirk of St Giles, somebody did – to the eldritch screech of 'Out, out, does the false loon dare say Mass at my lugg?' 'Clapping of hands, the hissing, the curses and exclamations which immediately followed rendered every sentence or attempted speech unintelligible.' The magistrates had the runagates put to the door and locked out, but

> then they became more furious and mad (as they were directed) crying and shouting saying 'Popery was now brought in amongst them'; dang at the doors and brake the glass windows with stones, with such noise that there was no more reading . . .

'Rascall women' cried out against the corpulent Bishop of Edinburgh as he quit the kirk, ready to stone him to death; he heaved himself into the Earl of Roxburgh's coach standing hard beside and they escaped with their lives only because, pursued by stones, the coachman careered down the High Street through the Netherbow at full gallop, the bishop's footmen running alongside with drawn swords. The experience of racketing at full tilt within a primitive seventeenth-century coach down the plainstanes in mid-riot scarcely bears thinking about. Such were the battle honours of what Edinburgh natives sardonically nicknamed the 'Stony Sabbath'.

A full-blown civic riot, ignited within seconds, lasted for days. It was the worst commotion to overwhelm the capital since 1596; yet again, the apparent cause religion, but it would be naïve to take Edinburgh too much at its own face value, and accept that even the slightest biblical phrase would have inflamed the meanest blue-gowned beggar. It stretches the imagination that the entire city would explode at a few hesitant words within the privacy of the cathedral. Edinburgh was already primed to detonate.

The Geddes riot, which the fanatics purloined for Presbyterianism with agonising consequences for the country, was the first popular expression of a thirty-year-old resentment against Scotland becoming a second-class country, and Edinburgh a provincial village; a vexation which finally overwhelmed decades of appeasement by the burgesses, who had been wholly preoccupied with raising the capital to a centre of seriously rich mercantile entrepreneurs instead. In 1603, James had departed to London promising undying love: 'There is no more difference,' quoth he, 'betwixt London and Edinburgh, yea not so much as betwixt Inverness or Aberdeen and Edinburgh; for all our marches are dry and there be no ferries betwixt them' (rapidly instructing the construction of a bridge at Berwick-upon-Tweed). He continued: 'Ye need not doubt but, as I have a body as able as any King in Europe, whereby I am able to travel, so shall I visit you every three years at the least, or often as I shall have occasion.' But once he had settled in London, the hunger to return to his habitat became less pressing. Smugly, he informed the English parliament on 31st March, 1607:

> Here I sit and govern [Scotland] with my pen; I write, and it is done; and by a clerk of the Council I govern Scotland now – which my ancestors could not do by the sword.

He managed only one return visit in 1617. His rule by the pen became characterised by petty interference, increasing remoteness and occasional flattery. In return for reneging upon part of his debts to the capital, he flattered Provost and baillies by accretions to their pomp; but accompanied them by a relentless trickle of minor but niggling infringement of the capital's powers, liberties, and elections. His triumphant return on 16th May, 1617 brought recollection to an old generation, and a vision to the new generation, of the status Edinburgh had enjoyed as capital city when King and court were in residence. Overblown panegyrics by William Drummond of Hawthornden reflected how much Scotland had lost without a head or chief patron to whom artists could address themselves.

Provost, the four baillies, the whole council of the town, with one hundred honest men besides, were all assembled to greet the King at the West Port, 'in black gowns, lined with black velvet, and their whole apparell was of black velvet'. He endured a harangue each from Provost Nisbitt and Town Clerk Hay in expectation of '500 double angels laid in a silver basin double over gilt' which he accepted 'with a mild and gracious countenance'. Hay, however, was not solely indulging in flowery flattery when he had said:

> The very hills and groves accustomed before to be refreshed with the dew of your Majesty's presence, not putting on their wonted apparel, but with pale looks, representing their misery for the departure of their Royal king.

Hay was making metaphorical comment about the state of Scotland in the King's absence. The Archbishop of St Andrews, Spottiswoode, offered a sermon in St Giles, whereafter 'the whole honest men of the town' conveyed the royal party to Canongate Cross 'called St John's Cross, where drawing forth his sword, the King knighted the Provost etc'. The King's stay was brief, and he never returned. His advisers were cast in adverse mould, and flattered the King's self-esteem by expressing amazement that such an erudite monarch could have sprung from such a primitive background. One such was Sir Anthony Weldon:

> The air might be wholesome but for the stinking people that inhabit it . . . their beasts be generally small, women only excepted of which sort there are none greater in the whole world. There is a great store of fowl too, as foul houses, foul sheets, foul linen, foul dishes and pots, foul trenchers and napkins . . . They have a great store of deer but . . . I confess all the deer I met withal was dear lodgings, dear horsemeat and dear tobacco.

The King dispensed inexpensive favours, and enjoyed a disputation with the professors of Edinburgh's Townis College (curiously held in Stirling) at which he praised their Latin pronunciation which reminded him of that of his old, long-dead tutor, George Buchanan. He was pleased with the progress in building the college, and the professors' determination to pursue the lamp of learning, 'a work so universally beneficial to our subjects, and of such ornament and reputation for our city in particular', and blessed their efforts, not with a grant of money, but with a grant of the title 'King James' College'. He took care to attract to himself no financial liability thereby: power without responsibility was certainly not the prerogative solely of whores.

He also tampered with the state religion of Scotland by the gradual restoration of bishops and archbishops to positions of authority within the Church, the subservience of presbyteries and committees of elders to them, and the heightening of solemn ritual. Dispossession and banishment faced ministers who dissented, and there arose a sullen resentment – particularly in Edinburgh, cradle of the Scottish Reformation, and the sole source of pure doctrine by direct lien with God. By subordinating its status as a religious centre to remote London decrees, the King was subverting the idea of Edinburgh itself. That the compromises were becoming untenable was evident to the otherwise blinkered Weldon:

> For the Lords Spiritual [bishops] they may well be termed so indeed, for they are neither fish nor flesh, but what it shall please their earthly God, the King to make them. Obedience is better than sacrifice, and therefore they make a mock at martyrdom, saying that Christ was to die for them and not they for him. They will rather subscribe than surrender, and rather dispense with small things than trouble themselves with great disputation. They will rather acknowledge the King to be their head than want wherewith to pamper their bodies.

A wet Edinburgh Sunday afternoon was best avoided, even in the seventeenth century:

> Their Sabbath exercise is a preaching in the forenoon, and a persecuting in the afternoon; they go to church in the forenoon to hear the law, and to the crags and mountains in the afternoon to louse themselves.

These bishops were not the great aristocrats of the pre-Reformation period. Since Scots nobles tended to regard the King solely as *primus inter pares*, James avoided them in his determination to elevate the cult of monarchy: he favoured instead the lesser sort – the middle men whom 'he might convict, and were hangable'. He promoted legal people and lesser lairds as a means of keeping the grandees at a distance. Thus rose to eminence Sir Thomas Hope, Lord Advocate in 1626, Sir Gilbert Primrose, Lord Balmerino, Tam o' the Cowgate (Sir Thomas Hamilton, Lord of Session) and people like him. Bishops came from the same class. King James's continued absence and continued tinkering provoked trouble, particularly after the introduction of the 'Perth Articles' to heighten the ceremony of church services. Despondent private prayer meetings in suburban villas near Sciennes sought divine assistance, and considered resistance.

Once Charles I succeeded to the throne and proposed to revoke all grants of Church land made since 1540, the resentment was fanned into flame. It hurt alike those new men of the middle rank whom James had nurtured (those he felt he could hang) the 'Lords of erection' whose titles derived from abbeys, priories and other religious properties, and the greatest in the land, most of whom had not accompanied the King south and remained dangerously idle as they pondered their new role in Scotland as landlords without any state or political function. Long accustomed to participating in power, Scots aristocrats were now detached from it, save for those who had become powder-puff mutants at the Court of St James. The Scots parliament met but infrequently, and then only to approve an agenda set in London. The Privy Council was bypassed, and General Assemblies were no longer summoned because, saith the King, there was nothing to discuss.

When, seventy years later, Andrew Fletcher of Saltoun was speaking against the Act of Union his perception of the relationship between Scotland and England during the seventeenth century was as appropriate to the 1630s as it was to his own time.

> All our affairs since the Union of the Crowns have been managed by the advice of English ministers, and the principal offices of the Kingdom filled with such men as the court of England knew would be subservient in their designs: by which means they have had so visible an influence upon our whole administration, that we have from that time appeared to the rest of the world more like a conquered province than a free independent people . . . So long as Scotsmen must go to the English Court to obtain offices of trust or profit in this kingdom, those offices will always be managed with regard to the court and interest of England, though to the betrayal of the interests of this nation . . . And what less can be expected, unless we resolve to expect miracles?

It pleased no one that it took the new King eight years to come north for his coronation. When he finally condescended to do so in 1633, he offered flattery, like his father, but insufficient to conceal serious political errors. His entry at the West Port was greeted with customary ceremony by the Lord Provost and about sixty baillies and councillors, all clad in well-furred robes and black velvet gowns. Only one harangue this time, in return for double the coin awarded his father – a gold basin containing 1,000 double gold angels, upon which he 'looked gladly' (truly did the Stewarts drool over coin). The procession then passed up the Upper Bow with

> a brave company of town's soldiers, all clad in white satin doublets, black velvet breeches and silk stockings, with hats, feathers, scarves, bands and the rest correspondent. These gallants had dainty muskets, picks, and gilt partisans and such like, who guarded His Majesty.

By the time he left the Tolbooth, he had tholed four speeches, and there was a fifth at the Mercat Cross at which 'His Majesty's health was heartily drunken by Bacchus on the Cross' the spouts of whose fountain were running with wine. At the Tron, a scaffold in imitation of Parnassus 'all green with birks', supported 'nine pretty boys [had they mistaken the King for his father?] representing the nine nymphs . . . where he had the sixth speech'. Within the structure itself sat two bands, a choir and organist, with an organ, who performed 'an excellent piece of music called *Caledonia*'. Drummond of Hawthornden was wheeled out for another panegyric with the overblown sentiment that mountains and trees would swivel on their sides to face the glorious visage of the monarch. The coronation took place at 2.00 p.m. on 18th June, 1633, in the Abbey Church of Holyrood (the ceremony modified by the addition of a sermon) with a splendour unknown to at least two generations of Scots.

> Upon the morn, Tuesday, about ten in the morning, the nobility came up to the castle in their furred robes; the king had his robe royal, who in order rode from the castle down to the abbey of Holyroodhouse, and first the Earl of Angus rode immediately before the King in his furred robe, carrying the crown betwixt both his hands . . . The Lords, with the rest of the nobility, all richly clad in scarlet furred robes, rode upon their horses, furnished with rich saddles and foot mantles, ilk ane in their own rooms, with the king down through the streets to the Abbey.

Two days later, the King and nobles rode from Holyrood up to the tolbooth, in the Riding of Parliament.* It was a gorgeous affair. Charles was on a chestnut horse caparisoned with 'a fair bunch of feathers' on its

---

* Spalding's description of the Riding of Parliament is the only detailed depiction of that ceremony when it was attended by the King:

> In the first rank rode the commissioners of burghs . . . well clad in cloaks, having on their horses black velvet foot mantles; secondly, the commissioners for barons; thirdly the lords of the spirituality; fourthly, the bishops who rode together . . . fifthly followed the temporal lords; sixthly followed the viscounts; seventhly the earls . . . eighthly the earl of Buchan . . . carrying the sword, and the earl of Rothes carrying the sceptre, riding side for side with other; ninthly the marquis of Douglas carrying the crown, having on his right arm the Duke of Lennox and on his left the Marquis of Hamilton; following them came His Majesty . . . and none rode without their foot mantles and the nobles all in red scarlet furred robes, as their use to ride in Parliament is . . . The heralds, pursuivants, macers and trumpeters followed His Majesty in silence . . . the Causeway was railed from the Nether Bow to the Stinking Style with stakes of timber dung in the end on both sides, yet so that people standing without the same might see well enough and that none might hinder the King's passage.

head, and a purple velvet foot mantle: the King was hatted, carrying his rod of state, and accoutred in King James IV's 'robe royal' of richly furred purple velvet laced with gold, which was so long that it hung well behind the horse, its train carried by five grooms. Timber stake barricades had been erected that 'none might hinder the King's passage'.

None might hinder the King's passage indeed. Parliament acquiesced to the King's proposal to elevate Edinburgh formally as capital of Scotland, although it now required to be dignified by a bishopric, with dean and twelve prebends, and a cathedral. St Giles lacked the necessary dignity divided, as it was, into several churches. Charles instructed that

> St Giles' Church (designed by us to be the Cathedral Church of that Bishopric) be ordered as is decent and fit for a church of that eminency . . .

The High Kirk as cathedral was to become a whole church again 'and not be indirectly parcelled and disjointed by walls of partitions', and the new dean was despatched to Durham Cathedral to inspect what improvements could be learnt therefrom.

On Monday, 24th June, the town hosted another sumptuous banquet for sundry nobles, courtiers, and court officers with music and much merriment; and, after dinner, Provost, baillies and councillors,

> ilk ane of them in other's hands, with bare heads, came dancing down the street with all sort of music, trumpeters and drums, but the nobles left them, went to the King and told him their good entertainment with joy and gladness, whereat the King was well pleased.

Edinburgh councillors dancing in the street must have been a sight of rare luminescence; but the pleasure that Scotland enjoyed during the King's visit simply served to emphasise how dispossessed it felt when he returned to England again. Once back in London, Charles sought to enhance ritual during the service even more, elaborate clerical dress, and – the last straw – to introduce a new liturgy. Edinburgh, primed to explode, chose the day of the reading of the new liturgy.[*]

John Spalding (Commissary Clerk to Aberdeen) doubted that Edinburgh had endured a spontaneous religious uprising, and preferred the conspiracy theory: 'They began at religion as the grounds of their quarrel, whereas their intention was only bent against the King's Majesty and his Royal prerogatives: and conform to that clandestine band, begins the disorder in Scotland.' Spalding doubted that the stool-throwing was spontaneous: nobles had 'devised a number of rascally serving women to throw stones at the reader'. Yet the extent of popular indignation can be gauged by the delivery of sixty-eight petitions for the liturgy's withdrawal. Renewed riot broke when the King ordered the petitioners to withdraw from Edinburgh, occasioned by the mobbing of the Bishop of Galloway with 'wild clamours and execrations' as he passed to the Privy Council. If Galloway thought that he would be safe having reached the Privy Council he was soon disabused: the Edinburgh mob had them all trapped:

> The Lords of the Privy Council sent to the Magistrates requesting their assistance. But the Magistrates stood in need of assistance as much themselves; for the disorderly rout which besieged the Privy Councillors controlled the streets that also surrounded the Town Council's chamber where the Magistrates were sitting; nay, even thronged into it and vowed their immediate destruction.

The Earl of Traquair, Lord Treasurer, desired to assist the magistrates, and left the Privy Council to do so, but the mob pounced upon him,

> pulled off his hat and cloak, broke in pieces the white rod which he bore as the badge of office, threw him down on the street and had he not been instantly raised by his attendants, who conveyed him back to the Privy Council, would undoubtedly have trodden him to death.

The King's reaction to the 'Stony Sabbath' was uncomprehending. The Privy Council was removed to Linlithgow, those thronging Edinburgh were instructed to return home, and all consideration of ecclesiastical matters was suspended. The Earl of Traquair returned from London to forbid 'all conventions, meetings, and groups of protesters under pain of

* (p. 72) The victory of proletarian power over authoritarian monarchy, as evidenced by the episode with the stool, was hugely appealing to the nineteenth-century Professor John Blackie, who liked to stride across the room singing a squib of his own composition, of which the following is a verse:

> And thus a mighty deed was done by Jenny's valiant hand
> Black Prelacy and Popery she drave from Scottish land;
> King Charles he was a shuffling knave, priest Laud a meddling fool,
> But Jenny was a woman wise who beat them with a stool!
> With a row-dow – yes, I trow! – she conquered by the stool!

Blackie always emphasised the last line by flinging a stool across the room.

treason'. In the teeth of widespread commotion, the Privy Council 'ratified and approved the King's proclamation'. Spalding commented bitterly: 'They understood not well what they were doing, to declare the nobility and body of the common people traitors in such a troublesome time.' Events moved speedily forward.

A National Covenant, reminding the King of a covenant signed by his father to protect the Kirk of Scotland and abjure Popery in 1581, was drawn up and prepared ready for the nation's signature. It rehearsed all the statutes of the previous seventy years in support of the Scottish mode of Presbyterianism, and affirmed the importance of Scottish parliament and Scottish statute against arbitrary royal rule from London. It was signed with immense solemnity amongst the splendid new tombs of the Greyfriars Kirk, by nobility and barons on 28th February, and by the ministers and burgesses the following day. It was a brave act. All signatories had thereby publicly declared themselves as part of what the King would undoubtedly view as a treasonable conspiracy: and their only security against a King propense to hanging was their collective defence.

The signing ceremony itself was overlain with symbolism (reviving echoes of that mystery that seems to accompany the 'winged citadel', the Summons of Plotcock and the Beggars' Summons), set as it was amidst the wintry table tombs of Greyfriars Kirkyard overshadowed by the castle. They could have chosen the more convenient, more spacious and newly paved Parliament Square, the Mercat Cross or even St Giles itself, just as easily.

> All ranks and conditions, all ages and sex flocked to subscribe to
> [the Covenant] with ardour, as if they believed that the insertion
> of their names in this parchment scroll did virtually enrol them
> in the book of life . . . few in their habits were disposed to resist
> it.

Our retrospective vision of this momentous event has always had the sepulchral air of people who must do what they must, even if the consequences were to prove terrible: as they did. All that the country had built up over the previous forty to fifty years, in particular its stately, wealthy capital, was to be put at risk of Civil War.

What kind of city had Edinburgh become? It is enjoyable to look at it through the eyes of John Taylor, the London waterboatman poet who trekked north in 1618, in imitation of his friend Ben Jonson, who was visiting Edinburgh, and William Drummond of Hawthornden at the same time (they met in Leith). Taylor arrived allegedly penniless (yet equipped with servant and horse) and passing through the Netherbow into the stone heart of Edinburgh, he sought a likely mark. His servant persuaded a burgess called John Maxwell to offer him 'unexpected and undeserved courtesy' and a loan of ten shillings: Maxwell took him to his house, caused the horse to be put in his own stable (there were evidently stables within the old city), whilst they discoursed over a 'pint of Spanish'. His guided tour began at the castle where his attention was drawn by 'Roaring Megg' (the cannon Mons Meg) which then lay dismounted. He was fascinated by its size: 'It is so great within, that it was told me that a child was once gotten there': in other words, it was a military fornicatorium. Nothing loth, Taylor wanted to try it out: 'I, to make trial crept into it, lying on my back, and I am sure there was room enough and spare for a greater than myself.' (A French visitor Jorevin de Rocheford, visiting in 1661, was given the same tale. 'Two persons have laid in it as much at their ease as in a bed.' It would have to have been a skinny romance.)

Taylor then accompanied Maxwell down the 'fairest and goodliest street that ever my eyes beheld', where he admired the 'buildings on each side of the way being all of squared stone, five six and seven stories high'. He was puzzled that the nobles' and merchants' houses were 'obscurely founded' down the closes, and ruminated why so many people in Edinburgh would wish to cling to a crag rather than expand on the flat and fertile ground around Leith: 'So this City had it been built but one mile lower on the sea side, I doubt not but it had long before this been comparable to many a one of our greatest towns and cities in Europe'; and presumably Maxwell, with thirty years of peace under his belt, had forgotten Edinburgh's painful history, and neither could predict what was soon to be unleashed. In Leith, Taylor found his 'long approved and assured good friend Master Benjamin Jonson at Master John Stewart's house: "I thanked him for his great kindness towards me, for at my taking leave of him, he gave me a piece of gold of two and twenty shillings to drink his health in England."'

Edinburgh truly achieved its status as capital between 1588 and 1638. It had earned its sorely afforded monuments. The majestic Tron Kirk, begun in 1633 just below the Black Turnpike, was built in response to the division of the city into four parishes in 1625, and, for almost a century, presented the most sophisticated façade in the High Street. The splendid ashlar-fronted, towered Parliament House was begun in 1632 by Sir James Murray of Kilbaberton on the site of the St Giles Prebendaries' houses forfeited to James in 1597. Of its cost of £127,000 Scots, some twenty-five per cent had been raised by public subscription, and the rest by the city: it may have been the King's idea, but it was not going to be his financial responsibility. The hillside offered capacious basements which were still proving useful a hundred years later:

> In the basement is deposited the public theatre or stage erected at the Mercat Cross 'on all publick rejoicings'; and the machine denominated the Maiden, for decollating state criminals at the Mercat Cross; the common gallows occasionally erected in the Grassmarket, and a number of leathern buckets, flambeaus, etc used in extinguishing casual fires.

In short, the city's junk room.

With the creation of Parliament House, the burgh had thereby created the first 'square' within the city, bounded on the south and west by the old graveyard and the new Parliament Hall, on the north by St Giles with its little timber bothies or 'krames', occupied by the goldsmiths and snuggled between the buttresses, and rather grand new tenements to the east. In 1643, these shops were ordered to be let only to goldsmiths, bookbinders, montremakers and mathematical instrument makers (the name montremakers for watchmakers reveals the extent of the French influence). Parliament Square became, according to Thomas Morer fifty years later 'the pride of Edinburgh . . . The yard is square and well paved, and beautified with good buildings round it.'

De Rocheford was impressed with the tapestry-hung Parliament Hall, but surprised that shopkeepers were allowed to 'sell a thousand little curiosities' in the Great Hall. Outside on the terrace, with its fine view over the Cowgate, a pavilion had been erected, with a garden.

The fashionable Lawnmarket was adorned with sumptuous merchants' mansions at the extremities of the closes on the western side – notably those of Robert Gourlay and John McMorran, high on the bluff overlooking the Grassmarket. The Grassmarket had become the service centre of the city, 'inhabited by many workmen and mechanics, who, though they do not ennoble that quarter, render it the most populous'. The West Bow clanged to the activities of the hammermen and whitesmiths, and a new stench joined the old familiars in that quarter of the city after 1600 – the rich whiff of maltmen that a frosty morning perpetuates even today.

On his arrival in Edinburgh in 1617, King James had been praised by the Provost for 'beautifying her also with a new erected college'. Great steps had been made with the Townis College since the burgh had purchased the site of the Kirk o' Field in 1582 (assisted with a legacy from Robert Reid and the library of advocate Clement Little). Its growth was piecemeal rather than to the magnificent plan which so ennobled the rival university in Glasgow. It inhabited the cloister of Kirk o' Field, in which Darnley had been murdered: the exploded north range rebuilt, and the Provost's Lodging converted into the principal's house. In 1617 a new library was added alongside the Duke of Hamilton's great lodging in the south wing. A smaller courtyard known as the Laigh Court had been added to the north in 1625, and in 1636 it had been graced with an entrance gatehouse with a Dutch steeple above. A fine new hall in 1639 completed an irregular double-courtyard campus.

The splendid towers of one of Scotland's stateliest Renaissance buildings rose not far to the west: those of the hospital endowed by George Heriot in his will of 1623 for 'the founding and erecting of an hospital within the said town of Edinburgh in perpetuity . . . to be employed for the maintenance, relief, bringing up and education of so many poor fatherless boys, freemen's sons of the town of Edinburgh'. Its master was abjured to bring up scholars and 'inferior officers in good manners; and therefore, that in all cases of misdemeanours as sparring, fighting, lying, spoiling of their clothes or chambers or the like, they receive due correction and chastisement'. The architect, whose portrait is still hung within the hospital, was William Aytoun who, about the same time, probably built the pretty pile of Peffermill for himself, beautifully set under the lea of Arthur's Seat (and later immortalised by Sir Walter Scott as Dumbie-dykes). Heriot's displays distinctive European influence in the arcading on the interior and much of the detail work around the entrance gates and the windows. With mordant wit, Aytoun selected a classical order for this hospital for 'fatherless bairns' known as 'Doric Bastardo'.

It was a time of much building in Edinburgh. The east wing of the palace of Edinburgh Castle had been majestically rebuilt, probably by the King's master mason Sir James Murray (who likewise built himself the splendid château of Baberton by Balerno). Holyrood underwent major repairs, possibly including the rebuilding of the great courtyards, south wing and the gallery in time for King Charles's coronation in 1633. Rarely occupied royal buildings, however, were not typical of Edinburgh at its mercantile zenith. Instead, the town blossomed with finely cut and chased ashlar-fronted *hôtels* for lairds, villas like châteaux in the immediate hinterland, new town houses and rebuilt tenements on finely dressed stone arcades.

Until the outbreak of the troubles in around 1638, Edinburgh prospered as never before or possibly since. The King's exodus to London had freed the capital from the remorseless aristocratic factionalism that had surrounded him. Had not James VI been perilously close to being kidnapped within his own Palace of Holyrood by the Earl of Bothwell in 1591? The lure (the King) had been removed from the tormented animals (the lords) who pursued him; and in the larger environment of London those who accompanied him south found their desperation defuse. Sporadic violence continued in the streets, but it was of a less serious degree than probably could be found elsewhere in Europe. With the customary exception of the Badlands of Buchan, Scotland was enjoying the longest period of stability it had known for centuries.

The court's absence released the energies of the lesser men, the professionals, and – above all – the international traders of Edinburgh. King James's crafty decree as to the constitution of Edinburgh's council in 1584 had quieted disruptive rivalry between burgesses and craftsmen, and stabilised city government. His decree was crafty: the aspirations of the crafts had been met by formalising and increasing their representation on the council as office bearers, whereas the fears of the burgesses were assuaged by ensuring that these changes were restricted so as to leave effective power with the latter. There was an unceasing demand to become burgesses: and the wealthier the latter had become, the more attractive seemed the favoured route of marrying a merchant's daughter. The pressure put upon such pulchritude led to a curiously offensive practice of inspecting the virginity of merchants' maidens prior to such marriages; its absence rendering the promotion to burgess of the suitor null and void (whether or not – it seems – the aspirant was the culprit, or simply an unsuspecting victim).

Early seventeenth-century Edinburgh merchants operated joint stock ventures, speculation and shipowning: and through Leith, they traded with all the countries of Europe and the Baltic. There was no sharp distinction between minor aristocracy, gentry and wealthy merchants, as successful entrepreneurs passed from burgh to countryside and countryside to burgh as may be. It was the period of the rise of the Hopes, the Trotters, Blairs, and the Foulis: Foulis of Ravelston (who built himself a splendid new Renaissance mansion in 1622 with extravagant interior carving work) was related to the family of Foulis at Colinton, but his success originated as a goldsmith and burgess of the city of Edinburgh. Edinburgh displayed the type of restlessness that characterised Glasgow in the following century as merchants sought licences and monopolies for trading, or for manufacturing.

Perhaps Edinburgh merchants overreached themselves in this unfortunately short high-noon of Edinburgh as a mercantile metropolis. Their trading patterns, money-lending, and venture capitalism were founded upon continued growth and confidence: which was shattered by the Civil War. Their ambitions were large. When the coastal waters were 'greatly pestered with pirates to the great hurt of the trade', in 1610, Edinburgh merchants fitted out their own navy to hunt them down, even so far as Orkney. Two years later, they ordered the construction of a paved causeway between Edinburgh and Leith, for the better passage of traffic, and another up to the Greyfriars Church gate. 'So much addicted to usury' were they at this time, they had offered James VI the opportunity of relief from his debt to them, in return for exemption from the then parliamentary maximum rate of ten per cent interest.

The town was on an expansive course. In 1636 it purchased the superiority of the Canongate, North Leith, Coalhill, and the Pleasance; and even in the midst of the troubles, in 1648, it purchased the West Port and Potterrow, later to add to Bonnyton Mills, Inverleith, the High Riggs, and Society. There was a new charity hospital beside Trinity College Kirk, a Grammar School in the Blackfriars Yards, a French school in the Cowgate (whose teacher in 1599 was curiously called Nicolas L'Anglois (Nicholas the Englishman), an English school and new markets.

The number of households within the city had doubled between 1580 and 1635, and plague was a constant visitor: it raged in 1604, and made a cataclysmic visitation in 1645. Self-preservation drove the council to worry about cleanliness. In 1621, it required thatch and timber roofs to be replaced with slate, lead or tile, and ordered stacks of heather, broom or whins or other fuel in the heart of the town to be removed out to 'remote parts'. It fulminated against the practices that had led to Edinburgh being known as 'a puddle of filth and filthiness':

> it oftentimes falleth out that in many streets and vennels of the said burgh, the filth of the slaughtered goods is in such abundance exposed to the view of the people that the closes and streets are so filled therewith, that there can be no passage had through the same.

With the erection of a 'pillar of hewen stone near the Mercat Cross with a seat thereon', the magistrates addressed themselves to the problem of unsuccessful capitalism: 'whereupon in all time coming, insolvent debtors would be required to sit on market day from 10 hours in the morning until 1 hour after dinner'. Before they could be set free, debtors would have to make or buy a yellow bonnet or hat to be worn by them during their time on the pillar, and all time thereafter so long as they remained bankrupt.

Viewing with alarm how the closes and catacombs of the capital had become the 'common receptacle of all evil and lewdly disposed persons, so that all virtue was suppressed, and all the poor of the kingdom have set themselves to no other thing but to continually beg', the council proposed the erection of a House of Correction for employing and punishing such 'pests of mankind'. Its purpose was to 'advance virtue, suppress vice, by compelling idle people to betake themselves to industry', and for the avoidance of doubt, its target population was specified as 'strolling poor, lazy beggars, idle vagrants and common prostitutes who crowded hither from all parts of the kingdom'.

Edinburgh's prosperity was generated by an élite of approximately 300 merchants who, by their shareholdings in the ships themselves, dominated, if not held a virtual monopoly of, Scotland's exports. Edinburgh's merchants maintained resident factors, often Scots expatriates, in European and Baltic ports such as Danzig, Dieppe, Paris, London and Bilbao. Those 'warm men' also acted as bankers to peripatetic Scots aristocrats on the hoof round Europe. Edinburgh entrepreneurs developed salt, coal, lead, herring packing, ropeworks and vinegar. Kings amongst these merchant princes were Patrick Wood, and Sir William Dick of Braid, both of whose fortunes collapsed along with the economy during the Wars of the Covenant. Dick had funded the young Montrose on his tour around France in the 1630s; acted as factor in Paris, and his reputation was kent through the banking centres of Europe. To judge from his tax payments, his income had been eighty times the norm for an Edinburgh burgess. He had a herring works in North Berwick, owned coal and salt works, farmed customs, and had granaries in Leith. It was said that when he agreed to fund the armies of the Covenant, great cartloads of bullion formed a procession from his courtyard virtually opposite St Giles out into the High Street. In return, it was said, for the 'sillie' bribe of being made Lord Provost, Dick lent the greater part of his fortune to the Covenanting army; Cromwell repudiated the loan, and Dick died in a debtors' prison in 1655.

The face of the High Street had changed. The timber extensions projecting forward into the street were rebuilt in well-cut stone supported upon arcades of which the sole surviving example is the house of Thomas Gledstanes, merchant. Its arcaded ground floor fronted timber booths and the new street-front rooms above acted as a frontage to older parts behind, with fine painted walls and ceilings. Comparable buildings are common today in the older towns of Austria and northern Italy. Altogether of a different order is the town house or *hôtel* of Sir Alexander Acheson in the Canongate: a U-plan courtyard house built of expensively cut stone, its principal apartments on the first floor: elsewhere in Scotland, that house would have suited laird if not lord. The tailors congregated in their new hall near the college in the pastoral suburb of the Cowgate.

Aristocratic grandiloquence was conveyed by Moray House, further down the Canongate: a house later to become notorious when the Marquis of Montrose, being hauled past on his way up to the scaffold, received some disdainful spittle from the Earl of Argyll's wedding party on the balcony. This magnificent *hôtel*, handsome, richly plastered principal apartments on the first floor, exemplified the stark contrast between town and country. A wall, modified only by windows and balcony, to the street; but an open courtyard to the south, with splendid views over formal gardens, garden buildings and the summerhouse in which the Act of Union was later to be signed, to Arthur's Seat. Over a hundred similar buildings – villas and castle-like lairds' houses (châteaux) – lay so close to the capital that they could be seen from the castle. It is not remarkable that a Renaissance capital should become thronged with the town houses and villas of those attracted to the nation's heart: but their extent is a mute legacy of the capital's largely unappreciated role as an international trading emporium. *

The Stony Sabbath put all this mercantile success in jeopardy. The signing of the Covenant in Greyfriars Kirkyard was a formal declaration of opposition – if not actually of war – by representatives of the general body of people within Scotland. It was then passed round Scotland for subscription by the people of other parts of the country; some of whom only subscribed on the amendment that their intention was not to be disloyal to the King. On 4th March, 1638, the burgh council thought 'this time of great danger' required the recruitment of 300 men to guard the town both day and night.

What had begun as a constitutional protest had been overtaken by extremists: and the more obdurate the King deported himself, the more it strengthened the hands of the zealots. Spalding was outraged that 'the Archbishop of St Andrews [Spottiswoode] an old reverend man, High Chancellor of Scotland is forced, for fear of his life, to flee into England for safety and refuge at the King's hands . . . the King was very sorry at their overthrow, but could not for the present mend it.' The glorious organs of the Chapel Royal which King James had ordered to be erected in 1618 were

> broken down masterfully, and no service used there; but the haill chaplains, choristers and musicians are discharged, and the stately organs altogether destroyed and made useless. These un-

* Many of Edinburgh's environing villas survive today, whilst others were rebuilt in succeeding centuries. They include Sciennes, Comiston, Croft an Righ, Prestonfield, Caroline Park, Liberton House, White House, Bruntsfield, Newhailes, Laurieston Castle, Baberton, Peffermill, Brunstane, Inch, Lochend, Craigentinny, Merchiston, Colinton Castle, Drylaw, Dalry House, Easter Dalry, Ravelston, Wester Coates, Pilrig, Pinkie House, Duddingston, Craigmillar, Carberry, Craig House, and Glenlockhart. Great losses to the capital have included the Grange, Saughton, Niddrie Marischal, Corstorphine, the Dean, Royston Castle (at Granton), Warriston, and Wrychtis House.

couth alterations bred horrible fears in the hearts of the country people.

In August 1638, the Marquis of Hamilton returned from the King with the offer to convene both parliament and General Assembly on the pre-condition that the Covenanters would 'break and dissolve their Band of Covenant'. They were not so stupid. Had they agreed, they would have forfeited their only protection, and been at the mercy of a chancy monarch. When, during the summer, Covenanters began to arm, the King dropped the precondition: the first General Assembly in twenty years would be held in Glasgow on 21st November, and a parliament in May 1639. The General Assembly took place in Glasgow Cathedral, admitted nobody who did not have a lead token indicating that he was a Covenanter, and on its fourth day, seized control from Hamilton. It deposed bishops, purged 'refusers to subscribe the Covenant, refract Ministers and other disobedients, and of all other matters', and decided to levy tax to pay for its army. Committees of leading Covenanters, barons, burgesses and ministers were established to abuse, so said Spalding, the King's lieges with 'grievous burthens, levy of men, money, horses, arms, taxations and other charges', to assist in the defence of the Covenant and religion.

At this juncture, Field Marshall Alexander Leslie returned to Scotland, clad in the European-wide reputation he had earned in the Thirty Years' War: 'by his valour [he] attained to this title Excellency, inferior to none but the King of Sweden, under whom he served amongst his cavalry'. Leslie took command of the military preparations:

> First, he desired cannons to be cast in the Potter Row by one Captain Hamilton; he began to drill the earl's men in Fife, he caused to send to Holland for ammunition, powder and ball, muskets, carabines, pistols, pikes, swords and all other necessary arms fit for old and young soldiers in great abundance. He caused send to Germany, France, Holland, Denmark and other countries for the most expert and valiant captains, lieutenants and other officers who came in great haste upon hope of bloody war, thinking, as they were all Scots soldiers that came, to make up their fortunes upon the ruin of our kingdom.

In March 1639, the Covenanters seized Dumbarton Castle and Dalkeith Palace: and as the King prepared to march north, he dispatched ahead a navy commanded by Hamilton. James Howell visited Edinburgh about this time, to find a funereal rather than triumphant atmosphere:

The Bishops are all gone to wreck, and they had but a sorry funeral: the very name is grown so contemptible that a black dog, if he hath any white marks about him, is called Bishop. Our Lord of Canterbury (Archbishop Laud) is growing here so odious that they called him commonly in the pulpit the Priest of Baal, and the son of Belial.

Leith had been fortified 'with infinite alacrity: not only mercenaries, but an incredible number of volunteers, gentry, nobility, nay the ladies themselves surmounting the delicacy of their sex, and the reserve so becoming to them, put their hand to the work happy, if at any expense, they could promote so pious a cause.' The pennants of an invasion fleet were again visible from High Street eyries on 2nd May: 'Four ships Royal and 26 other ships, well furnished with men, meat, munitions, captains and commanders', but storms and poor seamanship militated against success, and seaborne invasion (save one ship in Aberdeen) proved imaginary. The King's army paused at Berwick faced by 20,000 Covenanters camped at Duns, protesting that 'our desires are only the enjoying of our religion and liberties, according to the Ecclesiastical and civil laws of His Majesty's Kingdoms.' The two sides negotiated.

The Pacification of Berwick should have allowed calmer counsels to prevail but the fury of religious fanaticism had been released, and it was not going to cede the power it had so suddenly won. A General Assembly held in Edinburgh on 12th August abolished episcopacy and rejected parts of the liturgy including the Book of Common Prayer. Not surprisingly, when parliament met in Edinburgh at the end of the month, it sat without archbishop, bishop, Chancellor, or Clerk Register, 'for all had fled the land'.

The King's evident desire to wage total war upon Scotland was scrutinised carefully north of the Border. Edinburgh established a nightly watch of 400 men, raised new fortified mounds and trenches in the Causeway to defend the town against the castle if need be, and stocked sundry houses with sand and water against cannonade or fire. Two hundred men were despatched to guard Leith. The royalist commander of the castle, General Ruthven, misliking what he saw, ordered the downtaking of the new fortifications, and prohibited any further building, and the mustering and daily drilling of citizens within sight of the castle. Instead, he requested assistance with the repair of some of the crumbling walls of his fortress. An equable truce was reached: but once the citizens resumed their work at its expiry, constructing bulwarks in the gardens of Heriot's Hospital, across the causeway, and in 'sundry other parts within and about the town for the defence', and mounted cannon upon them 'for pursuit of the castle', Ruthven ordered his own cannon to open fire.

The King instructed the Provost and baillies of Edinburgh to proclaim the Earl of Argyll outlaw at the Mercat Cross 'that none of the King's lieges should answer or obey the said Earl' in retaliation for his support for the Covenant. The Provost felt unable to comply. He pled that

> in such troublesome times, the country being in uproar and afraid of the incoming of the sea and land armies, he durst scarcely hazard to make any such proclamation against the person of such a prime nobleman.

Besides, he questioned whether the act to deprive Argyll of his estate or dignities without advice of council and Scottish parliament was consistent with Scottish law. 'None of our noblemen are holden to answer but before his country, Council and Parliament and to be tried by his Scottish peers.' These were curious times that a Provost of Edinburgh could dispute constitutional issues with a King.

By the middle of 1640, Edinburgh was fast regressing to the pitiful condition of 1571:

> The castle of Edinburgh was now daily shooting at the town; few durst keep the Causeway, many fled the town for plain fear, with their wives, bairns, goods and gear, and some persons were shot and slain dead.

On 13th July, 'great bickering' led to the death of twenty of the town's guard, their dead bodies thrown over the castle wall 'to the great terror of the town's people, besides many others sore hurt'. It was Ruthven's revenge for the town's hanging a man called Baxter for convoying a packet of letters from the King up to him.

By 'daily taking our Scottish ships to the number of 80 small and great', the English navy was also throttling the trade of Leith. Yet instead of being plundered, the seized ships were taken carefully to Berwick, Newcastle, Holy Island and similar ports, where their goods were unloaded, inventoried, and put into store. Royal command insisted that they be seized: but the northerners 'always restored haill and sound to the owners, without loss of a groat'. It was a great kindness long remembered by the Scots, but trade was still severely prejudiced.

The phony war came to an end in August 1640, when General Alexander Leslie marched out with an army of 20,000, ten battery cannons, eighty field pieces, and 9,000 ells of canvas for tents and pavilions zealously provided by the city of Edinburgh. Spalding observed with amazement how all the silver within the city was melted down into good coin to pay the soldiers 'upon security of repayment in the current money according to weight'. The host crossed the Tweed on the 18th, and arrived at Newcastle twelve days later. Starving Royalists in Edinburgh Castle, 'scarce of fresh meat', disported themselves by sniping at a few poor haravesting peasants in the fields below. Their desultory malevolence assisted them little: castle rations were totally exhausted a fortnight later: 'having neither water, wine, beer, nor ale they could last no longer'. Once he learnt that Dumbarton Castle had also surrendered, the Governor, General Ruthven, resolved 'to seek a parley by drum', and

> rendered the castle upon condition that he and his soldiers should go honourably, carrying colours, burning matches, tuck of drum, with bag and baggage, and to march frae the Castle down through the town in good order and array. With some difficulty their conditions were granted . . .

Ruthven emerged with about seventy soldiers and thirty-two women. During the siege, about 160 people had perished in the castle 'through a sickness contracted by eating of salt meat, twelve thereof only being slayed all this time', and about 180 men, women and 'bairns of common people' slain in the town. But 'great skaith' had been done to the buildings by the cannon fire.

Sensing that their power was on the wax, fanatics flourished. Celebrations of Yuletide (Christmas) were suppressed, and merchants and craftsmen were charged, under pain of punishment, to go to work on Christmas Day 'to keep their booths, buy, sell and labour as on any other work day, all and every one, husbandmen and others. The booth-doors stood open, for fear, but there was little merchandise bought, far less work wrought.' Much of the extremity was inspired by the dreadful Andrew Cant, once minister of Pitsligo and Edinburgh, but now returned to Aberdeen. He began to cry and thunder out of the pulpit against anti-Covenanters; he would not suffer the people to pray when he prayed at sermon, but in their hearts to follow him, saying his outward prayers were sufficient for all; he refused to 'baptise bairns but after a preaching or lecture'. The following Christmas was also 'commanded to be a work day. Ilk Burgess to keep his booth, and ilk craftsman his work, feasting and idleness forbidden out of the pulpit . . . the people were otherwise inclined, but durst not disobey . . . the colleginers and other scholars kept the schools against their wills this day . . .'

In 1641, the Marquis of Montrose wrote to plead with the King: 'aim not at absoluteness: It endangers your estate and stirs up troubles'. The 'mighty distemper' into which Scotland had fallen could only be cured by 'Your Majesty's presence for a space in that kingdom', and for once, the King listened. Only now did a glimmer of what he had unleashed upon Scotland penetrate. He returned to Scotland in mid-year to seek an accommodation with the Scots so as to release his energies to deal with his disaffected English subjects. On 14th August, Charles I entered Edinburgh through the Water Gate with fewer than a hundred people in his train, and little of the ceremony of 1633: 'the King, somewhat melancholious after his travel, coming all the way post by coach, gave little ear to their speech.'

The following day he listened to a sermon 'after the Scottish fashion' in the abbey kirk, and then attended parliament: not the old parliament but a purged parliament. Nobles who had not subscribed to the Covenant, or the Acts promulgated by the subsequent parliaments and General Assembly, were expressly forbidden to take seats, and liable to be warded in the castle. Parliament met throughout the autumn:

> but mark this much, that the Covenanters had all their desire, and those who followed the King *simpliciter* were borne down from honours, dignities and places, and they, the Covenanters, had got all.

The King attempted to buy support by ennobling his enemies and faint echoes of pageantry and pleasure trembled in the air as the King hosted a banquet for the nobility in 'a Royal and merry manner', which the castle saluted with thirty-two shots of great ordnance.

After Charles's departure for England, Scotland marked time. It was not yet in irreversible decline, but it had forfeited its prosperity, and much of its spirit. The 'Presbyterian Pope' records an Edinburgh whore's reaction to the new dispensation:

> Wi bibles and psalm books they cant
> As ilka ane of them were sant,
> Wi' holy keckle, pegh and pant,
> And greet and grain,
> That every godly bowhead plant
> Gaze now to them,
> Repeating lectures, sermons, graces
> Telling soul-exercise and cases
> And making sic Wast country faces
> That I sair fear

> That we may a' resign our places
> If they thrang here.

Thrang here, unfortunately, they did.

In October 1643, Scots Covenanters bound themselves to English Presbyterians in a Solemn League and Covenant which proposed the abolition of both Popery and Prelacy, and the transformation of the Church of England to the Scottish model. Many of the original Covenanters, particularly now that they had got their parliament and General Assembly back, repudiated the new extremism. They sought to consolidate the concessions they had gained, rein in the extremists, and restore peace and prosperity. The Covenanters regarded them as turncoats; accommodation proved impossible and Civil War ensued.

Ably led by the Marquis of Montrose, they defeated Argyll in the west, took virtually the entire north of Scotland, and then vanquished central Scotland in the bloody battle of Kilsyth, in August 1645, which is said to have deprived some of the fishing burghs of Fife of their entire sea-going population. Edinburgh came under immediate threat. The town council

> caused proclamation to be made by beat of drum that none of the inhabitants presumed to leave the town without leave of the Magistrates, on penalty of £1,000, loss of their freedom and forfeiture of all their effects within Edinburgh to be applied in defence of the city . . . and for the greater security of the town in this time of imminent danger, whole householders, within the space of forty-eight hours, were to give in to the magistrates the names and quality of their several lodgers, under pain of £1,000 Scots and loss of their freedom forever.

The town wall was repaired, and two new gates were erected – at the bottom of Leith Wynd, and the other at the Pleasance, and the Trained Bands were ordered to stand guard from eight in the evening until six in the morning. Montrose, fresh from the scandalously bloody sack of Aberdeen by his 'Irishmen', addressed Edinburgh with the genial courtesy of a giant tiger:

> Loving friends, notwithstanding of your former miscarriages and continuance in this present rebellion, which might move us to use all the rigour and severity you have hereby justly deserved. These are to will and require you, in His Majesty's name and authority . . . that you will immediately after sight hereof, enlarge and put to liberty all such of our people as are prisoners with

you . . . which if you do, you shall be assured not only to have your bygone enormities passed and forgot, but to have all the favour and protection from us you can either expect or desire hereafter. But if you refuse or neglect, you shall oblige us to use all the just resentment against you and your town, by fire and sword that can be used against rebels and principal fomenters of so treasonable and unnatural rebellion.

The capital was in desperate straits. Drained of men of soldiering age, it had just suffered the worse plague in its history. Plague had seeped into the capital early in the year; and it was swiftly obvious that this was no ordinary visitation. The council had appointed Joannus Paulitius MD to visit the infected, from April, for which he was to receive £80 Scottish per month, but there was little even a doctor could do. By the dog days of August, bubonic plague was in full swing in the city: debtors were released from the Tolbooth with the consent of their creditors, all 'unfreemen' were expelled beyond the walls and no owner of a house in Edinburgh was permitted to let a house to any other than a citizen. The town's historian, William Maitland, concluded:

> For aught I can learn, Edinburgh never was in a more miserable and melancholy situation than at present; for by the unparalleled ravages committed by the plague, it was spoiled of its inhabitants to such a degree that there was scarce 50 men left capable of assisting the defence of the town in case of an attack; which the citizens never had more occasion to fear than at this time.

Edinburgh, being in no position to resist Montrose, ceded to his demands. But his threat proved ephemeral, for within months, Montrose's Highland soldiers who had stood him in such good stead whilst plunder was plentiful in the Highlands and in the north, deserted him as he marched south. Less than a month after Kilsyth, he was defeated at Philiphaugh, barely escaping with his life. A large number of the Royalist army and its adherents surrendered to promises of quarter offered by General Leslie: but they had reckoned without the appalling Andrew Cant. With others 'possessed with the same spirit', Cant roared from his pulpit 'bloody oracles before the people: that God required the blood of these men, nor could the sins of the nation be otherwise expiated or the revenge of heaven diverted'. The luckier ones were brought back to Edinburgh for judicial execution: the rest, including many camp followers, were hacked down in what became known as the Fields of the Dead.

After the execution of Charles I in 1649, Montrose returned from exile with a force of mercenaries in 1650, invading the north of Scotland. Defeated at Carbisdale, he was kidnapped at Ardvreck and brought as prisoner down throughout the north-east, through Dundee (which provided him with a decent suit of clothes) to Leith. He was then taken up to the Water Gate on a carthorse, surrounded with about forty prisoners of quality on foot. Once within the Canongate, Montrose was bound in a high chair and taken up through the town: and as he passed a wedding party of Argyll's at Moray House it is said that some of the guests took time off from their carousing to spit in his face. He had already been condemned to death, and his trial was simply a matter of pronouncing sentence: a special scaffold was erected between the Cross and the Tron with a gibbet thirty feet high to which he was conveyed in 'a scarlet cloak richly shammaded with golden lace'. He ignored the ministers beside him on the scaffold, who railed vehemently at him and protested that all he had done was his duty, obeying his prince's 'just commands'. Just before his execution he penned this poem:

> Let them bestow on ev'ry Airth a Limb;
> Open all my Veins, that I may swim
> To Thee my Saviour, in that Crimson Lake;
> Then place my pur-boil'd head upon a Stake;
> Scatter my ashes, throw them in the Air:
> Lord (since Thou know'st where all these Atoms are)
> I'm hopeful, once Thou'lt recollect my Dust
> And confident Thou'lt raise me with the Just.

Even the most fervent of Covenanters, like Archibald Johnston of Wariston who helped draft the original Covenant and was perhaps the leading intellectual strategist of the movement, were not anti-royalist as such: 'all the Royalists in Scotland could not have pleaded so much for the Crown and the King's just power as the Chancellor and Wariston did for many days together.' But who was to define what was the King's *just power*? Those responsible for the massacre of disobedients at Philiphaugh, for example, were vehement in the religion in which they had been nurtured. Wariston, to whom his religion was 'more than all the world', spent many hours each day in prayer, frequently three hours at a stretch; so exalted, that just before his execution after the Restoration, he confided to a friend that 'he could never doubt of his own salvation, he had so often seen God's face in the house of prayer.'

The Scots watched with dismay as the English parliament decapitated their monarch on 30 January 1649 without the Scots parliament's agreement, and promptly crowned his son. In so doing, they subjected Charles

II to unaccustomed humiliation by extracting an undertaking that he would abide by the Covenant. The manner of doing it so angered the King that Presbyterians were to pay for it dearly later in the century. The republican government in England found itself threatened with a bleeding wound in the north, and Cromwell was duly despatched to staunch it.

David Leslie's army boxed Cromwell in a disadvantageous spot with poor provisions near Dunbar. In August 1650, the Earl of Loudon, Lord Chancellor of Scotland, wrote to Edinburgh seeking sustenance for his army:

> The best service you can do to your brethren is to send out bread and cheese, or other meat, to give them for this night and the morrow morning, for they will seek no more until the Lord deliver us and them, or declare his pleasure in the contrary. Send out the Baxters with all their own bread, and Hors together; accommodate them all that you can, for truly they deserve it and God is hitherto with them to their comfort. Send us your provisions in by the other side of Corstorphine; we are drawn up from bewest Corstorphine meadow.

But it was a sadly purged army that Leslie led. He was compelled, against his better judgment, to relinquish his strong position, and force Cromwell to a fight; and on 3 September 1650 the Scottish army was routed at Dunbar: many killed and 9,000 taken prisoner. Some 1,000, those most free of wounds, sound of wind and limb, were to be transported as slaves. A further 1,000 virtual slaves were despatched to assist in the draining of the Fens in East Anglia, and 5,100 prisoners were discharged as unfit, many of them coming to swell the misery in the capital. Of the 2,000 balance who were marched down to Newcastle, barely 300 survived.

Cromwell reported to London of his great mercy at Edinburgh Castle which had held out for three months:

> I sent a summons to the castle upon the 12th [December]; which occasioned several exchanges and replies . . . indeed, the mercy is very great, and seasonable. It has pleased God to cause this Castle of Edinburgh to be surrendered into our hands this day at about 11 o'clock. I think, I need say little of the strength of the place; which, if it had not come in as it did, would have cost very much blood to have attained, if at all to be attained; and did tie up your army to that inconvenience, that little or nothing could have been attempted whilst this was in design.

In the list of the cannon which he had captured was 'the great iron murderer called Muckle Meg'.

The danger of future Scots disaffection or a Scots army was to be removed by a union between the two countries; and, in April 1652, an Act of Union was duly proclaimed 'with much solemnity at the Mercat Cross of Edinburgh, by beat of drum and sound of trumpet, and the Cross adorned with hangings'. Under threat of dismissal, all people at universities, colleges and schools in Scotland had to take a Test of Loyalty, agreeing to swear to 'live under and give obedience to the authority of the Parliament of England exercised in Scotland'. An English observer was puzzled by the Scots' ungrateful lack of enthusiasm:

> There was a very great concourse of people at the proclamation of it: after the reading whereof the [English] soldiers gave several shouts, as complying with the Parliament in this free conferring of liberty upon a conquered people: but so senseless are this generation of their own good, that scarcely a man of them showed any sign of rejoicing.

A sad change had come upon the country from twenty years earlier. Poverty and scarcity of money was increasing daily in 1657, causing people to 'sell their lands and estate [and] even their household gear, insicht and planishing and some of their clothes'. Daily in Edinburgh, and also in Canongate, rang the rouping bell to announce the compulsory sale of goods of a bankrupt.

Cromwell proved brisk with the rampant Presbyters: he could tolerate variety, but not fanaticism. In November 1653, his official newspaper recorded: 'Here hath been a thin meeting of diverse Hotspurs of the Kirk, to little purpose save thwarting and crossing one another, being of different parties and opinions.' In mid-1633, he despatched his colonels to close down the General Assembly, then meeting in Edinburgh. As the Moderator began to call the roll, the colonels 'desired them to be silent', and enquired by whose authority it met. After a wrangle, the Moderator was only permitted to hold his roll call if 'it were not longsome', but military patience proved short. He had barely begun calling the first presbytery, when the colonels interrupted: 'it would prove tedious, that we could not wait upon it, but desired him to remove and be gone, and if there were not, he had instructions what to do.' The Moderator then sought permission to have a prayer before the Assembly was dissolved, and seeming to obtain permission, began. Presumably the colonels were aware that an extempore Presbyterian Scottish prayer could extend several hours. After the Moderator had uttered barely five or six sentences, the colonels interpolated and 'desired them again to be gone'. Raising his voice, the Moderator carried on, but was forced at length to break off and quit the hall. The General Assembly was not to meet again for almost forty years.

CHAPTER SIX

LABORIOUS RESTORATION

The term Restoration is, so far as Scotland is concerned, inappropriate. Who was being restored to what? Charles II was already the crowned King of a country from which Oliver Cromwell had removed independence. Worse, during the latter part of the Commonwealth, some Scots had so prospered from the militarily imposed peace and justice that they opposed any dismemberment of the new arrangement. Dismembered, however, it was to be. Widespread if naïvely romantic Scottish joy greeted the return of Charles II: it was said that Sir Thomas Urquhart, translator and transmogrifier of Rabelais, was so overjoyed that he died of laughter. The town council of Edinburgh felt that it could run to the cost of a sumptuous banquet at the Mercat Cross, with general rejoicings elsewhere throughout the city. They sent the King a present of £1,000 sterling, and an obsequious address which produced its intended result. The King confirmed all Edinburgh's charters and rights, and gave them permission to impose a tax on beer, ale and wine.

So much did the people long for a new age to begin, that in future, the date of 29th May (the King's birthday) was to be held as an Edinburgh festival. Here is how it was celebrated in 1665:

> My Lord Commissioner, in his state, accompanied with his life-guard on horseback and Sir Andrew Ramsay, Lord Provost of Edinburgh, bailies and Council in their robes, accompanied with all the trained bands in arms, went to church and heard the Bishop of Edinburgh, upon a text as fit as well as applied for the work of the day: thereafter, 35 aged men in blue gowns, each having got 35 shillings in their purse, came up from the Abbey to the great church, praying all along for His Majesty. The sermon being ended, His Grace entertained all the nobles and gentlemen with a magnificent feast and open table.

At the Cross in Edinburgh, a green arbour had been planted and loaded with oranges and vines, and for eight hours wine ran liberally from its conduits 'to the great solace of the indigent commons there'. Castle cannons crashed, trumpets blared, drums rolled, the trained bands fired volleys (more or less into the air), bumpers of royal healths were drunk, and people joyfully acclaimed. The noise must have been frightful. Thereafter, the Lord Commissioner and the council went up to the castle where they were entertained with more wine and sweetmeats, and on their return, there were great numbers of bonfires. The joviality of ringing of bells and shooting of the great guns continued until midnight.

The jubilation was premature. The relationship between Scotland and the English crown, the cause of the original explosion in 1637, deteriorated after 1660. Although parliament met more frequently, the King exercised authority through commissioners with the power and the authority of a viceroy. Scotland's subservient role was painfully apparent to visitors like the Huguenot traveller Jorevin de Rocheford (of whom little is known), visiting probably in early 1661. The new palace block in the castle, he wrote, was

> pretty well built, which formerly served as the residence of the Kings of Scotland: and at present for the viceroys when the King of England sends any; for at the time I was there, there was only the Grand Chancellor [the Earl of Aberdeen] who had almost the same authority and power as viceroy.

The legality that Charles II was also King of Scotland, presumably not even mentioned by the garrison guide, had been rendered peripheral. Jorevin was much taken by the majesty, carvings and sculpture of Heriot's Hospital, its formal gardens used by the citizens as a place of recreation, its bowling green resembling 'a green carpet', and the kitchen garden stacked with a quantity of fruit trees. The High Street, 'so wide that it seems a market place throughout its whole extent', had been cleared of its fortifications. Holyrood, despite its half-burnt condition at the hands of Cromwell's soldiers, remained magnificent:

> In entering, you pass the first great court surrounded with lodgings for the officers; and from thence into a second, where appears the palace, composed of several small pavilions intermixed with galleries and turrets, forming a wonderful symmetry; but it has been much damaged by fire.

Meeting up with some Flemish and French fellow-Catholics, Jorevin was invited shooting over the whins and the sands of Portobello, retiring from the field, conquered and unwounded, but 'very much fatigued', with waterfowl, six large woodcock, a large leveret, six young wild ducks and two rabbits. Leith looked prosperous, exporting salt, fish, tin, lead and sea coal to Flanders, Holland, Denmark and Sweden and even France;

but it had shrunk to a village, in his estimation, occupied only by seamen and sailors. The Cromwellian citadel was 'almost ruined by [the waves], having undermined the bastions in such a manner that it is, as it were, abandoned, for there is no garrison to guard it'. From the fact that Jorevin records little destruction, it seems that Edinburgh citizens had used the last five years of the Commonwealth to repair damage. Equally, there is a dispiriting lack of ambition and flamboyance. One could infer that the stuffing had been knocked out of the place.

Save in personal licentiousness, life under viceroys was little more relaxed than life under the colonels: there was the apparatus of a reasonably efficient police state. All books required commissioners' consent before printing, and all articles in the new-fangled broadsheets or newspapers a licence from the Bishop of Edinburgh, or other member of the Privy Council. All innkeepers and burgesses were nightly required to submit to the authorities a list of strangers residing with them. For nonconformists, rebels or those beyond the establishment, the capital would have been claustrophobic if not dangerous.

In 1661, parliament revoked all Acts passed since 1633 including the hard-won concessions of 1637-9. Totem Presbyterians such as Johnston of Wariston and the Marquis of Argyll were executed as an example to others, and obedience upon oath was compelled from all ministers. Between 1661 and the execution of James Renwick in 1688, approximately one hundred noblemen, gentlemen, ministers and others, 'noble martyrs for Jesus Christ', were executed in Edinburgh, most of them buried in Greyfriars. During these decades of repression, extreme Covenanters looked back with nostalgia to the theocracy that ruled Scotland between 1649 and 1650. It had governed according to dictates which ministers received directly from God: and was accordingly of unexampled purity and unparalleled piety. They had fought for it with their blood, and were prepared to sacrifice themselves rather than renounce it.

For his part, the King had felt humiliated when he had had to treat with Presbyterians for his coronation in 1651. They were anathema to him now. Ministers who wrote to remind the King of his obligations to the Covenanters were imprisoned: and the King's powers to appoint officers, to summon parliament and to raise armies were increased. On 6th September, 1661, episcopal government returned to Scotland with the nomination of the minister of Crail, James Sharp, as Archbishop of St Andrews. The following year, all parishes whose ministers had been appointed since 1649 were declared vacant. Current incumbents had to apply for approval from the local patron, and confirmation by the local bishop. Approximately 270 ministers, the majority of them in the southwest of Scotland, refused and were dispossessed. Many of them, unable to sustain themselves, came to Edinburgh. An indication of how government pressure was maintained upon dissenters is the edict of March 1679:

> the Magistrates were strictly commanded to turn out of the city and liberties of Edinburgh, the wives and family of all the outed Presbyterian ministers, under the penalty of 1000 pound sterling for each of the said families that shall remain in the town after the twenty-fifth day of the approaching month of March.

Only one week's notice from the date of the order had been given 'for those unhappy families in the utmost misery and distress to prepare for their woeful departure'. Those refusing to attend the established church were fined, and meeting in 'conventicles' – that is to say private, Presbyterian meetings often in the remote countryside – was made illegal and punishable by death. Religion was not the point at issue: such disobedience was considered treasonable. The military was unleashed upon the south-west in 1663 and the unnecessary harshness of their actions provoked the rebellion known as the Pentland Rising three years later. The rebels never exceeded 1,100, many were armed only with their normal agricultural implements like scythes and pitchforks, and they looked to a contemporary 'rather like dying men than soldiers going to conquer'. They were defeated at Rullion Green by Thomas Dalyell of the Binns, eighty prisoners taken, twenty-one of whom were hanged at the gallows at the Mercat Cross.

When the Duke of Lauderdale was appointed King's Commissioner at Holyrood, he intended to enjoy his viceregal status in Scotland. His great country château of Thirlestane, by Lauder, enjoyed the same designer, Sir William Bruce, and the same European craftsmen that he used to remodel the Palace of Holyrood. Brunstane, his villa near Edinburgh complete with its new bathhouse, provided a convenient cottage for the capital. But under the direction of John Mylne, master mason, and Sir William Bruce, the burnt palace was transformed into something of truly regal splendour, built 'in exact ashlar, smooth as paper, close-jointed'.[*]

James Brome chanced upon Viceroy Lauderdale riding in state to open

---

[*] The description of the construction of Holyrood is so detailed as to leave nothing to chance. Take, for example, the specification for the main entrance: 'To make ane gate of the Doric order, two columns on each side of the said gate, with pedestal, base, column, chapterhead, and entablature of ane model according, to thirty-one foot height, rail, balusters, and pilasters with proper furnishing above, about and alongst the said entablature, which runs from tower and tower, as also above the cornice of the inside to the whole breadth of the court, the cornice enriched only with dentellie [dentils], the columns two part set off the porch and the porch three or four feet off the naked of the wall, the door within consisting of six foot and twelve foot, with ane architrave going round frieze and cornice.'

Parliament in 1669:

> and indeed it was a very glorious sight, for they were all richly
> accoutred and as nobly attended with a splendid retinue, the
> heralds of arms and other officers, that went before were wonder-
> ful gay and finely habited, and the servants that attended were
> clad in the richest liveries; their coaches drawn with six horses,
> as they went rattling along, did dazzle our eyes with the splen-
> dour of their furniture, and all the nobles appeared in the great-
> est pomp and gallantry.

Increasing consumption in the capital sat ill beside rural misery; and yet
another sumptuary Act controlling the expenditure on luxuries was
thought necessary in 1672. Five years later, coffee houses became
licensed for the first time in the city. Street lights became the thing when
the council decreed that every tenement should display a lantern and
candle at first storey level, which should burn from five o'clock in the
evening until ten at night, from the end of October to the beginning of
March.

So long as they behaved doucely and did not challenge the state, Lauderdale would tolerate even fanatics: but to the dispossessed, living in remote countryside sustained on little more than religious exaltation, their
misery almost entirely attributable to religious persecution, accommodation with representatives of Satan was inconceivable. The military were
deployed again, and the Conventiclers defended themselves with a number of sympathetic 'broken men of war'. After the murder of Archbishop
Sharp in 1679, disturbances in the south-west increased, urged on by
radical ministers like Richard Cameron (originator of the Cameronians).
After a surprise victory over John Graham of Claverhouse (Bluidy Clav-
ers) who had been brought in to lead the campaign at Drumclog, the
Presbyterians parked near Bothwell Bridge. The government despatched
an army of 5,000 regulars under the Duke of Monmouth, bastard son of
the King himself, which routed the Conventiclers, killed some 700 and
took 1,200 prisoner. Many were brought to Edinburgh and miserably
confined without shelter in Greyfriars Kirkyard from July to November;
and some were executed in the Grassmarket, in the manner suggested by
the licentious Duke of Rothes whose dismissal of one such was 'then e'en
let him glorify God in the Grassmarket'.

Prejudice against Conventiclers was matched only by prejudice against
witchcraft, the apogee of which was probably the execution of Major
Weir, a prominent member of town society living in the West Bow with
his sister. A person of unexampled piety, Major Weir confessed, when

well struck with years, that he had been guilty of the most ambitious deviations with his sister, of which sorcery was the chief. Whether he was addled, wandering with age, or even expressing regret at something he had not done, their elderly existence was soon snuffed out on the Castle Hill in 1678. Save for livid ghosts and phantasmagorical black dogs with glaring red eyes, their house remained uninhabited for generations.

In 1679, the capital seemed unexpectedly set to flourish once more. In haste to remove his brother and heir, James, Duke of York, from danger in London caused by his flagrant Roman Catholicism, Charles II dispatched him as viceroy to Scotland. The whiff of being the centre of a royal court returned to the Canongate. James was greeted with pomp and ceremony only little less than that accorded a King. He was magnificently entertained by the citizens ('at an expense which testified their loyalty more than their economy') and there was profligate issue of Freedoms of the City to his attendants.

Accompanied by his wife and daughter, Anne, James set himself to woo Scotland. Had the Scots not stood by his brother against England? If the worst came to the worst, would they not do the same for him? Since the country was, if anything, even more anti-Catholic than England, the task was just that much greater; and he began the process with splendour. Lord Fountainhall has left a good description of how 'our Court at Holyroodhouse' celebrated the Queen's birthday in 1681 with

> bonfires, shooting of cannons, and the acting of a comedy called Mithridatus King of Pontus, wherein Lady Anne, the Duke's daughter, and the Ladies of Honour were the only actors.

The Lady Anne, of course, became the Queen best known for being dead. The nobility, who had not been flattered (nor would have tholed being flattered) by Lauderdale, were gritumly attracted to a prince of the blood. Robert Chambers described how they warmed to the

> exquisite mixture of formality and condescension . . . They made parties, balls, and masquerades at the Palace, and are said to have treated those who attended them with the most engaging attentions. In a species of dramatic entertainment which they got up, in one of their private apartments, and which seems to have been of a similar description with Milton's Masque of Comus, they condescended so far as to act particular characters, and to direct the performance . . . The vast numbers of nobility and gentry that flocked around the Duke filled the town with

gaiety and splendour. It is said that old people, about the middle of last century, used to talk with delight of the magnificency and brilliancy of the Court which James assembled, and of the general tone of happiness and satisfaction which pervaded the town on the occasion.

It was possibly the only time in its history that the Palace of Holyrood, as rebuilt by Lauderdale, came close to being used as it had been intended.

During his residence, the Duke of York addressed himself to the condition of the capital, to which little save destruction and repair had happened since the 1630s. He suggested an extension of the regality to the north, and made a formal Grant of Encouragement to compel proprietors of lands required for any new bridge or extended regality to 'part with the same on reasonable terms', and that such lands should be 'erected into a Regality in favour of the citizens'. Since James wished to use Holyrood Abbey as a Catholic chapel, he encouraged the city to use Thomas Moodie's legacy to build a new church in the Canongate – and by this act, undid much of the good he had achieved. The Edinburgh mob lying restless within its catacombs was not prepared to tolerate overt Catholicism. Baulking at attacking the Duke of York himself, they attacked a known Catholic adviser – Sir James Dick of Priestfield, and burnt his house (which he repaired and transformed with public funds into the splendid Prestonfield House which we know today).

James's sojourn in Edinburgh accelerated the capital's emergence from its post-war misery. The Merchant Company was founded in 1681, and a piazza or open-air Exchange was constructed for the merchants in Parliament Square four years later. The Order of the Thistle and the Royal Company of Archers were revived and royal patronage extended to the foundation of the Royal College of Physicians. James was patron of the military engineer, Captain John Slezer, whose drawings of Scotland in *Theatrum Scotiae*, published in 1692, with text by Sir Robert Sibbald (Geographer-Royal, King's Physician, and primary mover in the establishment of the College of Physicians and the Royal Botanic Garden) comprise the most vivid and accurate record of late seventeenth-century Scotland.

Royal patronage also extended to the Physic Garden, then in the grounds of Trinity Hospital, which had been founded in 1675 by Sir Robert Sibbald and Dr Andrew Balfour, with the object of discovering what *materia medica*, in the way of herbs, Scotland was capable of producing. It proved a noble asset to the capital: a place where George Home MP would go for a stroll after dinner, or send to from the country for cuttings of herbs and flowers. The English chaplain Thomas Morer admired its 2,700 plants when he visited it in 1689, but regretted the absence of beauty or walks. The bookish might prefer the emerging Library of the Faculty of Advocates (precursor of the National Library of Scotland) much of whose credit may be attributed to Sir George Mackenzie of Rosehaugh, Lord Advocate (whose role as persecutor of the Covenantors earned him the nickname of 'bluidy Mackenzie'). A considerable legal thinker, Mackenzie was also author of *Laws and Customs of Scotland in Matters Criminal*, of the first Scottish novel *Aretina* and of several books and essays.

In addition to the customary tourist sights, Thomas Morer observed that the newer houses of Edinburgh were being built of stone: 'with good windows modishly framed'. He was curious that 'most of the houses . . . are parted into diverse tenements so they have as many landlords as storeys.' The wynds and closes were 'very steepy and troublesome, and withall so nasty (for want of bog houses which they very rarely have) that Edinburgh is by some likened to an ivory comb, whose teeth on both sides are very foul, but the space between 'em is clean and sightly'.

Nor was he over-impressed by the college – 'one small quadrangle and some other lodgings without uniformity of order' – although he admired the library. Morer particularly liked Leith, 'the warehouse of Edinburgh', which he found thriving, not just for its European trade, but because it had become the capital's playground: thither the citizens flocked 'by foot or by coaches to divert themselves, having no playhouse, music meetings or spring garden to tempt them to those superfluous expenses'.

It was to remedy the nastiness of the wynds that the King's master mason Robert Mylne soon became Edinburgh's first developer. From the wynds, closes and lands, he carved two unusual but highly desirable enclosed squares: Milne's Court in the still-fashionable district of the northern Lawnmarket; and Milne's Square opposite the Tron Kirk. Both were successful and profitable. Worried that Edinburgh was rebuilding itself to 'excessive incommodious and dangerous height' with 'slight and insufficient construction', parliament established building regulations specifying minimum thicknesses of wall at various storey heights.*

When the Duke of York became James VII in 1685, Edinburgh might well have hoped for a share in the glory. But when, instead, the Scottish parliament refused to endorse the King's aggressive Roman Catholic policy, James proceeded to impose it by using the royal prerogative. The Monmouth Rising in England was duly paralleled by one led by the Earl

---

* The thickness of side walls was to be three feet at the first storey above the causeway, two feet nine inches for the second, reducing to two feet at the fifth. If the walls were to be built ashlar, every tenth stone had to go through the wall as a binding stone. Cross-walls without chimneys were to be a minimum of ten inches thick.

of Argyll in Scotland, both of which ended in defeat and the execution of their leaders. The mob was roused once more. In 1686, the rabble was inflamed by public attendance at Mass and

> insulted the Chancellor's Lady and other persons of distinction when returning from their Chapel. The affront was resented with great severity. A journeyman baker, being ordered by the Privy Council to be whipped through the Canongate of being concerned in the riot, the Mob rose, rescued him from punishment, beat the executioner and continued all night long in uproar.

Soldiers from the castle brought down to quell the disturbance fired into the mob, killing two men and a woman, and the Privy Council, determined to enforce its authority, 'appointed a double file of musketeers and pikemen to prevent the sufferers from being rescued' when several condemned rioters were whipped. Tension ran so high that an indigent fencing master who proposed a toast of 'Confusion to the Papists' was hanged for his temerity at the Mercat Cross.

Edinburgh merchants must have watched with intensifying gloom as James permitted a Catholic printing press to be set up within Holyrood, Jesuits to open a college, the nave of Holyrood Abbey to be converted for the celebration of Mass with ceremonial use by the Knights of the Thistle. Once King James's wife, Mary of Modena, had given birth to a son, most Scots had supported his replacement by William of Orange, since a Roman Catholic succession remained unacceptable to the country. They had also been gravely alarmed at the King's use of his prerogative to relax restrictions against Roman Catholics. Arbitrary rule and Papist habits had been the triggers of the 1637 wars. When news of the invasion of William of Orange and of James's flight reached Edinburgh at the end of 1688, the mob attacked:

> Drums were beat through the city, the inhabitants assembled in great multitudes. They proceeded to demolish the Chapel of Holyroodhouse, but were opposed by a party of about 100 men stationed in the Abbey who adhered to the interests of James. The mob pressing forward, were fired upon by this party; about a dozen were killed and thrice as many wounded, upon which they fled for the present: but quickly returned with a warrant from some of the Lords of the Privy Council . . . they were headed by the Magistrates, Town Guard, trained bands and heralds at arms. The Captain of the party being defeated, some being killed and the rest made prisoners. Then there was nothing to resist their

fury. The Abbey church and private chapel were robbed and despoiled of their ornaments; the College of the Jesuits almost pulled in pieces, and the houses of the Roman Catholics plundered.

King William never visited Edinburgh during his reign, and was never crowned in Scotland. Sometimes, particularly during the Darien fiasco, he appeared wholly muddled over the fact that he was nominal King over two separate countries, seeming to favour the attack by one upon the other. So Edinburgh was not to be a beneficiary of the new regime.

Its remoteness was swiftly perceived, and it seemed to some as though religion had been safeguarded at the expense of sovereignty. Opposition to William swiftly coalesced into a Jacobite rebellion, which ended with the untimely death of Claverhouse at Killiecrankie, and with the defeat of the rump in the Haughs of Cromdale in May 1690. Scotland was governed once more at the end of a pen, and at the mercy of London politics. Even though directed at lawless Highlanders, the massacre of Glencoe, the following year, left an evil taste. The Scottish parliament became much preoccupied with 'the matter of Glencoe' and on 11th July, 1695 prepared an address to King William that Sir John Dalrymple had exceeded instructions 'therefore desiring His Majesty would dispose of him as he in his royall wisdome shall think fitt.'

Harvest failures combined with the effects of forty years' disrupted husbandry led to famine, particularly in the west and south-west of Scotland. Andrew Fletcher of Saltoun calculated that there were, about this time, some

> 200,000 people begging from door to door. These are not only no way advantageous, but are so very grievous a burden to so poor a country; and though the number of them be, perhaps, double to what it was formerly, by reason of this present great distress; in all times there have been about 100,000 of these vagabonds who have lived without any regard of subjection either to the laws of the land, or even those of god and nature.

He recommended deportation to the colonies as a suitable remedy. That tempted Scots to think that a colony of their own might not be a bad idea. William's own Commissioner encouraged the Scots parliament to believe the King would support such a venture.

> If you will find it will tend the advancement of trade that an Act be passed for the encouragement of such as shall acquire or estab-

lish a plantation in Africa or America . . . His Majesty is willing
to declare he will grant to the subjects of this Kingdom in favour
of their plantations and such rights and privileges as he doth
grant in like cases to the subjects of his other dominions.

On 26th June, 1695, the Company of Scotland was given a due monopoly of Caledonian imperialism, and a book was opened for subscribers to
register their names and shareholdings: 'The Books of the Indian and
Affrican Company wer opened this day,' wrote George Home on 26th
February, 1696. On the morrow, he went to the India Company room to
pledge of his £500, and found 'many subscribers of all sorts come very fast
in'. English merchants were also invited to contribute, and had subscribed £300,000 before the English parliament declared such sharehold-
ing an Act of Treason. All but four of the London shareholders withdrew
their investment. The Scots raised £400,000 sterling (a substantial proportion of the country's entire liquid capital), and in July 1698, 1,200
colonists sailed from Leith in five ships to land at Darien in the Isthmus
of Panama. First reports were good:

> The soil is rich, the air good and temperate, the water is sweet
> and everything contrived to make it healthful . . . the country
> certainly affords gold enough.

Aware of the Spanish claim to Darien, the English government then
declared that the Scots had 'gone upon a design which His Majesty was
in no way acquainted with and could therefore not approve of', and forbade governors of English plantations to lend any assistance; the
Governor of Jamaica wrote to the Spanish Governor of Cartegena, that

> although the Scottish nation recognises the King of England as
> its Lord, it is nevertheless a nation distinct from the English, and
> the English are in no way accomplices to this design . . . nor
> shall the Scots receive any aid from me.

The colonists were wracked with disease, particularly malaria, and were
unable to obtain any assistance. The Spaniards attacked in due course,
and in early 1700, the Darien colony was finally abandoned, at a cost of
some 2,000 lives, perhaps a quarter of a million pounds sterling, and the
greater part of the fleet. A semi-official enquiry into the disaster was held
in Scotland; and when its findings were published, a copy was burnt in
London by the Public Hangman, on the grounds that it was a breach of
their treaty with Spain and likely to damage Jamaican trade. The printer

of a comparable book was imprisoned in Edinburgh; but the mood of the crowd was such that it burned down the Tolbooth door to rescue him, lifting the gaoler's wig whilst they were at it. The four men who were tried for this outrage were pilloried at the Tron and pelted by the Edinburgh mob – but with flowers. It is said that the leader was due to receive a flogging, but since the executioner merely patted him gently, the executioner himself was sentenced to a flogging by the hangman of Haddington. The latter dared not face the capital, and bolted.

In the early years of the eighteenth century, the relationship between Scotland and England was at its nadir. Desperate to generate new trade to recoup the Darien losses and offset the appalling consequences of famine, Scots sought to expand their trade: the English reaction was to inhibit this at all stages. They passed an Act declaring the Scots to be aliens, shut English markets to Scottish produce, and fitted out ships to intercept Scots trade with France. A sign of the extreme animosities between the two countries was the fate of the unfortunately English Captain Thomas Green of the ship *Worcester*, driven for repairs into Leith Roads in March 1705. It took little misunderstanding and gossip for the capital to become convinced that this same captain and crew had been responsible for the capture of a Scottish vessel and the murder of its entire crew. Captain Green endured a full legal trial, and was found guilty of piracy aggravated by murder. The Lord Chancellor, doubting their guilt, sought royal intercession; the mob rose up, and Captain Green and two of his crew duly suffered on Leith Links on 11th April for a crime of which they were probably both ignorant and innocent.

There was only one way forward if Scottish mercantile interests were to survive: full union with England; and the period between the Darien disaster and 1707 was dominated by the Union debate. We now know, from the despatch of Daniel Defoe to the capital in 1704 to act as government informer, briber and a destabiliser of the Scottish interest, that England desired the Union more than Scotland. Strong measures if Scotland contained nothing worth having. In 1706, when it looked as though the Act of Union was chancy, Defoe set himself to create a spy ring with the following objectives:

1. To inform myself of the measures taken, or parties forming, against the Union and apply myself to prevent them. 2. In conversation and by all reasonable methods, to dispose people's minds to the Union. 3. By rational discourse, to answer any objections, libels or reflections on the Union, the English or their Court, relating to the Union. 4. To remove the jealousies or uneasiness of the people about secret designs here.

The deed was done in the Parliament House of Scotland. It caused such convulsion that some of the aristocratic pro-Union conspirators could write to each other only in codes lest their messages were discovered, and due revenge exercised. Defoe reported to his controller after a few weeks in post:

> I converse with Presbyterian, Episcopal dissenter, Papist and non-juror, and I hope with equal circumspection . . . God knows where the money is to pay for it! Today I am going into partnership with a Member of Parliament in a glasshouse, together with another in a salt-work. With the Glasgow mutineers I am to be a fish merchant, with the Aberdeen man a woollen . . .

In early 1707 he could report again: 'I have my spies and my pensioners in every place . . . I have spies in the Commission, in the Parliament and in the Assembly, and under the pretence of writing my History I get everything told me.'

As soon as the formal articles of Union became available in October 1706, Edinburgh erupted:

> The outer Parliament House and the square adjoining were crowded with an infinite number of people who, with hootings and execrations insulted the Duke of Queensberry, Commissioner, and every partisan of the Union, whilst those headed the opposition were followed with the loudest acclamations.

It was, perhaps, the zenith of the power of the Edinburgh mob, which could surge from its catacombs for days if not months upon end, to occupy the city and terrorise the pro-Union conspirators who, like Sir Patrick Johnston, a former Lord Provost, were fair game: 'By a narrow escape, he saved himself from falling a victim to popular fury.' Once the mob was 'absolute master of the city', troops took possession of the Netherbow and, later, of Parliament Square and the different lanes and avenues of the city, by which means the mob should have been quelled. But it was not. It grew in size, and surged up the High Street 'threatening destruction to all the promoters of the Union, and continued for four or five hours in this temper'. The politicans were shocked:

> Formerly they did, or pretended, not to believe the disposition of the people against the Union, but now they were thoroughly convinced of it, and terribly afraid of their lives, this passage making it evident that the Union was crammed down Scotland's throats.

The Marquis of Queensberry, the King's Commissioner, could only reach Parliament House from his carriage through two lanes of musketeers 'as if he had been led to the gallows'; and on his return to the abbey, his coach had to be protected by Horse Guards. Condemning the tumult, the Privy Council imposed instant curfew 'whenever the drum should beat', after which soldiers were authorised to fire upon and kill anybody in the street. Queensberry

> was constantly saluted with curses and imprecations as he passed
> the streets, and if the Parliament sat till towards evening, then to
> be sure he and his guards were well pelted with stones.

Sixty-six royal burghs petitioned parliament that the terms of Union protected 'neither our religion nor our civil interests and trades, as we now by law enjoy them'. The opposition to the Union was far more widespread and far more vehement than the opposition to the liturgy which had caused the conflagration in 1637: but it was being introduced with much better oiled sophistication. Riot as the mob might riot, grieve as Lord Belhaven and Fletcher of Saltoun might grieve, the 'parcel of rogues' signed the Treaty of Union. As they were doing so, they were so harassed, it is said, by the vengeful mob that they were hunted out of the safety of the summerhouse in the garden of Moray House (which survives yet), to an underground cellar bar, where the signatures were dry before they were discovered. The cellar was universally thereafter held in execration. It was indeed the end of an 'auld sang'.

The Union was not so complete as some of the English MPs had desired nor so advantageous to Scotland as most of those not in receipt of bribes had sought. Its one saving grace was that the laws and the religion of Scotland had been safeguarded; and it was upon that foundation that Edinburgh entered its next creation.

The Scots soon learnt that the Union was not all it had been cracked up to be and became resentful. The English mocked; but in 1714, Daniel Defoe, who was, perhaps, better placed to judge than many, responded on the Scots' side:

> England being the husband has married a wife . . . much inferior
> to him in quality. Good! But who promoted the match? Did his
> wife court him or draw him in? Was he heated with liquor and
> did it when he was drunk? Or was he hooked in, cheated or sur-
> prised into it? Did she manage him cunningly or imply agents to
> wheedle him in? . . . If this is the case in a real marriage of a man
> and a woman, she runs a great risk . . . but if on the other hand

she declined the match, fled from him, struggled vehemently with her friends who persuaded her to have him, and had her words of matrimony as it were crammed down her throat, she may indeed be blamed if she makes an ill wife, but he can never be excused if he makes an ill husband.

The English court, Defoe concluded, was the recipient of all the wealth and ready money of Scotland, 'which should otherwise have circulated in a home consumption to the encouragement of trade and the enriching of their own people'. By the time he wrote that, in 1714, it was of course far too late.

THE OLD METROPOLIS

After the Union with England in 1707, conventional wisdom has it, Edinburgh sustained a lengthy post-marital depression (later christened by Robert Chambers as 'Edinburgh's Dark Ages') only to emerge fifty years later to give birth to the Enlightenment. Physically, it remained little altered. The skin of the old city remained stretched tight around a rock-girt citadel erupting amidst pleasant farmland and villa plantation, which only the infirm would have been unable to reach in a fifteen-minute walk. Its north side was still guarded by the Nor' Loch (with its fat, edible eels), pretty noisome by mid-century, half filled up with the town's ordure running down into it. The hard edge of the city had been nibbled by suburban squatting, limited in extent, around the gates at Potterrow, Pleasance and Portsburgh.

Within the walls, there was to be mild refashioning. James Court arose in 1727, followed by new flats and houses in New Street and St John's Street in the Canongate. Rather more substantial changes were occasioned by the erection of smarter squares of terraced houses (neither wholly complete nor wholly square) by James Brown and John Adam in 'the London manner' beside the university, for those who sought the status of a house overlooking a patch of grass the size of a tennis court. Altogether more spacious and stately, George Square followed in 1766, occupying unbuilt ground beyond Edinburgh's boundary between the louche Bristo Port and Sir John Hope's recently planted Meadows, which he had planted over the drained Burgh Loch. The square's instantly fashionable, plain Scots houses were still insufficient in quantity to challenge the primacy of the Old Town.* That challenge was to come from the New.

So those travelling to Edinburgh to participate in the intellectual en-

---

* According to Robert Chambers, an invitation to dine in George Square, Edinburgh's Bloomsbury Square, was of such note that those thus privileged would stand erect in the High Street, and announce their fortune to an admiring throng by summoning a chair to convey them to their destination with unusual ostentation: 'My Kingdom for a chair,' they bellowed, 'going to George Square' (or some such).

quiry that had won the city European acclaim would have found no physical manifestation of the Enlightenment much before 1780. Hence the
surprise of so many visitors. When Matthew Bramble (Tobias Smollett's
alter ego) wrote of Edinburgh that it was a 'hotbed of genius', he spoke of
Old Edinburgh with its extraordinary concentration of people focused
upon the stone cloister of the High Street. If, during this period of seeming recession, the winged citadel had seemed to have furled its wings and
tucked its head beneath, a rumbling in its gut heralded regeneration. The
Enlightenment emerged from what appeared to be unpromising if not uncouth physical conditions. As the fourth-century poet Eubolus recorded
of Athens:

> You will find everything sold together in the same place at
> Athens: figs, witnesses to summonses, bunches of grapes, tur-
> nips, pears, apples, givers of evidence, roses, medlars, porridge,
> honeycombs, chickpeas, lawsuits . . .

so was it also of Edinburgh's High Street during the Enlightenment. Ironically, when the next generation of visitors ventured north, it was to
admire the physical manifestation of pure reason as exemplified in the
Athens of the North; failing to realise that they were, in effect, admiring
a whited sepulchre. The conditions were no longer appropriate for creativity.

Edinburgh had had to accept that it was no longer the focus of national
political events, nor the location of the stirring scenes which had kept its
plainstanes slippery with blood and wine over the previous two centuries.
Kings no longer ventured north to be crowned (no wine), and traitors
were no longer executed at the Mercat Cross (no blood), but at Tower
Hill in London instead. Although the city still resembled, as Defoe put
it, a gigantic castle, politically it was almost a cadaver.

The city escaped narrowly in the 1715 Rising, its inhabitants' loyalties
never tested because the challenge never came. Learning that a Jacobite
detachment planned to sail from Burntisland to Lothian, the council
ordered the city walls and gates to be repaired and fortified; the sluice on
the Nor' Loch to be dammed up, trenches to be dug, the Town Guard to
be augmented, trained bands to be armed, and 400 men to be raised and
maintained at the King's expense. There began a run on the Bank of
Scotland on 8th September, so great that the bank stopped payment
eleven days later, and ordered their notes to bear interest instead.

A secret plan to enter the capital by capturing the castle was conceived by Lord Drummond through 'a little broken merchant' Charlie
Forbes. Certain of the garrison had been bribed to throw down some rope

to an invading force concealed in the West Kirk (St Cuthbert's). The rebels were to attach grappling irons which the suborned sentries would then pull up and fix. Forbes had also undertaken to commission ladders. Grappling irons were hoisted as planned, but Charlie Forbes, diplomatically drunk in a howff, failed to turn up with the storming ladders. He arrived too late, just as the watch was about to change: the bribed sentry hollered out 'Enemy!' to save his skin, threw off the grappling irons and discharged his piece. The threat evaporated.

The next flicker was the Porteous Riot – an Edinburgh event which revived the mystical overtones which had manifested themselves at the signing of the Covenant, in the Stony Sabbath, the Beggars' Summons and the Summons of Plotcock. Captain John Porteous was the bumbling and choleric captain of what the poet Robert Fergusson called 'The Black Banditti' – the City Guard. In 1736, Porteous's detachment faced the task of guarding two smugglers who had been sentenced to death, one of whom escaped during the final service in St Giles. Sympathy lay with the other. As Porteous and his men escorted him to execution in the Grassmarket, a regiment of regular soldiers then quartered at Edinburgh was paraded in the street as extra security. Porteous took great exception to this sign that he and his men were not thought capable of guarding the smuggler adequately. The sympathies of the crowd for the prisoner at the gallows inspired a mild mobbing, the odd howl of execration and occasional lump of excrement which sair affronted the Porteous sense of dignity. In furious overreaction, he impelled his men to fire into the crowd. About sixteen were killed or wounded, including a boy watching from a tenement window. Having exceeded his authority, Porteous was duly arraigned, tried, and sentenced to hang for murder. A bloody but unparticular incident; but influence at the court in London led to the granting of a stay of execution, pending likely reprieve, and the captain remained warded in the Tolbooth pro tem.

Once rumours of a reprieve filtered down the wynds and the closes of Old Edinburgh, Porteous's fate was sealed. The city had suffered: it had then exercised its lawful jurisdiction in trying and condemning the culprit; and it was not prepared to have its authority set at nought. Up from the wynds and closes, for the first time in thirty years, surged the Edinburgh mob in unusual silence, led by masked people who remained unknown, but were thought to include some of the leaders of Edinburgh society. They located Porteous's cell, pulled him down from the chimney up into which he had scrambled in terror, and marched him silently up the Lawnmarket and down the West Bow. When one of his slippers fell off, it was properly replaced. They liberated some rope from a rope shop, leaving more than its cost behind on the counter, and – failing the gibbet which was presumably stored as usual in the basement of Parliament Hall – hanged the captain in his nightshirt and slippers from a dyester's pole in the Grassmarket. Such was the eerie and the compelling power of this silent doom-laden procession, it seems difficult to believe Scott's story that the body was hacked by weapons. At sunrise, Edinburgh had returned to its normal routine as though nothing had happened, save for the swaying curiosity in the Grassmarket and the broken door to the Tolbooth.

Edinburgh had reasserted its sovereignty. Poor Porteous, undoubtedly richly deserving his fate, was a victim of a thirty-year resentment at the city's relegation to the political periphery. A hundred years before, similar feelings of resentment caused the Stony Sabbath and a national catastrophe. In these more enlightened times, they led solely to the death of the captain of the City Guard. As Edinburgh exuded silent satisfaction, London waxed wrath, decreeing the suspension of the city council, wild penalties for those involved, high bribes for informers, and the destruction of the Netherbow Port. It was but a storm on a dyester's pole: the ringleaders were never caught, the Netherbow remained a few years yet, and the town council duly reinstated.

Edinburgh viewed the '45 with detachment. It appealed to the role of political capital of Scotland that it had relinquished, and the whole affair was characterised by an extraordinary sense of make-believe. Only mildly alarmed at the first rumours of a distant Highland army, Whigs became seriously dismayed when it proved sufficiently successful as to reach the Lowlands. A troop of volunteers (a good number ministers of the cloth) under the captaincy of George Drummond enjoyed marching and counter-marching in the College Yards, artillery practice, and catching nosegays thrown by ladies in the High Street. It marched out of the West Port to join the regular army at Corstorphine only to find that the dragoons had retreated towards Leith, leaving them bare and exposed: so they marched back again. Convinced that the picturesque but otherwise tatterdemalion Highland army of 1,800 soldiers 'the half of them only armed . . . averse to approach the walls and afraid of cannon', would be terrified by an efficient and brisk show of defence at the city walls, the volunteers then rushed to the barricades. That worldly cleric, Rev Alexander Carlyle (later of Inveresk and nicknamed Jupiter in consequence of his noble physiognomy, considerable height, fine embonpoint, and immense circle of friends) formed part of a troop of twelve men defending the Port at the bottom of Leith Wynd. They had the insouciance one normally associates with gamekeepers protecting pheasants. But once they realised that the regular army was never going to arrive, their fervour abated. They disbanded and returned to their homes, anxious lest they might be marked down for extinction by the invaders.

Was Lord Provost Archibald Stewart an ardent Jacobite and playing a double game as Carlyle and his cronies were certain? In August, he had written to the Marquis of Tweeddale that the 'town was never better affected nor more peaceable than at present. Nothing shall be neglected on my part to preserve the people in their duty towards their King and Country; and we trust in God that no threat or danger shall ever reach us.' Emergency measures had been introduced: the walls and the gates had been repaired and cannon placed on them; ditches had been dug – even to the extent of men being employed 'on the Sabbath as well as on other days'; 200 muskets and bayonets, cartridges, flints, barrels of gunpowder from the Governor of the castle had been distributed amongst the volunteers; innkeepers and others who let lodgings were enjoined to give to the authorities exact lists of strangers residing in their houses each night; and cash at the banks was removed into the castle.

Lord Elcho, who later horrified Carlyle after the Battle of Prestonpans by his air of 'savage ferocity', has left us this note: 'The Prince told them he was going to send a detachment to attack the Town and lett them defend it at their peril; that if they did the consequences would be bad, and if they did not, he intended no harm to the Old Metropolis of His Kingdom.' The town council determined that without the regular army it could not resist, and agreed to 'capitulate on the best terms that could be obtained'. But the Prince forestalled them. On 17th December, 'the Prince order'd Young Lochiel with 800 men to March and attack the town. There came out some time after another deputation of Six Counsellors . . . They Gott the same Answere as the first.' The coach returned the unsuccessful ambassadors to the city, but as the Netherbow guards opened the gates to let it emerge again, Lochiel's men 'rushed in, secured this and the other gates of the city, took possession of the main guard, made the soldiers on duty prisoners, and seized upon the arms and ammunition belonging to the city'. A few hours later, the Highland army arrived in the King's Park and encamped near Duddingston. The Prince lodged in Holyrood House.

The air of fantasy which pervades the Jacobite occupation of Edinburgh is symbolised by the vision which graced the proclamation at the Mercat Cross of Edinburgh announcing Bonnie Prince Charlie's regency on behalf of his father King James:

> Ride a cock horse
> To Embro Cross
> To see a fine lady
> On a white horse

It was the dazzling Mrs Murray of Broughton: what a beauty, sword challengingly disposed across her limbs, with what a magnificent seat upon what a noble white charger! If e'er there was a romantic fantasy, it was the notion that the solid Hanoverians would retire gracefully to permit the bloodless recovery of their Scottish throne by these gallant Stewarts and their white-horsed *inamorata*.

Distant echoes of ancient Holyrood revelry once more reverberated up the Canongate. The Prince held levees in the palace and inspections of troops in the park. Reported rapine was absent, and exortion minimal: 'Such was the simplicity of these poor Highlanders, that it is said some of them presented their pieces at passengers and, asked what they wanted, answered "a penny" with which they went away satisfied.' Those who had waited forty patient years for the capital to sail out of its doldrums regarded the Jacobite occupation as a wonderland. Great indeed was the dismay on both sides upon the killing of the ostentatious Colonel Gardiner at the Battle of Prestonpans after only eleven of his regiment had followed him into the fray. Real death was not the sort of thing that was meant to happen.

Notions of romantic balls and fashionable levees at Holyroodhouse are at slight variance with Alexander Carlyle's admittedly whiggish description of Prince Charlie's court as 'dull and sombre. The Prince was melancholy; he seemed to have no confidence in anybody. Not even in the ladies who were very much his friends . . . He was thought to have loiter'd too long at Edinburgh . . . his army wanted clothing and necessaries, the victory at Preston put an end to his authority.' The Prince may have sensed that the city's support had more the substance of a fashion show, frill or frolic, than of a countrywide uprising behind him. The Jacobite episode was not an Edinburgh episode, but one forced upon it. Glad that the '45 was over but concerned at reports of brutality following Culloden, the city remained equally aloof from the Hanoverians: and protective towards Archibald Stewart, their Lord Provost, when he was taken to London for trial for 'neglect of duty, misbehaviour in public office, and violation of the trust and duty of his Office'. The city rejoiced wildly on 2nd November, 1746 when he was found not guilty.

More pantomime was yet to come. Down marched the public hangman from the castle, accompanied by the town's chimney sweeps, each carrying Jacobite standards from Culloden, which the hangman was to burn with ceremonial formality at the Mercat Cross. The procession was protected against another insurrection by the City Guard and an English regiment. The behaviour of the English army of occupancy was less relaxed than had been the Jacobites', although less damaging in Edinburgh than it appears to have been in Stirling, Aberdeen and Inverness. The Jacobites had prohibited all rejoicing at the victory at Prestonpans on the grounds that both sides had been the King's subjects: a sentiment that does not appear to have commended itself to King George's generals. On Prince Charlie's birthday on 20th December, 1746, they instructed a search through the Canongate, Leith and outlying areas of Edinburgh 'for ladies and other women dressed in tartan gowns and with ribands' under express orders from the Justice Clerk and from that thug Lord Albemarle (Commander in Chief in Scotland). If any such were found, they were to be seized, made prisoners, and hauled before Albemarle for interrogation. Much merriment ensued. Only one person, apparently, was thus seized and paraded: Miss Jean Rollo, a statuesque dame wi' a lang pedigree. Given her speedy release, we can only surmise who came off best in this encounter. They were probably relieved to see her posterior.

Prince Charlie's Holyrood levees marked Edinburgh's last major appearance in national politics. Even the Edinburgh mob began to lose its nerve, erupting less frequently, and never again to the degree that it might threaten governments. The proposal to end discrimination against Roman Catholics tempted it out in February 1779 to burn one Popish chapel and plunder another. 'Next day they renewed their depredations, destroying and carrying off the books, furniture etc of several Catholic priests, and others of that persuasion. The riot continued all that day, though the assistance of the military was called in to preserve the peace; but happily, the last extremities were not resorted to, and no lives were lost.' It rose again on the King's birthday in 1792, allegedly in the interests of reform, to burn Henry Dundas in effigy. This great body of people, once led by deacons of their trades, had been relegated to a swarm of the lower orders surging across the North Bridge to shatter a few windows; or playing a noisy role during the Reform agitations of the early decades of the nineteenth century.

The consequences to Edinburgh of Parliament's departure in 1707 had been serious enough: it had lost its capital status, and the civic inactivity which lasted virtually until 1746 implies a sense of marking time. Its citizens had been reluctant to face the loss of its national political role. Visitors to the Canongate during this interregnum felt a sense of desolation and lost magnificence comparable to descriptions of Pompeii. 'The prime Nobility built their palaces in this street, and those that were oblig'd to attend the Court took lodgings here,' wrote John Macky in 1723, 'so that nothing can be suppos'd to have suffer'd so much by the Union as this street.' The epitaph to Lucky Wood, the Canongate tavern-keeper, lamented that: 'the Canongate was the greatest sufferer by the loss of our Members of Parliament.' In 1753, Edinburgh's historian William Maitland found it 'a piteous case . . . many of the great lodgings have fallen down, whilst others are ruinous.'

Instead, the city tinkered with housekeeping, and addressed itself to fires. A fire in the Meal Market on 3rd February, 1700 reduced much to ruins as George Home recorded: 'There was burnt, by the earliest computation, betwixt 300 and 400 families . . . from the Cowgate to the High Street all is burnt, and hardly one stone left upon another. The Commissioners, President of Parliament, President of the Session, the Bank, most of the Lords, Lawyers and Clerks were all burnt . . . Twenty thousand hands flitting their trash they know not where . . . many ruefull spectacles, such as [Lord] Crossrig naked, with a child under his oxter, happing for his life.' So the magistrates appointed 'twelve men to be called by the name of Firemasters, and each Firemaster to be empowered to name 6 assistants to himself to be ready at all times on the occasion of fire . . . each Firemaster to have in his hand a baton, and each assistant a leather cap on his head with a cross-iron bar on it, a badge of pewter on the front made with lugs nailed to the shaft, and a sledgehammer with a handsaw.' Not before time. A great fire in the Lawnmarket in 1725 burnt so quickly that even the furniture could not be saved, and a public subscription was required for the relief of the sufferers.

The council sought petulantly to contain the roaring, untrammelled nature of the time by enforcing Sabbatarianism and proper observance. It deplored the fact that on Sundays in 1719, the citizens would 'take their recreation in walking through the fields, parks, links, meadows, with other places where they resort in companies, to find their own pleasures. And by entering into taverns, alehouses, milkhouses, gardens or other places, to drink, tipple or otherwise mis-spend any part.' To them, the height of impiety was 'not to be ashamed of washing in waters . . . on the Holy Sabbath'. Religious policemen, first active in the late sixteenth century, survived under the title 'Seizers'. One such, in holy zeal, became inflamed at the sight and sound of the blackbird of 'an honest Jacobitical barber' which was left outside on the Sabbath to sing his favourite air 'The King Shall Enjoy His Own Again'. This was a manifestation not just of impiety, but of treason. The Seizer seized both bird and cage, and lodged them with the City Guard. But such fanaticism became unfashionable as the old enthusiasts were superseded by the easy-going moderates.

The mode of living in Old Edinburgh, with as many landlords as storeys, was – according to its first historian, William Maitland – European: 'the said houses or apartments, being so many separate dwellings, are ascended to by public stairs like the Chambers of the Inns of Court at London and the City of Paris in France (from the latter I am persuaded that the Edinburghers learnt both their method of building and manner of dwelling).' In protest at Sir Gilbert Elliott of Minto's *Proposals* to construct a New Town of villas in the neo-classical manner, he rushed to the defence of the ancient virtues of Edinburgh living in 1753:

> the buildings here, elsewhere called houses, are denominated lands; and the apartments, in other places called storeys, here called houses, are so many freeholds inhabited by different families, whereby the houses are so excessively crowded with people that the inhabitants of this city may justly be presumed to be more numerous than those of some towns of triple its dimensions. Nor is it, in this town, deemed mean to dwell or lodge in highest apartments; for even merchants and bankers transact their affairs on the third and fourth storeys; and many persons of distinction lodge higher . . .

Had Edinburgh remained capital, the seat not just of parliament but also of royalty, the wealth and patronage dispensed by the court would have inevitably caused continuous rebuilding, as it had in London. Without it, changes to Edinburgh's fabric before 1760 were few. The most distinguished was an ample court of buildings north of the Lawnmarket begun by James Brownhill, a wright, in 1727 which he named James' Court after himself. He attracted custom by broadcasting the availability of his own scavenger (dung collector) to prospective occupants, and by holding balls and assemblies. The view from its north wing, over a beautiful avenue of trees to the Forth, was judged unequalled.

Those making nocturnal visits to taverns and clubs down wynds and closes had less to fear for their personal safety than in almost any comparable European city; for in Edinburgh, the *apaches* who haunted the streets of Paris were suborned and tamed by being made cadies. Those 'very useful blackguards', to whose presence visitors ascribed the absence of theft or violence, acted as messenger boys and guides: they were taxi cabs on foot. If you wanted somebody, you called a cadie: if you wanted something delivered, you called a cadie. 'Though they are wretches, that in rags lie upon the stairs and in the streets at night, yet they are often considerably trusted . . . and have seldom proved unfaithful. These boys know everybody in the town who is of any note.' The year 1714 witnessed the institutionalisation of the Cadies' Company whose regulations required a member to 'behave himself decently, and shall not use any unbecoming language to one another, much less to any other persons; neither shall they curse or swear by faith, conscience or the like, much less profane the Lord's name . . . whoever shall be fighting with any, beating his neighbour, or keeping a correspondence with thieves, pickpockets, or debauched persons, or shall by paper or pamphlets in a clan-destine manner, shall lose his privilege.'

So despite its decaying, catacomb-like appearance, Hugo Arnot con-sidered Edinburgh to be a peculiarly safe place to inhabit. 'In no city of its bulk are the persons or properties of the inhabitants so free from pre-datory assault. A street murder is a thing unknown in the memory of man. Robberies are very rare . . . A person may walk the streets any hour of the night without dread of disturbance.' The howffs, and their French *prix fixe* menus, earned his praise:

An Edinburgh tavern (if a good one) is the best of all taverns. The custom of charging so much for every dish is not known in Scotland: the rule is, so much per head. It cannot fail to surprise an Englishman to see two complete courses, containing every-thing nice in season, and frequently a dessert of excellent fruits, at the rate of half a crown a head. But the great article from which the landlord expects his profit is the wine, which is there drunk in greater quantities than in England. The tavern is much frequented in Edinburgh, although by no means to such a degree as formerly. Within these fifty years, hardly any sort of business was transacted but in a tavern.

A hostelry of the better sort, such as this, was a cut above those in which Arnot found the roaring boys 'when disposed to enjoy a frolic. These are called the oyster cellars, a sort of alehouse where the proper entertain-ment of the house is oysters, punch and porter; but whereas supper may be had . . . equal to any in the taverns, most of these oyster cellars have a sort of long room, where a small party may enjoy the exercise of a country dance, to the music of a fiddle, harp or bagpipe. But the equivocal character of these houses of resort prevents them from being visited by any of the fair sex who seek the praise of delicacy, or pique themselves on propriety of conduct . . . The claret is in general excellent, and equal to any that is to be had in London.'

Arnot suffers from the glow of partiality, for not all were of such sweet-ness and light. Edward Burt supped in an Edinburgh tavern in around 1754: 'The cook was too filthy an object to be described; another English gentleman whispered me and said, he believed, if the fellow was thrown against the wall, he would stick to it.' Oysters were not the preserve then, as they are now, of the rich: but were a genuinely popular treat – as may be inferred from Robert Fergusson's poem 'Caller Oysters':

> Whan big as burns the gutters rin,
> Gin ye hae catcht a droukit skin,
> To *Luckie Middlemist's* loup in,
> An' sit fu snug
> O'er oysters 'an a dram of gin,
> Or haddock lug.
> When auld Saunt Giles, at aught o'clock,
> Gars merchant lowns their chopies lock,
> There we adjourn wi' hearty fock,
> To birle our bodles,
> An get wharewi' to crack our joke,
> An' clear our noddles.

Fergusson conjures up an image of friendly, cheerfully crowded, cosy drinking-houses populated by companions quaffing oysters as they shelter from the stone-cracking frost and searing winds outside; places that enfolded you with companionship rather than alcohol guzzling. Then the ten o'clock drum or bell, and the inhabitants scurried elsewhere with some trepidation for supper or for four more hours of drinking and supper. Fergusson paints a vivid picture of Edinburgh at night, as patrons pursued paths home, their scalps tickling with apprehension lest anything land on them to, as Dr Johnson put it, render the wig flaccid.

> Thro' ilka gate the torches blaze,
> And globes send out their blinking rays.
> The usefu' cadie plies in street,
> To bide the profits o' his feet;
> For by thir lads Auld Reekie's fock
> Ken but a sample o' the stock.
> O thieves that nightly wad oppress
> And make baith goods and gear the less . . .
> Frae joyous tavern, reeling drunk,
> Wi' fiery phizz and ein half sunk,
> Behad the bruiser, fae to a'
> That in the reek o' gardies fa' . . .
> Whan feet in dirty gutters plash,
> And fock to wale their fitstaps fash;
> At night the macaroni drunk,
> In pools or gutters afttimes sunk:
> Hegh! What a fright he now appears,
> Whan he his corpse dejected rears!

Edward Burt was more explicit: 'We supped very plentifully, and drank good French claret, and were very merry til the clock struck 10, the hour when everybody is at liberty, by beat of the City Drum, to throw their filth out of the windows. Then the company began to light pieces of paper, and throw them upon the Table to smoke the room, and, as I thought, to mix one bad smell with another.' Burt was guided to his lodgings down a wynd by a cadie,

> who went before me to prevent any disgrace, crying out all the way with a loud voice 'haud your hande'. The throwing up of a sash, or otherwise opening a window made me tremble, while behind and before me, at some little distance, fell the terrible shower. Well, I escaped all danger, and arrived, not only safe and sound, but sweet and clean at my new quarters; but when I was in bed, I was forced to hide my head between the sheets; for the smell of the filth thrown out by the neighbours at the back of the house came pouring into the room to such a degree that I was almost poisoned with the stench.

Conditions for the Edinburgh poor who failed to clamber up the tree of aptitude remained indifferent. The city was 'greatly pestered with beggars', which may explain the generous number of its charitable institutions, such as the Trades Maiden Hospital – founded 'for the maintenance and education of the daughters of decayed merchants', or the Orphan Hospital, designed to assist 'the unhappy and deplorable conditions of the many poor helpless and distressed infants of indigent parents who, through great poverty, being brought up in ignorance and vice, become a burden and reproach to their country'. Charity was strictly regulated. The fifty-four men and women occupying Trinity Hospital were reduced to forty because the capital could not sustain the number: but each of them had 'a convenient room with a proper furniture to lodge in. The men have yearly, each a hat, two neck cloths, two shirts, a pair of breeches, one pair of shoes, and a pair of stockings, and every other year, a coat and a waistcoat'. Each person's daily allowance of food was 3 English pints of ale, 10 ounces of household bread, porridge for breakfast and – from August to January – roasted mutton two days a week, boiled mutton with broth two days a week, boiled fresh beef and broth two days a week. Male children and grandchildren of decayed merchants who were entertained at Watson's Hospital, were 'apparelled in the modern dress in a very handsome manner, more in all respects like the sons of gentlemen than charity children. Their diet, porridge with ale or buttermilk for breakfast (no buttermilk in winter), mutton and lamb alternately roasted or boiled with broth, with plenty of greens and roots according to season.'

Famine still afflicted the poor. The winter of 1739-40, 'of the hard frost', brought weather so remarkably severe 'and the cold so intense, that above Alloa the Forth was entirely frozen over. There was even a crust of ice at the Queen's Ferry. The mills were stopped, and as a consequence there was a great dearth.' Deep snow prevented coal from reaching Edinburgh, and several people perished from cold. Public contributions were levied, private donations sought, and banks lent money without interest so that the poor could be sold food at 'easy rates'. Another bad harvest in 1741 caused prices to rise so much that, despite the magistrates regulating official prices to ensure that the market was properly supplied, 'the people became tumultuous, broke in upon and plundered several granaries.' Once they had attacked the magistrates, troops were sent to disperse them, and only did so by firing at the mob: 'killed one and wounded several'.

'The beauty of this noble street' (the High Street) was unpleasantly obstructed by markets until they were relocated downhill to the north towards the end of the century, and remained eclipsed by obstructions such as the city wells, conduits, the Luckenbooth Row, the Mercat Cross, and the town's guardhouse. It was still the forum of the city and the meeting place for its residual merchants, but lacked its ancient ceremonial and ritual; and the Mercat Cross itself, the focus for such ritual, was soon to be removed as an impediment to traffic. The regal splendour of the capital's former processional had been reduced to a noonday cannon, a peal of bells, and a troop of soldiers cocking their muskets on the occasion of the King's birthday. Holyrood, partially occupied by the Dukes of Hamilton, was largely neglected: and the roof of its abbey church, the bones of Scotland's Kings having been left scattered beneath, finally collapsed in 1768 under the weight of an incompetent re-roofing with stone slabs.

What was life in the Old Town like? Looking back from 1792, the bookseller William Creech recalled with roseate and not wholly accurate fondness what Edinburgh had been like thirty years before. In 1763, people of fashion dined at two o'clock and returned to business in the afternoon. Wine was seldom seen at the tables of the middle rank, and gentlemen attended the drawing rooms of ladies in the afternoon, to drink tea and enjoy agreeable society. Church-going was fashionable, and few would dare to be seen strolling in the street during the time of public worship on Sundays. A fine fellow was someone who had a well-informed and accomplished mind, elegance of manners, and no debts. Opportunities for women were lesser, their education restricted to the sewing and pastry school. But the city was safe for them: 'young ladies,

Above The Winged Citadel: The Old Town of Edinburgh from St Anthony's Chapel drawn by Thomas Hearne in 1779. (*Charles McKean*)

Below Edinburgh from Calton Hill c.1680 drawn by Captain John Slezer. Note the Nor' Loch at the foot of the Castle. The spires, in descending order are of St Giles, the Tron Kirk, and the Netherbow Port, followed by the Canongate Tolbooth and Holyrood. (*Charles McKean*)

Above Old Parliament Square, St Giles Church, and the Parliament House of Scotland on the left, as they would have been c.1805. Painted by Hendry Duguid. (*National Galleries of Scotland*)

Below The original sixteenth-century palace of Holyrood House, the Escorial of Scotland, drawn by James Gordon of Rothiemay in 1647. The right-hand tower was not built until the 1660s. (*RIAS Collection*)

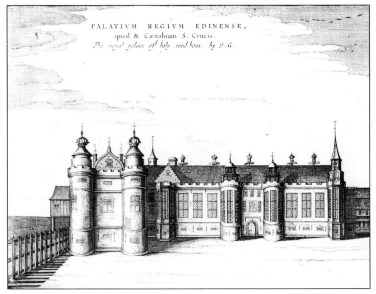

Above The Palace of Holyroodhouse
as rebuilt by Sir William Bruce.
Drawn by Thomas Hearne in 1779.
(*Charles McKean*)

Right Libberton's Wynd, more or less
on the site of George IV Bridge,
drawn by Walter Geikie. (*Edinburgh
Central Library*)

Above The Devil Rides Out: the Gaberlunzie Man's drawing of demon coaches and headless horses of Major Weir thundering down the West Bow. Spoof picture c.1840. (*Charles McKean*)

Right The Netherbow Gate from the east c.1750 prior to its demolition. Edinburgh's only major gateway faced eastwards toward the "auld ynemie" of England. Even at midday, sunlight barely reached the Causeway. These were the great gates that were girt struck at ten o'clock every evening, entombing the natives within. Artist unknown. (*Edinburgh Central Libraries*)

Below Sketch from Walker's Hotel by Major General John Brown in 1791 of a naked, young Princes Street on the right, St Cuthbert's Church in the distance, and the Castle on the left. (*The National Library of Scotland*)

Above The West Bow drawn immediately prior to its demolition. (*RIAS Collection*)

Below The Old and New Towns in the early nineteenth century. (*Charles McKean*)

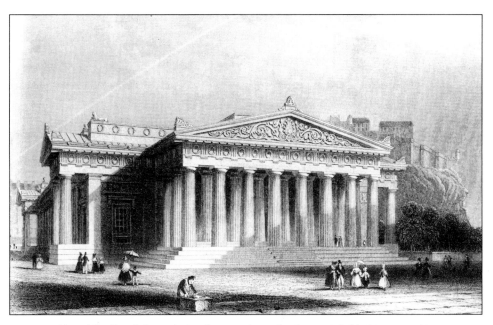

Above The Royal Scottish Academy as drawn by George Meikle Kemp in 1834. Symbol of the Athens of the North. (*Charles McKean*)

Below The divided psyche of Edinburgh is symbolised by this view of Calton Hill: the chasm of the railways to the right balances the National Monument on the left. They sandwich a cemetery, a prison, a monument to David Hume, and the Royal High School. (*Edinburgh District Libraries*)

Above Moray Place soon after completion (*Charles McKean*).

Below Capriccio: the monuments of Edinburgh c.1862 drawn and compiled by David Rhind. A maverick fantasy rendering Edinburgh more Athenian than Athens, more Salzburgian than Salzburg, and more Neapolitan than Naples. (*RIAS Collection*)

Above The head of the Bow: the Lawnmarket in late nineteenth century faced by Mylne's Court, the old timber buildings of the Bow on the right. (*RIAS Collection*)

Right Charlotte Square: amongst the most princely town houses to be constructed anywhere in Britain, this end pavilion terminates the east of Robert Adam's north facade of Charlotte Square. (*RIAS Collection*)

Above A typical Geddes view of contented children occupying repaired if dilapidated houses in Mylne's Court. (*Edinburgh Central Libraries*)

Left The western New Towns: from Charlotte Square (right middle), to the Moray Estate (centre), down into Melville Street and St Mary's Cathedral, this aerial view emphasises the supreme order and regularity of the early suburban expansion of Edinburgh. The higglety-pigglety clutch of buildings by the trees on the left is the Dean Village. (*Aerofilms*)

Above Royal visit of King Olav passing down the High Street towards the Netherbow. Note the windows thronging with inhabitants of buildings which have now been replaced or demolished. (*Scotsman Publications*)

Opposite top Port of Leith in early 19th century. (*Charles McKean*)

Opposite below Homes fit for heroes: peripheral council housing during the 1930s seeking to maintain old Scots traditions. (*RIAS Collection*)

Above Just gone midnight: the New Year crowds thronging outside the Tron Kirk. (*Scotsman Publications*)

Opposite top A lost tradition: the great Grassmarket bonfire with something specal about it. Most of the children have gone now. (*Scotsman Publications*)

Opposite below The Grassmarket revives: the Fringe Saturday flea market. (*Edinburgh Central Libraries*)

Balloons over the Winged Citadel. (*Scotsman
Publications*)

even by themselves, might have walked through the streets of the city in perfect safety at any house; and no person would have presumed to speak to or interrupt them.'

The inhabitants became aware of the growing incompatibility between their rising aspirations and the Old Town's inconveniences, and as the century wore on, began to retreat to the 'spacious streets and houses more large and commodious' in the New Town to the north. The Assembly Rooms, in Old Assembly Close (and recently relocated there from the Upper Bow) were insufficiently fashionable. Hugo Arnott complained that the dancing room was 'neither elegant nor commodious. The door is so disposed that a stream of air rushes through it into the rooms; and, as the footmen are allowed to stand with their flambeaux in the entry, before the entertainment is half over, the room is filled with smoke almost to suffocation.' The lanes and alleys of the Old Town remained so narrow and steep that the only access for wheeled carriages from the south to the High Street was up St Mary's Wynd. Impossible for wheeled vehicles, old Edinburgh simply would not pander to the citizens' longing for gentility. There was 'only one stand of coaches in the city; thither the coaches repair between 8 and 9 in the morning; about 3 in the afternoon they commonly disappear, and when once put up, the owners will on no account set the horses again to a coach.'

Nor did the great merchant princes of early seventeenth-century Edinburgh burgeon any more. The expansion of ports like Port Glasgow and Dundee had reduced Leith's national role, already in decline after the Union had severed or at least damaged its links with its traditional trading partners in Holland and France. There was no mercantile siller to finance the fine building which had so distinguished the city a hundred years previously – before its flirtation with trade had ended in tears and bankruptcy. The proportion of merchants, and their importance within Edinburgh society, had slumped drastically by 1707, whereas that of lawyers increased more than commensurately. Once government departed for London Edinburgh was set to remain a partial capital focused solely upon the law and the Church; and there seemed little to prevent it from becoming the echo of a larger version of Stirling, Dunfermline or Linlithgow.

No longer 'considerable for trade', Edinburgh depended 'chiefly for support on the College of Justice, and the seminaries of education and the inducements which, as a capital, it affords the genteel people to reside in it': inducements which include 'excellent water and a plentiful variety of vegetables at a moderate price', and sturdy and robust Highlanders for use as servants, porters and chairmen – all circumstances which 'must be undoubtedly conducive to health'. Not least, Mr Bell in the Pleasance made 'the best strong beer of any brewed for sale in Scotland'. From time to time, 'country gentlemen, even of good Scots fortunes' came to lodge in the capital whilst their children were being educated at school or university. Considering the latter's old double-courtyard buildings to be outdated, and aware that the city was 'so embarrassed in its funds that it is impossible for her to advance a sum sufficient to build a new college', Arnot proposed that the college should be relocated within the Palace of Holyroodhouse instead.

Once the proposed imitation of London's Vauxhall pleasure gardens at Comely Garden had been dismissed as 'wretched, for which neither the climate nor the gardens are adapted', the week-long Leith Races represented the peak of popular entertainment which attracted highest and lowest. 'I never saw,' wrote Jerry Melford in Smollett's *Humphrey Clinker*, 'such a concourse of genteel company at any races in England as appeared on the course of Leith.' He attended a ball and dinner held by the Cadies' Company 'to which they formally invited all the young noblemen and gentlemen that were at the races . . . reinforced by an assurance that all the celebrated ladies of pleasure would grace the entertainment with their company'. Indeed, Jerry could have obtained, had he wished, an 'impartial list' of those ladies for an advance scrutiny. It can be little surprise, therefore, that the ensuing company of lords and lairds, 'courtesans and cawdies' should enjoy round after round of toasts before dancing, including one to the 'Beggars' Benison' (beggars enjoyed the blessings of manhood as much as lords: and that notion was so potent in eighteenth-century Scotland that a secret society was founded with that title: the Beggars' Benison of Anstruther).

Since the sands were thought 'heavy and fatiguing for the horses, especially if they are not of a strong bottom', the races moved eventually to Musselburgh and lost much of their popular appeal. For during the races, Leith had assumed the character of a carnival or fair, with 'public diversions every night'. The prizes included a piece of plate of fifty guineas' value, donated by the city of Edinburgh itself.

Stench was no stranger to the capital: to the sweetness of the Pleasance Brewery was added the sourness of nightly sewage disposal, and a whiff of corruption emanating from the Greyfriars Churchyard. Arnott found it so crammed with graves, one upon the other, 'that the sexton frequently cannot avoid, in opening a ripe grave, encroaching upon one not fit to be touched. The whole presents a scene equally nauseous and unwholesome. How soon this spot will become so surcharged with animal juices and oils that, becoming one mass of corruption, its noxious streams will burst forth with a fury of pestilence, we shall not pretend to determine.' Plague emanating from decomposing bodies was only prevented, he thought, by the coldness of the climate, the acidity of the coal smoke, and the extraordinary violence of Edinburgh winds.

Arnot took a team to inspect the Tolbooth, that totem of Old Edinburgh which Sir Walter Scott would christen the 'Heart of Midlothian', and came away appalled. There was no ventilation, water nor privy: filth was thrown into a hole at the foot of the stair leading to a drain 'so completely choked as to serve no other purpose but filling the gaol with a disagreeable stench'. Those of the twenty-nine prisoners, five women and five boys, some debtors, some malefactors, who had been unable to pay for the relative freedom of moving from chamber to chamber, occupied rooms 'destitute of all accommodation and very nasty. All parts of the gaol were kept in a slovenly condition; but the eastern quarter of it (although we had fortified ourselves against the stench) was intolerable . . .' The iron room used for condemned prisoners contained three boys 'confined for about 3 weeks for thievish practices. In the corner of the room we saw, shoved together, a quantity of dust, rags and straw, the refuse of a long succession of criminals. The straw had originally been put in the room for them to lie on, but had been suffered to remain till, worn by successive convicts, it was chopped into bits of 2″ long.' The apartment above contained two under-twelves. 'We had no leisure for observation; for no sooner was the door opened, than such an insufferable stench assailed us from the stagnant and putrid air of the room as, not withstanding our precautions, utterly to overpower us.' It was the underbelly of the Enlightenment.

CHAPTER EIGHT

MEN OF GENIUS

The eighteenth century comprised Edinburgh's finest years: more glorious than the mercantile Renaissance city of the early seventeenth century, more magnificent, even, than when it was known as the Athens of the North in the early nineteenth century. For the city flourished as a different kind of capital – a capital of the intellect, the product of which is now called the Scottish Enlightenment. It was a city that, uniquely in Europe, made an aristocracy of aptitude.

Once government departed for London, Edinburgh was obliged to fall back upon Scots law and the Scottish Church to validate its capital city status. During the legal session, litigants, plaintiffs and defendants were attracted to the capital to battle, with writs in court, issues they might previously have battled with broadswords on the heath. The law expropriated Parliament House for courts and the Laigh Hall below for the Advocates' Library; and a conspicuous feature of capital living was the residence and omnipresence of Law Lords in the High Street and its closes during the session: and their active participation in the clubs and debating societies as part of the nation's élite. They were internationalists, these lawyers, like the doctors. Scots medicine and Scots law were both more closely thirled to the continent of Europe than to England, and it was not unusual for high-flyers to study at the universities of Paris, Utrecht or Leyden.

The Church of Scotland also regarded Edinburgh as its natural centre. It governed public worship, doctrine and spiritual discipline through its annual General Assembly, to which representatives came from all the airts and pairts of the country. When reflecting over the role of the Church in Edinburgh's eighteenth-century achievement, Dr Alexander Carlyle was driven to remark on the high proportion of Enlightenment luminaries who were ordained Church of Scotland clergymen, even if their nominal posts were those of university professors.

Independent Scottish intellectual identity was underpinned by the number of Scottish institutions and professional bodies – from the Royal College of Physicians to the Society of Antiquaries – which had risen to fourteen residing in Edinburgh by the end of the century; and these in turn were supported by the charitable and educational bodies of which there were a comparable number.[*] They were liberated by the absence of court and parliament, freed from the pressures of placemen, and uninhibited by the presence of the greatest aristocrats. Such organisations offered manifold opportunities for ambitious men to flourish. These men of aptitude formed Edinburgh's aristocracy. The resulting atmosphere of intellectual freedom was more or less unique in the eighteenth century: a man was what he did. Only in Edinburgh could a poor Laurencekirk schoolmaster with a bent for grammar be elevated to become 'The Great Grammarian' – the title earned by Thomas Ruddiman. A great grammarian he may well have been; but it was his very good fortune to be in Edinburgh, where, as a result of the exotic nature of its society, he was absorbed into the nation's élite.

In their existential, empirical and slightly agnostic city, effort was respected and birth treated as incidental, save to snobs; for natives who necessarily lived cheek by jowl developed an informal *modus vivendi* with an absence of class-consciousness rare at the time. It persisted long enough to be observed by the London journalist Robert Mudie in 1822, who praised the 'relative superiority of the humbler classes over those whom chance, ancestry or office has set up into the high places': and was the core of Edinburgh's intellectual success.

That the classlessness was more apparent than real, however, is evident from the way in which people kept a keen eye on who they were and whence they had come. Even David Hume expends disproportionate effort in his brief autobiography to establish kinship with a lairdly branch of the Homes, as though to enhance the stature he had acquired by the

---

[*] Edinburgh was the seat of the Courts of Justiciary, the Courts of the Exchequer, the Court of Admiralty, the Commissary, Lyon and Sheriff Courts, the Customs, and the Post Office. By the end of the century it had a Register Office. The Court of Session, around which much of Edinburgh's life revolved, had two sessions per annum, summer and winter, the recess between becoming a recess for the capital as a whole.

Charitable bodies added to the capital included the Royal College of Physicians (1681), the Merchant Maiden Hospital (1695), the Trades Maiden Hospital (1704), the Literary Society (1718), the Royal Infirmary (1729), the Orphanage (1732), Watson's Hospital (1738), the Observatory (1741), the Charity Workhouse (1743), the Society for the Relief of Ministers' Widows (1744), the Company of Golfers (1744), the Royal Academy of Exercise (1764), the Dispensary (1776), the Society of the Sons of the Clergy (1791), the Blind Asylum (1795), Gillespie's Hospital (1796), and the Magdalen Hospital (1797).

National institutions and bodies of learning included the Botanic Garden (late seventeenth century), the Advocates' Library (late seventeenth century), the Speculative Society (1764), the Royal Medical Society of Edinburgh (1778), the Society of Antiquaries of Scotland (1780), Natural History Society (1782) and the Royal Society of Edinburgh (1783).

effort of his brain. The Atheist, as he was christened by religious hardliners, was generous to a fault and exceedingly good company. Robert Adam's mother had forbidden her son to bring the Atheist to disturb her peace; but after he had done so *incognito*, she concluded: 'The large jolly man who sat next me is . . . the most innocent, agreeable, facetious man I ever met with.' The innocent mirth and agreeable raillery which Carlyle most enjoyed in Hume's company are attributes of which few Edinburgh philosophers could be accused nowadays.

Ruddiman's career illustrates the opportunities the capital could offer a man of ability. Initially editor, copyist and printer, his reputation was established by the publication of his *Rudiments of Latin Tongue* in 1714. He set up as printer with his brother, responsible for Allan Ramsay's poems and the *Caledonian Mercury* newspaper, latterly becoming printers to the university. In 1730 he was appointed Keeper of the Advocates' Library, a position in which he was succeeded by David Hume in 1751. Through occupants like these, Keepers of the Library played a role central to the Edinburgh meritocracy. Conceivably, poor schoolmasters might have risen in society elsewhere; after all, Samuel Johnson's background was no less humble. Could the same, however, be said of a wigmaker?

Sixteen-year-old Allan Ramsay was apprenticed wigmaker in 1700, and opened his own shop, probably in the Grassmarket, in 1710. Books proved more attractive, and he moved first to Niddry's Wynd and thence in 1726 to new premises in the Luckenbooths, under the curious sign of the heads of Ben Jonson and William Drummond (where the bookseller William Creech was soon to come to roost). He used his new premises as the location for Scotland's first circulating library. In 1721, Ruddiman had printed some eighty poems which Ramsay had gathered or written for the Easy Club, one of the earliest such gatherings upon which Edinburgh's Enlightenment was to be founded. Three years later appeared the two-volume *Evergreen*, an anthology of early Scots poetry, and the first of five volumes of the *Tea-Table Miscellany*, a preliminary organisation of Scottish poetic culture comparable to the way Stair and Mackenzie had codified Scottish law. Ramsay opened Edinburgh's first playhouse, the New Theatre, at the foot of Carrubber's Close in 1736, for what he called 'her maist rational diversion', and was livid when it had to be closed once the government forbade theatre performances outside London. He protested that it reduced the Scots capital to the status of 'ilk clachan town'.

In 1738, he built himself an octagonal villa on the green slopes of Castle Hill, promptly dubbed the 'Goose Pie' by reason of its shape (it still survives embedded within Ramsay Garden). It would be erroneous to assume, however, that once this respected polymath had moved to his Goose Pie upon Castle Hill, he had completed that curiously British sequence of beginning in trade and seeking to end up a gentleman. For his son became a notable artist. Although Edinburgh would well respect an artist for his attainment, the occupation was then socially only little better than that of a wigmaker. Had Ramsay been moved by a desire for social standing, he could have followed the lead of William Adam, who purchased the ruined tower of Dowhill for his son Robert so as to endow the latter with the cachet of 'Robert Adam of Dowhill'. Allan Ramsay of Goose Pie gained his repute by what he did, not by his origins nor a spurious landed title.

The intelligent classlessness that contributed so much to the Enlightenment was curiously symbolised at the sign of Palladio's head in the Lawnmarket. Here was to be found the Looking Glass and Cabinet Warehouse of one of the most accomplished of mid-eighteenth-century cabinetmakers, Francis Brodie, deacon of his trade. His choice of the (albeit fictionalised) physiognomy of Andrea Palladio, the sixteenth-century Veneto architect and inspiration of eighteenth-century British Palladian architecture, as the centrepiece of a cabinetmaker's letterhead implies serious cultural aspiration. But then, why not? This cabinetmaker was the son of a Writer to the Signet, and direct descendant of the Thanes of Brodie (whom his artist brother went north to paint). Indeed, he was married into the Seafield family. Thus – if the term had any relevance in Enlightenment Edinburgh – he could be called a well-connected cabinetmaker.

His son, a partner in the business, likewise rose to become deacon, and town councillor; and he adopted – or perhaps inherited – the aristocratic indulgence of embracing a brace of expensive mistresses. His expenditure soon outstripping his cabinet-making income, Deacon William Brodie, an elegant, cultured, well-dressed and witty man, diversified as locksmith and established a low-life gang who would rob the premises for which he had fitted locks. The gang was interrupted in the robbery of the General Excise Office for Scotland in Chessels Court in 1788. An informer soon led the authorities to his accomplices, and Brodie fled to Flushing. An incautious postcard home brought arrest, forcible return to Edinburgh, trial and execution.

Brodie retained his dapper and elegant appearance throughout his confinement in the Tolbooth, where one visitor to his cell was astonished to find him carolling the song "Tis Woman Seduces All Mankind' from *The Beggar's Opera*. On his last night, the facetious Deacon drew up a last will in an almost grotesque parody of Sir David Lyndsay's 'Testament of the

Papyngo' 230 years earlier.*

As Deacon of Wrights, he had been called upon to improve the gallows, and ironically was to be the victim to test the success of his own modifications. As he clambered up the scaffold 'he inspected the thing with a professional air, and seemed to view the result of his ingenuity with a smile of satisfaction.' It was widely rumoured that beneath his neck stock he had fitted himself with a wooden neck band with the intention of cheating death; and immediately he was cut down, his body was conveyed by his workmen to Brodie's Close, his employees 'instructed to use all their endeavours to procure re-animation – which they did, it is also affirmed by some, with effect. But these are reports which it would be difficult to authenticate.' Perhaps he survives as one of the unseen denizens of the High Street, which – according to Chambers – included coaches parading up and down the Bow at midnight, drawn by six black horses without heads, and driven by a coachman of the most hideous appearance, whose flaming eyes placed at an immense distance

---

* Having a Royal successor to my means and estate, nothing else to dispose of but my good and bad qualifications, I hereby dispose of them as follows:

1. To . . . John Grieve, I bequeath my political knowledge in securing magistrates and packing the Corporation . . .
2. To Deacon T D, I bequeath my good breeding and sobriety, which may prevent his being kicked out of Company, for his petulance and ill-manners, as was lately the case at Archer's Hall.
3. To my late landlord . . . I bequeath my whole stock of economy, pride, and self-conceit, knowing he has very little of his own.
4. To the Magistrates of Edinburgh, present and to come, I leave and bequeath all my knowledge of the law, which may prevent their being under the necessity in future of borrowing from any of the clerks, who are as ignorant as themselves.
5. My charity and good deeds I humbly bequeath to the Ministers of the Church of Scotland, with this injunction, that they will not retain them amongst their hearers, but put them in practice themselves.
6. To William Creech, bookseller, who has favoured the public with an account of my trial, I give and grant my honour and gratitude.
7. To Hamilton the chimney sweeper, I freely bequeath my dexterity at cards and dice, trusting when he gets a pigeon, that it will enable him to refund himself of the money which he has prosecuted me for.
8. To my good friends and old companions Brown and Ainslie [two of his three accomplices] I bequeath my villainy and whole other bad qualities, not doubting by their own will secure them a rope at last.
9. And lastly, my neck being now about to be embraced by a halter, I recommend to all rogues, sharpers, thieves and gamblers, as well in high as in low stations, to take care of theirs by leaving of all wicked practices, and becoming good members of society.
Signed: William Brodie, October 1st, 1788

from each other in his forehead, looked for all the world like the night-lamps of a modern vehicle.

The shape of the Old Town compelled over 23,000 people of all classes to live contiguously, people inescapably clamped together within tall sandstone cliffs. As a consequence a deep *nostalgie de la boue* – a fondness for low life – is present in much Enlightenment life. Whereas the milk-white 'Rape of the Lock' by Alexander Pope was condemned as overly indelicate for London's gentler sex (the poem laments the unauthorised snipping of a maiden's lock of hair) the poets of Edinburgh celebrated the real thing. Allan Ramsay apostrophised whores, brothel-keepers and innkeepers; Robert Fergusson innkeepers, oyster-sellers and fishwives; and Robert Burns – in his 'Merry Muse of Caledonia' – all manner of gay bawdy. Although by no means their sole preoccupation, it was central to their creativity. Even judges were condemned by succeeding generations for being too coarse on the bench: but the term coarse implies a misunderstanding of the nature of Enlightenment Edinburgh. Integral low life played an essential role in the development of a rounded perception of the human condition. The understanding of man was not to be achieved by contemplation from an isolated study, but by the seething proximity of all classes, answerable to nobody but themselves.

The Enlightenment milieu was comprised mostly of graduates, frequently clergymen, enriched by the ambitious and, perhaps, by an intelligent younger son of a noble, a laird or a military man. Superior aristocrats, though they celebrated and dined, are rarely numbered amongst the *illuminati*. Deliberate in its search for talent, particularly medical talent, the city offered generous salaries to attract the best doctors to the university to ensure the furtherance of its medical reputation. It was, after all, a Lord Provost – namely George Drummond – who had been behind the creation of the Royal Infirmary as a teaching hospital; and that hospital maintained a pre-eminence throughout Britain for almost a century partly because men of skill were attracted by the incomparable benefit that by settling in the capital they would become assimilated into a national élite with European audience.

The intellectual oligarchy which ruled the city during the eighteenth century followed the lead given by seventeenth-century precursors, notably Sir Robert Sibbald, prolific author and antiquarian who had acted as catalyst in the foundation of both the Royal Botanic Garden and the Royal College of Physicians, Viscount Stair, who codified Scots law, and Sir George Mackenzie who founded the Advocates' Library. David Hume, Adam Smith, Henry Home (Lord Kames), Drs William Cullen and Joseph Black and Professors (*inter alia*) Robertson and Blair earned Edinburgh a European reputation for law, philosophy, agricultural improvement, rhetoric and medicine. In *Guy Mannering* Sir Walter Scott illustrates the breadth of that oligarchy when Col Mannering received notes of introduction from his advocate Pleydell:

> Mannering was gratified to see that they were addressed to some of the first literary characters of Scotland, 'to David Hume Esq', 'to John Home Esq', 'to Dr Ferguson', 'to Dr Black', 'to Lord Kames', 'to Mr Hutton', 'to John Clerk Esq of Eldin', 'to Adam Smith Esq', 'to Dr Robertson', – a remarkable circle of friends for a busy member of the Bar.

Those self-same greyhairs which might one evening join the roaring boys in a tavern, attend the Masonic Lodge, or visit Johnnie Dowie's tavern to enjoy the latest in Robert Burns's *Cloacina* (literal shithouse – or bawdy verse), might the very next day be sitting in judgment on a prisoner's life, or disputing with the most sceptical the most advanced of philosophical tenets. The *illuminati*, nonetheless, forgetting how much of Edinburgh's sixteenth-century history had been directed by powerful women, found it hard to accept women as their equal. They did not take to bluestocking Lady Mary Wortley Montague, nor she to Edinburgh. Perhaps Carlyle felt threatened: 'she despised the women, and disgusted the men with her affectation. Old Edinburgh was not a climate for the success of such imposters.' Yet history remembers her with rather greater facility than it remembers him.

At the peak of the Enlightenment, Edinburgh might best be considered as a city-scaled university: its quadrangle the High Street, much suitably arcaded as a proper cloister should be, and its wynds and closes the stairs and chambers. The college itself - whose great entrance tower faced down College Wynd across Jamaica Lane – was physically peripheral. Nor were the undergraduates restricted to their double quadrangle out by the Flodden Wall: for the college was not residential, and its votaries lodged promiscuously (literally and figuratively) throughout the Old Town. David Hume lived in Riddle's Court off the Lawnmarket (prior to moving down to the Canongate and thence to James Court); and Adam Smith in the town house of Maules of Panmure behind the Canongate. Henry Home, Lord Kames, would be found at the courts in the Parliament House, Allan Ramsay and William Creech at the Luckenbooths, Thomas Ruddiman in the Advocates' Library, and Robert Fergusson, during his brief flame of glory, down Anchor Close in the Cape Club. That the entire city of Edinburgh operated as a college underlies the famous comment made in the 1750s by Mr Amyat, 'King's Chemist and a most sensible and agreeable English gentleman', who observed to

Creech: 'Here I stand at what is called the Cross of Edinburgh, and can, in a few minutes, take 50 men of genius and learning by the hand.' The capital of Scotland had transformed itself into a vast campus, outstanding in faculties of law, divinity, philosophy and medicine.

The university analogy holds good for almost all aspects of the city's extraordinary achievement. There were newspapers, magazines, learned journals and books,* and cultural stimulus was provided by the Musical Society founded in 1728 to provide weekly concerts in the delightful Palladian St Mary's Chapel. In 1762, they moved to Robert Mylne's new concert hall in Niddry's Wynd, designed 'after the model of the great opera theatre at Parma'. The music generally performed was 'a proper mixture of the ancient and modern. In every plan, there are one or two pieces of Corelli, Handel, or Geminiani.'

Well lubricated by print, debates continued long after classes, down in the dens, cellars, clubs, pubs and whorehouses. The bulldogs of this university, the porters and the wardens, were represented by the City Guard, a body which could unknowingly number amongst it one of Gaeldom's greatest poets – White Duncan, Duncan Ban McIntyre. As would be the case in a college, the town bell was 'girt struck' at 10.00 p.m., and the great doors of the Netherbow (so like collegiate doors) swung closed.

The city attracted visiting intellectuals. An indication of how unique the city was considered within Europe is given by the aristocratic French naturalist, Faujas de St Fond, who came in 1784 to admire a capital where literature, science and art were held in high esteem. 'The City is honoured, also, by the great men it has produced in almost every kind of distinction; while the fame of its professors has attracted to its walls foreigners from all parts of the world.' De St Fond found a peculiar calm in Edinburgh, particularly appropriate for the natural and 'proper place for the sciences', which he attributed to the absence of tumult, of parliamentary discussion, the noisy bustle of commerce and of 'the multiplied objects of distraction and pleasure'.

He visited scholar after scholar: saw Dr Howard's natural history collection, Dr Black's 'quartzified wood' and newly invented portable furnace, Dr Aitken's machinery 'for facilitating difficult births' and, above

---

* The *Edinburgh Courant*, later the *Scots Courant* then the *Edinburgh Gazette*, was founded in 1703. The *Caledonian Mercury*, printed by Ruddiman, followed in 1720, and the *Edinburgh Evening Courier* in 1748. The *Edinburgh Advertiser* arrived in 1764, then the *Scots Magazine*, the *Edinburgh Herald*, the *Weekly Journal*, *Ruddimans' Weekly Magazine* (1768), the *Edinburgh Magazine & Review* (1773), and the *Edinburgh Magazine* (1785). The *Medical Essays*, for the Society for the Improvement of Medical Knowledge, were launched in 1731, became *Medical Commentaries*, then *Annals of Medicine*, eventually to become the *Edinburgh Medical & Surgical Journal*.

all, the punch bowl of Dr Cullen, 'perhaps the oldest and certainly one of the most celebrated physicians in Europe', whose reputation had attracted to the city 'a multitude of foreigners who have come from all parts of the world to receive instruction in that learned school'. After a plain but plentiful meal, the Frenchman was 'somewhat astonished' to watch a great bowl of punch being brought in. Cullen explained that the drink 'was not only suited to his age, but that a long experience had convinced him that, taken in moderation, it was very salutary for the inhabitants of Scotland, particularly towards the end of the autumn and in winter when the cold damp, which generally prevails in this climate, prevents the equilibrium of the perspiration'.

The Frenchman acquired a taste for the brew:

> This humid and penetrating atmosphere had, for some time, affected myself in a very disagreeable manner, notwithstanding the active life which I led. I am persuaded, that it is one of the causes of that sombre melancholy which so often affects the English. In vain I took exercise, in vain I tried to divert myself pleasantly in the enquiries and occupations suited to my tastes; I found that the mists, the frequent rains, the daily winds, passing suddenly from heat to cold, a certain sharpness in the air, which one feels better than one can describe it; above all the disappearance of the sun, which fogs or clouds constantly eclipse at this season, plunged me into an involuntary melancholy, which I should not have been able to endure for long. From time to time, to raise my spirits, I was told that the sun was about to appear; but I was more than once tempted in my ill humour, to reply to them, as Caracciolo, the Viceroy of Sicily, did to an English nobleman, who desired him to look at that luminary in London, 'Your English sun, my lord, very much resembles our Sicilian moon.' Tried to find myself in this condition, I at last adopted the regimen of Doctor Cullen. Each day after dinner I took a glass of punch, composed of rum, sugar, lemon juice, a little nutmeg and boiling water, and I soon found myself quite well.

Easy familiarity between the classes was fostered by strong drink, whose significance to Edinburgh was celebrated by Robert Fergusson: 'great God of Aqua Vitae! Wha sways the Empire of this City'. Minor drunkenness may be inferred from a 1721 town council interdict against 'all persons from being in taverns, cellars etc after 10 at night, under penalties under the discretion of the Magistrates according to the degree of contumacy. Constables were ordered to seek out and ward persons found drunk in the street.' Two of Allan Ramsay's best poems were addressed to ale-wives called 'Lucky' – Lucky Wood, the Canongate tavern-keeper, and Lucky Spence, the Canongate madam. The death of Lucky Wood inspired a dirge:

> Oh Cannigate! Poor eltrich hole!
> What loss, what crosses does thou thole!
> London and Death gars thee look drole
> And hing thy head;
> Wow, but thou has e'en a cauld coal
> To blaw indeed

Lucky Spence recruited 'young lasses that had a little pertness, strong passions, abundance of laziness and no forethought' for her brothel. To such winsome creatures, Ramsay gave the following advice:

> When e're ye meet a fool that's fow
> That ye're a maiden gar him trow
> Seem nice, but stick to him like glew;
> And whan set down,
> Drive at the jango til he spew,
> Syne he'll sleep soun.
> Whan he's asleep, then dive and catch
> His ready cash, his rings or watch

Then follows what Robert Chambers would undoubtedly have condemned as 'gross indecency'.

Lord Cockburn remembered the custom of judges in his youth fortifying themselves with wine and biscuits if the trial was likely to be extended: 'When the business was clearly to be protracted . . . black bottles of strong port were set down beside them on the Benches with glasses, carafes of water, tumbler and biscuits; and this without the slightest attempt at concealment.' Henry Mackenzie, author of *The Man of Feeling*, recalled that the common way of proclaiming the arrival of a cargo of claret at Leith, before Scottish claret's exemption from duty ended about 1780, was by sending a hogshead of it through the town 'on a cart with a horn: and anybody who wanted a sample or a drink under pretence of a sample, had only to go to the cart with a jug, which, without much nicety about its size, was filled for 6d.' People were known by the quantity of wine they could consume. It was not uncommon for each person to drink several bottles of claret during those long evenings, beginning at 4.00 p.m. and, with an intermission and change of venue at 10.00 p.m., continuing beyond midnight. Dr Alexander Webster was described by Carlyle as 'a five-bottle man . . . he was held to be excellent company even by those of dissolute manners. This had [brought] on him the nickname of Dr Bonum Magnum in the time of faction; but never being indecently the worse of liquor, and a love of claret to any degree not being reckoned in those days a sin in Scotland, all his excesses were pardoned.' Carlyle himself was not averse to a drop. It is told that one of his servants watched admiringly as the minister left Pinkieburn on his way home: 'there he gaed, dacent man, as steady as a wall, after his ane share o' 5 bottles o' port.'

Long liquid evenings required participation, debate and thought, with alcohol the facilitator. The howffs and the catacombs of the Old Town became performing spaces for clubs. Clubs throughout Europe might propose countless toasts, but Edinburgh clubs addressed themselves, in addition to toasts, to politics, philosophy and poems. Visitors to Edinburgh, accustomed to the easy-going card and concert parties that prevailed in most other European cities, found themselves willy-nilly plunged into serious debate in a variety of what could only be described as low dives. It was in a tavern, then, that novelist Tobias Smollett supped with Jupiter Carlyle, John Home, Mr Hepburn of Keith, Mansfeld Cardonnel (the Commissioner for Customs) charming them and a few others with his genuine humour and 'very agreeable conversation'; the fictional result appeared in *Humphrey Clinker*.

The clubs which met in such taverns acted as the focus for Enlightenment debate; and their importance lies in their deliberately mixed membership bridging disciplines and interests. Their value lay in the encouragement to share knowledge and to debate it. However immersed Hume, Ferguson or Smith might have been in their own studies, the ambience of the clubs compelled them to surface and to develop the capacity to share their knowledge and philosophies with people laymen in that subject. Indeed, the very existence of such groups fitted the vision of community that Ferguson proposed in his *Essay on the History of Civil Society*.

The Cape Club coalesced down Craig's Close within the oddly titled Isle of Man Arms and its apogee during the 1760s attracted among others Robert Fergusson, Deacon Brodie, and Alexander Runciman. There were the customary fatuous rituals and titles, with something libidinously ambiguous in their oath of allegiance to the huge steel poker which acted as a contemporary sceptre. In 1754, the Enlightened – the *illuminati* as it were – formed the Select Society, inspired by Allan Ramsay, painter: select by reason of its restricted membership of thirty. It met in the Advocates' Library to luxuriate over intellectual papers with 'Warm suppers and excellent claret'.

Two years later, a different group of wags adopted the less salubrious Carriers Inn at the foot of the Bow, under the title of 'Diversorium', and what began as a joke by Carlyle for private conspiracy during the General Assembly soon attracted others like wasps to honey. In poured *illuminati* such as John Home, Sir Gilbert Elliot, David Hume, Lord Elibank and Principal Robertson. Six years later, mine host Thomas Nicolson 'a confused, rattling coarse fellow' and his comely wife Nellie had removed near the Mercat Cross; and there, in 1762, was launched the Poker Club, which lasted over twenty years and comprehended 'all the literati of Edinburgh and its neighbourhood', with the rump of the Select and the Diversorium. Carlyle recorded: 'It was these meetings in particular that rubbed off all corners, as we call it, by collision, and made the literati of Edinburgh less captious and pedantic than they were elsewhere.' Club meetings began with dinner soon after 2.00 p.m., wine restricted to sherry and claret, and the reckoning was called at 6.00 p.m. Each session would appoint a new chairman and an assassin, 'in case any officer of that sort should be needed'. Nicolson quarrelled with club members in 1769, and they removed to Fortune's where dinners were more showy but not better; and the price trebled. So, in due course, the Poker split, and the Tuesday Club emerged from the ruins.

Attendance at such clubs was recognised as a privilege, and Carlyle was pleased to record two unsolicited references as to their value in his *Memoirs*. Sir Alexander Dundas declined an invitation by d'Alembert to attend a club in Paris on the ground that he dined weekly at a club in Edinburgh 'composed, he believed, of the ablest men in Europe'. General James Murray was dragged reluctantly to the club by his father, Lord Elibank, fearing 'a parcel of pedants descanting on learned subjects out of my range of knowledge; but instead of that, I have met with an agreeable, polite and lively company of gentleman in whose conversation I have joined and partaken with the greatest delight.'

The Mirror Club, patronised by the legal fraternity in Stewart's Oyster House, was so successful that it spawned the *Mirror*, a magazine edited by Henry Mackenzie during 1779 as a short-lived Scottish *Spectator*. It was at the establishment of Dawny Douglas, down Anchor Close, however, that the most famous of all, the Crochallan Fencibles, were to be discovered. Their celebrity derived in part from their generous welcome to Robert Burns when he arrived in Edinburgh in 1787; and it was for them he compiled his anthem to bawdy verse, 'The Merry Muse of Caledonia'. Its very name Crochallan, derived from a Gaelic song about Colin's coos (*chro Chalien*), was a parody on titles of the Scottish regiments raised in the depopulating Highlands for use against American rebels. Each mem-

ber assumed a new persona with a club title or great office. The douce solicitor, William Dunbar, was metamorphosed when he assumed the duties
of Club Colonel: throwing off restraint he became (in Burns's phrase)
'rattlin' roarin' Willie'.

The printer and antiquary William Smellie, creator of the *Encyclopaedia Britannica*, whose printing works were located conveniently close by,
introduced Burns to club membership:

> Shrewd William Smellie to Crochallan came,
> The old cock'd hat, the brown surtout the same;
> His bristling beard just rising in its might
> 'Twas four long nights and days to shaving night;
> His uncomb'd grizzly locks, wild staring, thatch'd
> A head for thought profound and clear, unmatched;
> Yet tho' his caustic wit was biting – rude,
> His heart was warm, benevolent and good.

Johnnie Dowie's howff down Liberton's Wynd enticed Robert Fergusson, David Herd (the collector of Scottish songs), the painters David
Martin and Henry Raeburn, and Robert Burns. Its rooms in the vaulted
lower storeys of the great tenements were so small that the tavern was
nicknamed 'the coffin'. According to Chambers: 'Johnnie sold good ale,
and his dens were chiefly resorted to by persons who wished to enjoy
themselves in a moderate way.' It is yet again an indication of the social
camaraderies of the city that when Dowie retired, he had acquired a fortune of £6,000, and a son at the rank of Major in the army. Not slow to
take advantage of a famous acquaintance, the tavern's title was later
modified to Burns' Tavern (late Johnnie Dowie).

A last vignette of Enlightenment Edinburgh is contained in one of the
two letters written by the ageing William Creech, bookseller, to Sir John
Sinclair of Ulbster in 1793, for use in the latter's Statistical Account. It is
the lament of a man out of step with his time. Ichabod! Ichabod! The
city's glory had indeed departed: luxury and licentiousness, rapine and
robbery had made 'remarkable progress indeed' since 1763. People of
fashion now dined at four or five o' clock, no business was done in the
afternoon, and even tradesmen offered wine in copious quantities and
good variety at dinner. Drawing rooms were becoming deserted, and
attendance at church was in decline: evenings were 'frequently loose and
riotous'. All poor Creech could see was a decline in church-going, adultery on the increase, divorcees received into society, the number of
brothels increased some twentyfold, and the women of the town more
than one thousandfold. Street robbery, housebreaking and theft had

become astoundingly frequent, and cockfighting endemic. The 'fine fellow' of 1792 'ridiculed religion and morality as folly and hypocrisy . . . was very jolly at the table of his friend, and would lose no opportunity of seducing his wife or of debauching his daughter'.

Eheu fugaces . . . labuntur anni! Was this the note to which the cadaver of Old Edinburgh was to make a final twitch? No. Let us leave the last word to John Wesley who, on an earlier visit, had considered the city the filthiest he had ever visited. When he revisited in May 1788, he wrote in his diary: 'I still find a frankness and openness in the people of Edinburgh which I find in few other parts of the Kingdom. I spent two days amongst them with much satisfaction.'

With the Enlightenment, Old Edinburgh replaced the loss of parliament with an intellectual creativity that earned the city European renown. Once it had developed its philosophy, it conjured up a new city, planned to Enlightenment principles, that would become the wonder of the age. But that new creation was to be a Frankenstein, the cause of the death of Old Edinburgh, bringing to an end the conditions – particularly the density and the social intermingling – that had enabled the Enlightenment to flourish in the first place.

CHAPTER NINE

A SPLENDID AND MAGNIFICENT CITY

The last twitch of the corpse of the Old Town took the form of a party. It was held in their house in the Luckenbooths in 1819 by the eccentric brothers Fergusson, George, former Governor of Grenada, and his elder brother James of Pitfour. A singular manifestation of their family's reputation for idiosyncrasy, according to Robert Chambers, was

> their pertinacity in clinging to this old-fashioned mansion. It had been built and fitted up by their respected father, and it would have been a change as bitter as death to have parted with it. They despised the prevailing rage of emigration, and continued to hold out against every temptation that the New Town could offer. The shivering Laplander never hugged himself more heartily amongst his snows, or more thoroughly condemned the accounts of warmer skies and richer soils, than did these old gentlemen felicitate themselves upon the comfort of the Luckenbooths, and laugh at the prospects of newer and more airy mansions.

Edinburgh society showed a vast degree of interest in the occasion and turned out *en masse* for the Old Town's last rout.

> It was certainly a wonderful sight to see this long-neglected and plebeian street thronged with the vehicles of fashion, and full dressed ladies from the west end of the town alighting amongst the druggets and the huckabacks of the Luckenbooths . . . Much was the Old Town beholden to him; for he clung to it while life permitted him, and postponed the date of its ruin 30 years! No person of his rank now remains within its precincts. The commercial and working classes have overrun all its stately lands, while the fading and melancholy traces of its former population are fast hurrying to oblivion. Alas! How rapid is the march of time.

The death of Enlightenment Edinburgh had been achieved in barely six decades.

The Whig establishment had viewed the end of the Jacobite Rebellion in 1746 with satisfaction: it yawned, stretched, and determined to tackle the development of Scotland which had languished in abeyance so long as the Jacobite question had remained unresolved. The transitory nature of the Prince's pantomime levees and their Culloden aftermath was conclusive evidence that neither King nor Parliament was going to return. Either the capital was to regenerate from within, or it would perish; but it was not until the collapse of a six-storey tenement in September 1751 that an urgent survey of the condition of all the others was undertaken. It revealed such prevalent neglect that further demolition ensued before the tenements tumbled of their own accord.

The ruins prompted a review of the Old Town's future. Some 23,500 citizens (not including beggars, broken men and others of the catacombs) huddled within the walls in endemically overcrowded conditions, rising in places to a density of 700 persons per acre (thus equalling the worst of nineteenth-century slum Glasgow). Twenty-seven different households inhabited Mary King's Close, ranging in degree from a gentleman, two Writers (lawyers), three merchants, to two glovers, two ale-sellers, two shoemakers, a journeyman weaver and a chairman. Narrow and somewhat down-at-heel, Mary King's Close attracted less quality than its near neighbour, Advocates Close, which enjoyed two Law Lords, a dowager, a benchful of merchants, and sank only as low as a vintner and an aleseller.

No easy extension to the westward, as was the case in both London and Glasgow, was possible in Edinburgh. George Drummond, Lord Provost for the third time (he was to be thus elevated thrice again), now had the chance to realise an objective which he had nurtured since his first election in 1725 – to build a new town on the empty fields to the north.

Proposals to extend the regality of Edinburgh to the north, first mooted around 1680, with the support of the Duke of York, viceroy in Holyrood House, had withered with his departure. A renewed prospectus is contained in a 1726 letter from the exiled Earl of Mar, loser of the battle of Sheriffmuir, to his son Thomas, titled his 'Legacy to Scotland'. A frustrated architect and planner of genius, Mar had come close to completing one of the most ambitious baroque palaces and garden in northern Europe at Alloa; and he addressed himself to the poor condition of the capital. His preference was to rebuild the city from scratch on a well-connected flat site. Scotland, he concluded reluctantly, was too poor to afford the cost. Consequently, the inaccessibility of the Old Town ridge should be ended by new streets, and bridges between Halkerston's Wynd and Moultrie Hill, to the north, and between St Mary's Wynd and the Pleasance, on the south. Houses and gardens were proposed for the neighbourhood of what was to become George Square, and the Water of Leith should be diverted at Coltbridge to run through and cleanse the Nor' Loch. Gardens would lead from this new canal up to 'many fine streets' built on either side of 'a single large and long street' on the line of the Long Gait. Once parliament returned to Scotland, the nobility and gentry required by the government and the courts of justice would be encouraged 'to make fine buildings, (stone being near).' These ideas closely resembled what Drummond set out to do.

Drummond's mouthpiece was the egregious Sir Gilbert Elliott of Minto, and his method the publication of a set of *Proposals* in 1752. Shrugging off the '45 as 'the rage of faction in this country' the *Proposals* focused upon business. Edinburgh was not in a fit condition to seize the opportunities for the development of trade since it lacked appurtenances worthy of a capital city. There was a 'great deficiency of public buildings', and the steepness, narrowness and dirtiness of the Old Town with its 'scanty and paltry accommodations' were driving an otherwise reluctant Scottish aristocracy to endure an 'obscure life' in London. If they were to be tempted back to enjoy the splendour and magnificence to which they were entitled in Scotland, Edinburgh required to emulate London's neat private houses, and 'the beauty and conveniency of its numerous streets and open squares, of its buildings and bridges, its large parks and extensive walks'. Revealing that the *Proposals* represented the community at large, Minto summarised the plan thus:

> The magistrates and town-council, the college of justice, and several persons of rank who happened to be in the neighborhood of this place [therefore propose]
> 1. To build an exchange 'upon the ruins on the north side of the high street'
> 2. To 'erect upon the ruins in the parliament close' a building for law courts, the town council 'several registers', the advocates' library etc
> 3. To obtain an act of parliament for extending the royalty; to enlarge and beautify the town, by opening new streets to the north and the south, removing the markets and the shambles, and turning the North Loch into a canal with walks and terrasses on each side
> 4. That the expense of these public works should be defrayed by a national contribution.

The new houses facing broad streets in the English manner were to be reserved for 'people of fortune and a certain rank': professional men, businesses of all kinds, the courts and all places of public resort remaining behind in the Old Town. He envisaged an aristocratic suburb, a Berkeley Square, 'thinly inhabited . . . and that too by persons of considerable rank', as was the case in Berlin (or perhaps, nearer home, like the new suburban streets of individual, detached, Palladian villas then under construction for the fabulously wealthy tobacco lords of Glasgow). The *Proposals* claimed that investment in new construction would generate an enhanced prosperity, and were at pains to reassure the citizens that the proposed suburb could not possibly damage the life of the Old Town. That Drummond's vision had become something altogether more sumptuous by 1763, may be inferred from his comment to Thomas Somerville as they both stood gazing north across Barefoot's (or Bearford's) Parks from a top-floor window in the new Exchange (now the City Chambers) in the Royal Mile: 'Look at these fields. You, Mr Somerville, are a young man and may probably live, though I will not, to see all these fields covered with houses forming a splendid and magnificent city.'

A splendid and magnificent city indeed: and one of the ironic fascinations in considering what happened next is to watch how those original *Proposals* became subverted. The London-based aristocrats remained aloof and never came back; the New Town was indeed peopled by professionals and, latterly, by men of business. Inevitably, places of resort like the Assembly Rooms followed their market from the Old Town to the New. Despite Elliott's reassurance to the contrary, the heart of Edinburgh was drained of those who had comprised the Enlightenment. Once the New Town became crowned by four extensions north, east and west, spangled with prodigious neo-classical monuments to culture, learning and to pleasure, it had grown a personality infinitely more stately than the Old. With the transformation of Calton Hill into a northern Acropolis, Edinburgh became the Athens of the North. The shift from one to the other can be seen as the single most important physical change in the capital's history.

Work began on a new Exchange in the High Street in 1753; the Nor' Loch drained six years later, the North Bridge begun in 1765 and Edinburgh finally extended its regality over the northern fields in 1767. (Not before time: by 1820, its already overcrowded population would have doubled yet again). In 1766, an unknown but well-connected architect, James Craig, had been adjudged winner of the council's design competition for the layout of a New Town on Barefoot's Parks. Craig's original plan was something in the form of a Union Jack. It was 'order'd', probably by William Mylne, and the result represented perfect reason loaded with the symbolism of unity between Scotland and England imposed upon an incomparably romantic setting. St George's (later Charlotte) Square to the west faced up a wide avenue (George Street) to St Andrew Square to the east. Parallel one-sided streets flanked the parallelogram – St Giles Street (changed at the King's request to Princes Street) downhill to the south, and Queen Street downhill to the north overlooking country to the Forth. The blocks were chopped by Frederick, Castle and Hanover Streets, and crossed by smaller streets for shopkeepers and artisans, christened Thistle and Rose to complete the conceit. Statues at street intersections emphasised the formal geometric symmetry that was to be imposed upon the landscape.

This plan has startling similarities to those described in Lewis Mumford's analysis of the decline of Greek cities like Miletus in the sixth century BC. A thriving middle class sought 'small elegances to compensate them for any empty political life' in the creation of new towns to a chequerboard pattern, with streets of uniform width and city blocks of fairly uniform dimensions. Rectangular open spaces were simply empty blocks. No effort was made to adapt or change the pattern to suit a topographic feature like a hill or a bay. Similar characteristics are to be found in Roman forts, possibly in the *bastides* (fortified towns) which the English planted in Anjou and in Wales, and even – to a much smaller scale – in the pattern of minor parallel streets flanking a principal one, leading to a main square with an axial church, used for the new agricultural towns then being planted in Buchan and Moray. As the classes of Edinburgh were segregated into geographically distinct streets, social exclusion became embedded in the forward development of the city.

The only monuments planned for the new housing estate were the two churches planned to face each other down George Street from the West End (St George's) and from the east end (St Andrew's). But the site for St Andrew's was swiftly snaffled by Sir Lawrence Dundas who commissioned the stately Sir William Chambers to build him a villa thereupon it (now the Royal Bank of Scotland). St Andrew's Church became relegated to the middle rank of the first block of George Street. It was an early triumph of adventurism over good planning.

The symbol of the authorities' confidence in the New Town was General Register House, funded by the government from the proceeds of Jacobite forfeited estates. (Ironically, the Forbes of Pitsligo were a prominent forfeited family and yet Sir William Forbes of Pitsligo was to become principal banker behind the New Town.) Designed by Robert and James Adam to face axially up North Bridge in 1772, Register House was far and away the most sumptuous construction in the capital. Virtually opposite it lay the 1769 Theatre Royal – the first place of resort in the New Town. Almost as soon as the new bridge opened, the theatre had settled in Shakespeare Square (where the Post Office now is) in advance of the population. Thus did the ridiculous outface the sublime: for the barn-like theatre with its shorn portico had all the architectural quality of a second-rank 1930s cinema.

Before the results of its architectural competition were known, the council induced John Young to take a stance in what has now become Thistle Court with £20: and Young's pair of small semi-detached provincial Scots houses are unlike anything later permitted by Craig's plan. David Hume built himself a house in the south-west corner of St Andrew Square opposite that of the eccentric Earl of Buchan. According to Carlyle, 'the street leading south to Princes Street had not yet got its name affixed, but he got a workman early one morning to paint on the corner stone of David's house "St David's Street" where it remains to this day.' Both Robert Chambers and Sir Daniel Wilson relate a different story, but Carlyle's account, being contemporary, is more likely to be accurate.

The Scots were initially deeply uncertain about the large Craigleith stone houses built, as Captain Topham observed, 'after the manner of the English'. He was entertained by the 'irrational prejudice' Edinburgh folk 'retained in favour of a little dark confined tenement on the sixth storey'. Perhaps as a consequence, what appear to be rows of terraced houses with their graceful circular bow windows that plunge down the side streets of the New Town are concealed tenement flats providing for the enduring Scots preference for flat-living. Sir Walter Scott lived in one such at 39 Castle Street.

Strict feu conditions imposed a homogeneity of scale, colour and material upon pleasing terraces of plain, dour, tall, well-built Scots houses which began to creep westwards down George Street from St Andrew Square. As you could guess from their stately windows, they promised the incomparable attraction of new-fangled reception rooms, the genesis of a social formality impossible in the Old Town. James Craig's notion that the central bays in each George Street block would be dignified by something grander never flourished, although some of them were later occupied by the Physicians' Hall, St Andrew's Church, and the Assembly Rooms.

Aspirations rose as building progressed westward: plainness was overlain by fanciful decoration on the façade, to the extent that by the last block before Charlotte Square, the unity of George Street had been lost. In 1791, the Lord Provost invited Robert Adam to design elevations for all four sides of Charlotte Square, even although it was intended that individual builders still would construct their own plots conform to that design. The north side has immense swagger. Nine houses of differing sizes lie behind a single palace-front block, of which Bute House at the centre is the largest, identifiable by its columns and pediments (it is now the official residence of the Secretary of State for Scotland).

Henry Skrine, on his 1793 tours round the north, was vastly impressed:

> We were most agreeably surprised to find ourselves transported into the most regular and superb city that any country can boast; the streets all intersect each other at right angles, and the buildings are of the finest stone, constructed in the most perfect uniformity.

Progress was far from smooth. Because the Nor' Loch was not properly drained, enclosed and planted with trees until 1821, Princes Street suffered from being a narrow carriageway overlooking a dump, which may explain why it *never* had the cachet of George Street. It was rapidly overrun by shops and businesses. Moreover, when the second New Town broke ground downhill from Queen Street on the Heriot estate, the first was still incomplete. Grass grew between its cobbles.

In the meantime, improvements to southern Edinburgh were in hand. The North Bridge suggested the usefulness of another bridge on the same latitude streaking southwards over the Cowgate to the countryside beyond. James Brown, developer of Brown's Square, impertinently suggested that two well-fed magistrates could scarcely pass each other in some of the wynds 'without manifest inconvenience'. Within five months of James Craig winning the competition for the New Town, William Robertson, Principal of the University, memorialised the town council to remind it of its southern obligations. Praising the great improvements which were still going forward – the magnificent bridge, streets and squares to the north – he lamented the 'neglected state' of the university fabric, which was 'generally accounted a dishonour to the City of Edinburgh and to this part of the kingdom'. He sought, not the minor repair and alteration of the double-courtyarded Renaissance university, but its total rebuilding 'according to a regular plan and in a decent manner on the ground where it stands at present'.

In 1785, Lord Provost Sir James Hunter Blair (a banker as corpulent as Brown might ever have conceived) obtained a new Act for a south bridge, the rebuilding or improvement of the university, better water supply, enlarged public markets, a further increase to the regality, and the formalisation of the Earthen Mound into a carriageway. For this, he earned immortality in the names of Hunter Square (which surrounded the sadly truncated Tron Kirk) and Blair Street. For reasons of cost, he rejected Robert Adam's ceremonial colonnaded southern entrance to the city and his southern parsimony reinforced northern Edinburgh as the fashionable side of the capital.

Robert Adam, 'whose interest was great in Edinburgh', designed a new double-courtyard university in 1789, whose foundation-stone ceremony with its great 'civic and masonic pomp' was observed by the young Harry Cockburn on a half holiday from the High School. It remained 'an immense ruin' seventeen years later, the money having run to only the entrance façade and the north-west quadrant. A monument, thought John Stark (another of Edinburgh's annalists), to vanity, a weakness he assessed as the principal failing in the Scottish national character:

> In no instance has this characteristic feature of the people discovered itself in a more striking manner than in the transactions of the citizens of Edinburgh. When in 1763, the improvement of the city, by the extension of its boundaries and the erection of new public buildings took place, the people entered into the scheme with an enthusiasm which is hardly to be paralleled. Since that time the city has been extended to more than double its former size, and the streets and buildings of this new part of it present an appearance for regularity, elegance of architecture and general magnificence which has raised the external appearance of Edinburgh above all the cities of Europe. But Scottish vanity is most conspicuous in the public buildings. When forming the plans of many of these, it was on a scale of magnitude which the poverty of the country prevented them from executing.

Robert Adam's scheme for a new law courts, town hall and library (one of the 1752 *Proposals*) would have tightly enfolded St Giles with a smart, Venetian windowed cloister. But it did not progress. Instead, the council occupied the Exchange in 1811, some sixty years after the merchants of Edinburgh had spurned it, and the King's architect Robert Reid joined the new Library to the old Parliament House behind a single tedious façade which erased the latter's 1633 Renaissance personality. The Signet Library within was designed by William Stark (whom Sir Walter Scott regarded as Scotland's finest architect) with appropriate magnificence. The east side of Parliament Square reached its present frigid grandeur after the second of two disastrous conflagrations in 1824, which broke out in a land halfway between the Tron Kirk and Parliament Close. The buildings in Parliament Square were reduced to a burnt shell: but it was the destruction of the steeple of the Tron Kirk that fascinated Cockburn:

> We ran out from the Court, gowned and wigged, and saw that it

was the steeple, an old Dutch thing, composed of wood, iron and lead, and edged all the way up with bits of ornament . . . there could not have been a more beautiful firework; only it was wasted in the daylight. It was one hour's brilliant blaze . . . the fire seized on every projecting point and played with the fretwork, as if it had all been an exhibition.

At a quarter to twelve, the steeple expired, and Sir Walter Scott greeted the tumble of its clock 'with a profound heave. Eh, Sirs! Mony a wearie wearie sermon hae I heard beneath that steeple!'

In 1815, parliament voted an annual grant of £10,000 for the next seven years to ensure completion of the university, and after an architectural competition, the young William Playfair was appointed to execute a single large courtyard with its stupendous Upper Library. The method of funding gave Cockburn a lever when he was lobbied by students. He requested his MP friend Thomas Kennedy to delay payment of the last instalment:

> some damnable underhand influence has, in spite of a resolution of the Senatus, expelled from the College all the Debating Societies except the Speculative, and perhaps one or two more. Literary societies of students which have met academically for 30 or even 50 years, are now in tatters. The lads have put their case into my hands . . . now I rely on your not letting the dogs get their grant til they satisfy us here on this point.

Power always rests with those with money: the societies were restored to the university, and the college received its cash.

Cockburn amused Kennedy with his tales of how the new university was making out, and in 1826 entranced him with the spectacle of Dr Thomas Charles Hope's lectures to ladies on chemistry.

> He receives 300 of them by a back window, which he has converted into a door. Each of them brings a beau, and the ladies declare that there was never anything so delightful as these chemical flirtations. The Doctor is in absolute ecstasy with his audience of veils and feathers . . .

Demand by the Enlightenment occupants of the Old Town for 'Space! Space! Air! Air!' had proved unstoppable. The second New Town, downhill from Queen Street, was centred upon Edinburgh's most formal street – Great King Street – which strides from Drummond Place in the east to Royal Circus to the west, in immense palace-fronted blocks of a truly Roman frozen grandeur. It was followed by a third to the east of Calton Hill, in which even Great King Street was outmarched by the legion of stern classical houses drawn up along the length of Royal Terrace; by a fourth, once the Earl of Moray redeveloped his villa into an aristocratic enclave; and a fifth westwards along Melville Street. The combined New Towns were greater in extent, as Sir Robert Matthew pointed out in 1970, than the united conservation areas of Chester, Chichester, York and Bath.

It had not been long before Craig's original plan was adjudged too frigid and insufficiently picturesque for such a fine site. Lord Cockburn thought that it compared poorly to the irregularities by which he had been entranced on a continental trip in 1823. It

> demonstrated an unfortunate propensity to avoid whatever had distinguished the place we had fled from. Hence we were led into the blunder of long straight lines of street, divided to an inch . . . every house being an exact duplicate of its neighbour.

The splenetic London journalist Robert Mudie, who came to cover George IV's visit in 1822, found the long streets of plain stone buildings forbidding and very heavy, as though they were constructed 'with the intention of being as inaccessible and dark as possible'. He thought that the 'cold eternity of stone and lime' was evidence of the 'ambition of the Athenians . . . to make every four stone walls a joint stock company'. So each new extension of the New Town was infected by a desire to be more picturesque; and the leader of the picturesques was the fragile William Stark, whose plan for the eastern New Town exploited slope, contour, view, and even existing trees to maximum effect. After Stark's death, those principles were followed by his pupil William Playfair to the extent of the occasionally curving contoured crescent.

John Stark has left a vivid description of the citizens settling into their new quarters. He lamented the end of concerts in St Cecilia's Hall and how 'the enchanting strains of Corelli and the sublime compositions of Handel had given way to the weekly concerts of Scottish church music where harmony and melody are alike unkown.' The 'vitiated taste of the present' was satisfied solely by an annual concert in the Corri's Rooms. Concert-going may well have been displaced by private music which flourished in the drawing rooms. Spacious art exhibition rooms had been opened by Henry Raeburn and Alexander Nasmyth in York Place, and by Watson in James' Square. The interior elegance of the Assembly Rooms in George Street and the 'fine display of beauty' evident at card parties and dancing assemblies was ample compensation for the defects of its architecture.

Plentiful provisions reached the new fruit market – 40,000 pints of strawberries and gooseberries in season – and tourists would enjoy a visit to the new fish market:

> It is well known that Edinburgh fishwomen have an absurd custom of demanding, at first, about three times the price they expect and do accept for their fish. This gives rise to much quarrelling and much wheedling, in which all the eloquence of Billingsgate may sometimes be recognised, with the change only of the broad Scottish dialect for the Cockney twang.

Stark doubted that Creech's dire predictions of moral collapse of 1792 had been fulfilled in the succeeding fourteen years, although he admitted an increase in the luxury of the table. The more opulent and wealthy tradesmen and merchants now attended little to business in the afternoon. 'The bottle is preferred to the amusements of the drawing room', but 'the torrent of vice, which stopped, else by this time on the same average of increase, the number of prostitutes would have amounted to that of the present population of the City.' Housebreakings and robberies remained mercifully rare, execution of criminals seldom, and public cockfighting matches virtually extinct. The Regency beau, thought Stark, was

> an object of laughter rather than censure, of pity rather than of reprobation. He can drive a coachful of ladies, equal to the most experienced coachman . . . But in other parts of education, he is not deficient: he excels in those tropes or figures of speech which the vulgar call swearing . . . as to the fair sex, the elegant society of the stable is preferable to that of the drawing room, and to lounge among brother fine-fellows in the coffee house or the tavern, is superior to the company of ladies . . . he pays his debts of honour much in the same manner as the fine fellow of 1783; and like him can drink three bottles of wine, kick the waiter, knock down the watchman with good grace.

It was not until roughly 1815 that Edinburgh began to metamorphose its New Towns from an opulent suburb into the Athens of the North (a foolish phrase, thought Cockburn, likely to bring mockery upon the capital). Comparisons between Edinburgh and Athens had originated in the late eighteenth century, but became frequent once the artist Hugh

'Grecian' Williams had exhibited canvases of Athens which he had painted in 1816, the purpose of which appeared to be the proving of the comparison. Similar canvases of Edinburgh from the Pentlands clinched the argument. Imaginative wishful thinking transformed an aristocratic housing estate into what Stark called the City of Palaces.

There was a ready market for a new Athens within the British Isles. Edinburgh offered a surrogate experience of both classical and romantic landscapes to those accustomed to a Grand Tour through Europe, but who had been trapped by the French Wars since the early 1790s within the safety of the 'wooden walls of England'. After Waterloo, Edinburgh set out to justify its new title, and the common purpose of recreating the physical and intellectual characteristics of Periclean Athens on the shores of the Forth focused upon Calton Hill as the Acropolis. Thomas Hamilton's original perspective for the Royal High School on the side of Calton Hill, in 1829, was more Athenian than Athens itself, and could have been painted by Grecian Williams. Athenian inspiration affected even fashion as curling and frizzing ladies' hair was dropped: 'under the influence of the Grecian revival, they began to wear it loose, confined over the brow with a bandeau or fillet allowing it to fall on the shoulders in a mass of curls'. The amphora as fashion-plate! Every visitor had to contribute a mite: even Queen Victoria noted of Calton Hill in her diary that 'Albert felt that even the Acropolis could not have been finer.'

The money and desire to achieve great monuments coincided with a flourishing of native architecture: genius from William Playfair and William Burn, bravura in James Gillespie Graham, and solidity in Robert Reid, William Sibbald, Thoams Bonnar and Archibald Elliott. It could be supposed that the Scottish élite provided enlightened and wealthy patronage within a supportive climate of opinion to enable its architects to outstrip their European counterparts: and in 1840, they combined to form the Institute of the Architects of Scotland.

Most Athenian patrons, however, like those in our own dull sublunary times, were committees rather than committed individuals: Committees of Trustees, Committees of Council, and Committees for the Boards of Manufacturers. Chicanery was rife. As soon as Playfair was invited to enlarge the Royal Institution at the bottom of Hanover Street, William Burn briskly attempted to persuade the client to seek a site higher up the Earthen Mound: a new site implied a new architect. Playfair's clients rejected the 'extraordinary nature of this unsought advice', and Playfair informed the aggressor: 'According to the gross conceptions of ordinary men, whose minds are cast in a common mould, such a procedure is liable to misconstruction.'

Whilst the public admired their designs, the architects resembled squalling tigers with their tails tied together. Playfair considered the architecture of Burn 'blotted the landscape'. The *Scots Magazine* dismissed Robert Reid's new St George's Church in Charlotte Square (now West Register House) as 'cool and deliberate bad taste'; Thomas Hamilton was condemned by Playfair as a man 'full of intrigue and vulgar taste'. Of James Gillespie (who married a Graham heiress, called himself Gillespie Graham and had himself painted in full baronial fig, styling himself 'architect in Scotland to the Prince Regent' without any authority to do so) Burn growled, 'There was nothing Gillespie would hesitate about, and therefore his conduct surprises no-one.' The Institute of the Architects of Scotland had a first life of barely five months.

The glory of modern Athens lay in its monuments rather than its houses: its processional ceremonial routes like Waterloo Place leading to Calton Hill, George IV Bridge and associated Victoria Street, educational institutions like the Royal High School and the Edinburgh Academy, charities like John Watson's and the Orphan Hospital, professional institutes like the Royal College of Surgeons and the Royal College of Physicians, and national institutions like the Royal Institution (now the Royal Scottish Academy) and the National Galleries of Scotland. It was symbolised, more than by anything else, by the monuments on the top of Calton Hill – the Observatory, the monuments to Professor Playfair, to Dugald Stewart and to Burns, and to the Acropolis, and the National Monument.

Athenian monuments formed part of what was called the neo-classical or Greek revival. But the Greek temple had no windows, and spaces within would have to be toplit. Since users received little in terms of usable internal space, Grecian architecture was somewhat short of utility. Most of the money was spent on an impressively columned pedimented façade (as was the case in the College of Surgeons), leaving little more than a hut behind. Each project ran into controversy over both siting and cost. To begin with, clients were persuaded to pay for the building that they desired; but by mid-century, they desired only the building they could pay for. The earlier results were incomparably splendid.

Calton Hill was opened up by the creation of Waterloo Place, which required the extravagant engineering of Regent Bridge over Leith Wynd, the expense of which was almost equal to the total cost of the first New Town. Everybody must have been relieved that the construction of Regent Road could be achieved by poor relief labour. (It was one of several poor relief projects which also included walks over Calton Hill, paths through Salisbury Crags, and the clearing of old quarries and whin bushes in Bruntsfield Links.) The opening of Regent Road to create a formal entrance to Edinburgh, however, inadvertently proved the last straw for the

Canongate, which now lost its role as Edinburgh's ancient entrance from the east. Robert Chambers lamented:

> Instead of profiting by the comparative retirement which [the Canongate] acquired on that occasion, it seems to have become the more wretchedly squalid, from its being the less under notice – as a gentleman dresses the least carefully when not expecting visitors. It is now a secluded and in general meanly inhabited suburb.

Only 'one person of condition', Sir William Bannatyne occupying Whitefoord House, remained in the entire street by 1833.

The continuing demand for poor relief, it was suggested in 1817, could be merged with Scottish national aspiration by the erection of a National Monument to commemorate Scottish heroism in the 'unparalleled victories' of the Napoleonic Wars. An Athenian committee, formed in 1819, recommended that a monument in the form of a replica of the Temple of Minerva Parthenon be erected on the summit of Calton Hill. No longer a simple work of poor relief, nor even just another military Valhalla: the proposal was based on no less grandiose a premise that since the Parthenon was the sole fount of architecture, then the Athens of the North required one as well.

From the *Edinburgh Review*'s sublime exposition of the matter, architecture had evidently transcended its private nature by 1822 to become the heart of Scotland's developing culture. Those who, even twelve months previously, had been unable to distinguish between the various classical orders, 'can now talk of the Parthenon, and of peristyles, and cells, and intercolumniations and pediments, with all the familiarity of household words'. The anonymous author (presumably Francis Jeffrey) placed his considerable weight behind the Parthenon. It would put an end to the 'examples of the progress of bad taste and of the imitation of bad models', particularly the copying of the 'peculiar taste' of buildings like Heriot's Hospital which, in the editor's view, should be preserved as no more than a historic curiosity. What he wanted was the Parthenon:

> We are confident, that after this building shall have been 20 years displayed, no architect, not even a stone mason will repeat, even in Gothic architecture, such things as we now see everywhere risen and, we fear, still rising about us.

He was certain that had Pericles been able to use glass roofs, he indubitably would have, thereby nullifying any problems caused by a windowless box. The interior of the National Monument should instil a sense of sublime into the national soul, and its architecture inform all subsequent buildings. Above all, wrote this wild rational romantic, the unmatched landscape of Edinburgh *required* to be enhanced by the greatest product of human endeavour.

> It is the peculiar boast of Edinburgh, the circumstance on which its marvellous beauty so essentially depends, is that its architecture is its landscape; that nature has done everything, has laid every foundation, and disposed of every line of its rocks and its hills, as if she had designed it for the display of architecture. It will also be the boast of our Parthenon that whilst it is the eye and centre of one of the noblest architectural landscapes of Europe, it will be everywhere supported by forms which will give to it additional importance and additional picturesque effect.

The committee raised a public subscription of approximately £24,000, and sought a design from the acknowledged expert on Greek architecture, C R Cockerell, who selected the young Edinburgh architect William Playfair to be his assistant. The anticipated government support was not forthcoming, and King George IV and his ministers studiously avoided the foundation-stone ceremony which took place during his celebrated Scottish jaunt in 1822. Cockburn wrote to his friend Kennedy to solicit support in parliament:

> I know no Whig here and no sensible Tory who is not most anxious to see Edinburgh graced by so noble and so cheap an edifice . . . we only want a public guinea for each of the 20,000 private ones we have raised ourselves . . . to give us a lift; our ultimate views are to give its interior a Westminster Abbey for Scotland, a noble and useful design, rendering the edifice more interesting than even its architectural beauty. So give us the Parthenon and let us keep our principles.

The contract began in 1826 to workmanship of Playfair's customary superlative quality, the massive stones for the columns from Craigleith Quarry requiring twelve horses and seventy men each for their transport. Three years later, the money was exhausted with only twelve columns to show for it. Notwithstanding, what was built was exactly that which the contract drawings specified *should* be built. In other words, it was a deliberate intention from the very first to build only the small section that we can see. It is therefore a deliberate folly: if money was insufficient to achieve the military Valhalla that had been hoped, at the least it could be used to crown Edinburgh's Athenian aspirations.

Moreover, the *Review*'s wish that it would act as a cultural beacon to guide subsequent architecture was indeed realised through the experience Playfair, as the assistant, had gained from working with Cockerell; palpable, for example, in the way he expanded the Royal Institution into the forceful Doric temple that we now know as the Royal Scottish Academy. With his later National Gallery of Scotland on the Earthen Mound immediately to the south, Thomas Hamilton's noble Royal High School, and a number of similarly illustrious classical monuments, Edinburgh had earned both its Attic title and its status as a cultural capital of Europe.*

It is tempting to ascribe the capital's slide towards bankruptcy in 1833 to this surge of extraordinary building. Cockburn lamented:

> Alas! Our poor bankrupt City! It is a great misfortune, not merely to creditors but in reference to all public proprieties . . . the Provost is going up to beg and weep. Be gracious to him. He seems to me to be by far the best Provost we have had for a very long while.

But the city's indebtedness had been growing since the seventeenth century, and accelerating since the late 1790s. The oligarchic and private nature of the city operations meant that few knew the facts. So alarmed were burgesses that they might have a personal liability for debts over which they had no control – debts that by 1819 were rising to a quarter of a million pounds – that they arranged for the matter to be examined by the House of Commons. The outcome was the publication of the city's accounts for the first time, which revealed a shortfall of income in the year 1818 of almost £16,000. Not surprisingly, anxiety over city finances played a prominent part in the commotion for burgh reform. There had been overspending on the Royal High School, and Regent Bridge proved enormously expensive; but the last straw was caused by borrowing from, amongst others, the government to finance docks in Leith. In 1833, the Commissioners on Municipal Corporations reported of Edinburgh that, *inter alia*,

---

* In 1828, one of Edinburgh's newspapers catalogued the capital's assets by way of proof of its nobility. It claimed 700 teachers, 400 advocates, 800 Writers to the Signet, 86 accountants, 40 physicians, 70 surgeons, 100 apothecaries and 400 sedan chairmen. There were 70 churches, 2 theatres, 13 courts, 42 insurance offices, 7 libraries, 11 hospitals, 60 charitable institutions, 25 literary societies, 80 public houses and 850 streets and lanes. The legal fraternity comes close to equalling all other occupations, and you were three times more likely to get drunk than became literarily improved.

officers were multiplied and salaries raised; a spirit of litigation prevailed, great profusion took place in the expenses of civic parade and entertainments, and extravagant sums were expended on public buildings and other works, as ill-adapted in general to their object of embellishing the city as they invariably were disproportioned to its expense.

On 29th August that year, trustees for the creditors of the city were appointed to regularise the city's affairs within four years. Profligacy was over. So also, as the result of municipal reform, was the old, oligarchic, self-electing council. Not a single sitting member retained his seat.

So what was it like to live in a gigantic, city-sized building site that endured over thirty years? Sir Walter Scott was a victim in November 1825:

> I had a bad fall last night coming home. There were unfinished houses at the east end of Atholl Place, and as I was on foot, I crossed the street to avoid the material which lay about. But, being deceived by the moonlight, I stepped ankle-deep into a sea of mud (honest earth and mud and water, thank God) and fell on my hands . . . I was absolutely rough-cast.

Far from being excluded from the New Town, professionals like Scott were (as they remain today) its backbone – promiscuously interrelated with intellectuals and minor lairds. Queen Street, for many the least fashionable of the New Town streets, seemed from its earliest years to attract money and the law. To take three houses at random, numbers 26, 27 and 28 were occupied in turn by an advocate, a minor laird who was also a banker, and a banker. The quality of doorways, plasterwork and timberwork, curved dining rooms, libraries, stairwells graced with splendid cupolas and delicate plaster cartouches, and elegant drawing rooms on the first floor, was high. It was to number 11 Queen Street that the advocate Grant of Rothiemurchus came to spend the winter of 1815 with his family. His daughter Elizabeth was unimpressed: 'the most disagreeable house possible, on the front of which the sun never shone, and which was so built behind that there was no free circulation of air through it'. Because the four good rooms on each floor did not intercommunicate, there was insufficient room for evening parties, 'and so during our stay, nothing could be given but dinners'. Nor did the street inspire that stern moralist John Ruskin, who fulminated against its 678 identically plain windows 'altogether void of any relief by decoration'. Not a bad window – indeed, manly and vigorous: 'but I cannot say it is entertaining'. His Scots audience might well have been puzzled at the concept that they should be entertained by windows. The austerity of Queen Street, however, reinforced Ruskin's prejudice against the unnatural tedium of classicism.

A last attempt to seduce those elusive aristocrats back from London was made by the Earl of Moray on the cliffs above the Water of Leith. 'An open field of as green turf as Scotland could boast of', remembered Cockburn,

> with a few respectable trees on the flat, and thickly wooded on the bank along the Water of Leith . . . that well-kept and almost evergreen field was the most beautiful piece of ground in immediate connection with the town . . . It would be some consolation if the buildings were worthy of the situation; but the northern houses are turned the wrong way, and everything is sacrificed to the multiplication of feuing feet.

Cockburn was too jaundiced. The baroque grandiloquence of the Moray estate, designed by James Gillespie Graham, is quite the grandest single piece of development in Edinburgh's history. With the railings and gates designed to exclude all inferiors, it offers the conclusive evidence, if evidence was ever needed, of the social divisions within newly dispersed Edinburgh.

The New Towns finally ceased building around 1851, almost a century after Minto's *Proposals*. The hugger-mugger of Old Edinburgh life had been rationalised: the indigent were in a Bridewell; the guilty in a new prison; the maniac in a new Bedlam; servants in the mews, shopkeepers and tradesmen in Thistle Street, Rose Street and their likes; commerce in Princes Street, middle classes in George Street, and professionals in Queen Street and Heriot Row. Those below the Plimsoll line remained in the Old Town.

Once new houses had replaced corncrakes, washerwomen occupied unused spaces as bleaching greens, lighters lit lamps, and coalmen delivered coal. Scott commented in his journal how the new houses had brought fog to Edinburgh: 'this (January 18th 1827) is another vile day of darkness and rain, with a heavy yellow mist that might become Charing Cross – one of the benefits of our extended City; for that in our atmosphere was unknown until the extent of the buildings below Queen Street.'

The New Town brought not just fog. It brought to the surface Edinburgh's latent class-consciousness. At the beginning of the nineteenth century, Henry Mackenzie had been amused to record one Edinburgh oyster wife patronise a neighbour as 'but a poor low-lifed creature, being only in the mussel line'. But in striking contrast to Enlightenment Edinburgh, snobbery appears to have become endemic in the Athens. Scott, for example, encouraged the Ettrick Shepherd James Hogg in his literary ambitions, but found the social habits of this 'rustic genius' difficult to accept. One night, Scott invited him back to his house in Castle Street. His son-in-law, the acid John Gibson Lockhart, records:

> When Hogg entered the drawing room Mrs Scott, being at the time in a delicate state of health, was reclining on a sofa. The Shepherd, after being presented, and making his best bow, forthwith took possession of another sofa placed opposite to hers, and stretched himself there upon all his length; for, as he said afterwards; 'I thought I could never do wrong to copy the lady of the house.' As his dress at this period was precisely that in which any ordinary herdsman attends cattle at the market, and as his hands, moreover, bore most legible marks of a recent sheep smearing, the lady of the house did not observe with such perfect equanimity the novel usage to which her chintz was exposed. The Shepherd, however, remarked nothing of all this – dined heartily and drank freely and, by jest, anecdote and song afforded plentiful merriment to the more civilised part of the company. As the liquor operated, his familiarity increased, and strengthened from 'Mr Scott' he advanced to 'Sherra' and thence to 'Scott', 'Walter' and 'Wattie' until, at supper, he fairly convulsed the whole party by addressing Mrs Scott as 'Charlotte'.

Sofas and chintz are not artefacts one associates with Enlightenment flats. Whereas in the Old Town there had been no averting of eyes, the New Town became virtually a petrified euphemism. The primness and prudery against which Robert Louis Stevenson was to react so wildly entered Edinburgh's bloodstream: signified by a compulsive need to be decorous and well uniformed in hats, gloves, and suchlike impedimenta. To a degree quite impossible in the High Street, a New Town address was a precise indicator of status: those in Moray Place at the pinnacle, followed by Charlotte Square and Great King Street. An address in Cumberland Street would indicate a middling kind of person, and in Young Street, a better kind of tradesman. Drones lived in the mews, the lanes, above or beside coach houses. It remained the case in 1901, as the celebrated architect Sir Robert Lorimer explained to a colleague:

> I regard it as being just as important for me to be in the centre of things as for a doctor to be in Charlotte Square! You want to

keep in touch with all those pot-bellied WS and people, you know what human nature is. If you are prosperous they will employ you, and if they think you are small beer and live away at Murrayfield or Stockbridge or somewhere they will let you severely alone.

If the Scotts may have looked down upon Hogg, that was nothing to how Elizabeth Grant of Rothiemurchus regarded the Scotts. Forbidden the attentions of a poet on the grounds that a scribbler was no fit companion for a Grant of Rothiemurchus, Elizabeth revealed herself to be a snob in her *Memoirs of a Highland Lady*. Her Edinburgh social round closely resembles Jane Austen's Bath, with the comparable society of minor aristocracy, military chaps and some senior professionals. Although she never met Scott, she felt able to conclude: 'His family were all inferior. I have often thought that this was the reason of the insipidity of his ideal gentleman and ladies – he knew none better.' Lady Scott she dismissed as an aristocratic bastard with a mother of low degree (which sits ill alongside the fact that her father was the Master of the Military Academy at Lyons) and dismisses her as 'very silly and very foolish . . . a most unfortunate mate for such a man'. Such an exercise in snobbery would have scarcely been credible in the Old Town, and would certainly not have been tolerated.

The social contrast between Old and New Towns struck most visitors from the 1790s, and their reaction is well represented by that of the American journalist Nathaniel Willis in September 1834:

> A more striking contrast than exists between these two parts of the same city could hardly be imagined. On one side a succession of splendid squares, elegant granite houses, broad and well-paved streets, columns, statues and clean sidewalks, thinly promenaded and by the well-dressed exclusively – the kind of wholly grand and half deserted city, which has been built too ambitiously for its population; and, on the other, an antique wilderness of streets and 'wynds' so narrow and lofty as to shut out much of the light of heaven; a thronging, busy and particularly dirty population; sidewalks almost impassable from children and other respected nuisances; and altogether, between the irregular and massive architecture and the unintelligible jargon agonising the air about you, a most outlandish and strange city. Paris is not more unlike Constantinople than one side of Edinburgh is unlike the other. Nature has properly placed a great gulf between them.

Oh, no it hadn't. It was not nature that did it: it was man.

Cockburn grieved over how changing fashion in the New Town had caused a dislocation of traditional habits: it

> altered the style of living, obliterated local arrangements, and destroyed a thousand associations, which nothing but the still preserved names of houses and places is left recalled. It was the rise of the New Town that obliterated our old peculiarities with the greatest rapidity and effect. It not only changed our scenes and habits of life, but, by the mere inundation of modern popu- lation, broke up and, as was then thought, vulgarised our pre- scripted gentilities.

In 1833, Robert Chambers perceived that Edinburgh had become

> two cities not less differing in appearance than in the character of their various inhabitants. The fine gentlemen, who daily ex- hibit their foreign dresses and manners on Princes Street, have no idea of a race of people who roost in the tall houses of the Lawnmarket in the West Bow . . . and in some of the sequestered closes and back courts of the Old Town, there may at this very day be found specimens of people bearing nearly all the charact- eristics of 17th century Edinburgh . . . the one is like the gay sur- face of the summer sea, covered with numerous vehicles of com- merce and pleasure; while the other resembles the region below the surface, whose dreary wilds are peopled only by the wrecks of such gay barques and by creatures of inconceivable hideousness and surpassing horror. In short, 'the march of intellect' proceeds along the South Bridge, without ever once casting a side look to the Cowgate.

It was a litany to be repeated until the Cowgate became sanitised. In 1865, Alexander Smith recommended visitors to

> stand on the South Bridge, and, looking down, instead of a stream you see the Cowgate, the dirtiest, narrowest, most dense- ly peopled of Edinburgh streets . . . The Cowgate has fallen into the sere and yellow leaf of furniture brokers, second-hand jewell- ers, and vendors of deleterious alcohol . . . the Cowgate is the Irish portion of the city. Edinburgh leaps over it with bridges; its inhabitants are morally and geographically the lower orders. They keep to their own quarters and seldom come up to the light of day. Many a man has never set foot in the street; the con-

158

dition of the inhabitants is as little known to respectable Edinburgh as are the habits of moles, earthworms and the mining
population.

An identical conclusion was reached by Robert Louis Stevenson barely a
decade later:

> Social inequality is nowhere more ostentatious than at Edin-
> burgh . . . to look over the South Bridge and see the Cowgate
> below full of crying hawkers is to view one rank of society from
> another in the twinkling of an eye.

The first New Town was a pure product of the Enlightenment: but as
years passed and building continued, it became transformed willy-nilly
into something much more glorious – into the Athens of the North. The
genius loci, the spirit of the place, the landscape, and indeed the weather
all conspired with suitable romanticism to make the New Town a capital
of European quality to rival the old one. The city, and many private individuals, risked bankruptcy and obloquy in order to acheive that aim.
But achieve it they did, creating the cynosure of northern Europe to
which any cultivated person aspired to come as part of their education.

The achievement had been at the signal cost of damage to the city's
soul. If it was in Edinburgh, as Sydney Smith said, that people were
metaphysical even while making love, perhaps intellect itself had been
over-valued. The condition of the Old Town of Edinburgh, the new
class-consciousness, and the petrified social divisions were direct consequences of the way in which Enlightenment Edinburgh tackled the
necessary problem of the city's extension. It embedded geographically
distinct social polarisation in the city, which has been Edinburgh's bane
ever since.

As Lewis Mumford wrote of the real Athens: 'as the inner life of the
Greek city disintegrated, the outer aspect of the city showed a far higher
degree of formal order and coherence.' The Athens of the North was
dangerously close to being a magnificent husk; but it yet had a romantic
song to sing.

CHAPTER TEN

ALL SORTS OF LITERARY IDLERS

Only while it aspired to be Athens of the North was Edinburgh intrinsically literary, although, as the country's capital, it was naturally the occasion of much writing generated by the court. With the exception of Dunbar's celebrated flyting of Edinburgh merchants, around 1503, exhorting them to cleanse the capital in time for the marriage of King James IV to Margaret Tudor, the country's abundant Renaissance poetry had only an incidental connection with Edinburgh. The magnet of royalty, instead, remained the target of poetic effusion – from Sir David Lyndsay of the Mount and Sir Richard Maitland to the group known as the Castalian Band which clustered poetically around James VI with pastorals and eclogues of an ambivalently Scottish tune. William Drummond of Hawthornden's relation to Edinburgh was no greater than the coincidence of the proximity of his family seat.

Fine printing thrived early in the capital. In 1507 James IV had granted a printing patent to Edinburgh burgesses Walter Chepman and Andro Myllar who opened a printing works in the Cowgate to print books of laws, Acts of Parliament, chronicles, Mass books, breviaries, and legends of Scots saints; soon followed by the poems of Henryson and Dunbar. So here lay the destination for scholars seeking publication. 'In time of vacance', James Melville recorded, he visited the dying George Buchanan, accompanied by his uncle Andrew Melville (The Blast) and Thomas Buchanan. Buchanan was then arranging for the publication of his *History of Scotland*. 'When we came to his chalmer, we found him sitting in his chair, teaching his young man that served him in his chalmer to spell a, b, ab; etc.' Andrew Melville's observation, 'I see, Sir, you are nocht idle' earned a truly Presbyterian riposte: 'Better this,' quoth he, 'nor stealing sheep or sitting idle, which is also ill!'

For the next century, sermons, memoirs, diaries, journals and records of travellers comprised the capital's principal literary output. By the eighteenth century, however, printing and publishing expanded with the demand from professors and the literati for the learned tomes and weekly journals which fed the Enlightenment. In 1752, the city had the extraordinary number of fifty-seven booksellers, binders and printers, most of them clustered at the centre of the High Street, by Parliament and Craig's Closes. Creative literature had made a stumbling appearance with a now forgotten novel by Bluidy Mackenzie, and Allan Ramsay's pastoral, *The Gentle Shepherd*, which he counterbalanced with poetic strophes to brothel-keepers. The devout were distressed at the threats to morality offered by Ramsay's poems; worse, by his enthusiastic advocacy of the theatre (mercifully quickly banned by the government), and – worst of all – by his lending library. The dairiest Wodrow confided his gloom to his book:

> profaneness is come to a great height, all the villainous, profane and obscene books and plays, printed at London by Curl and others, are gote down from London by Allan Ramsay, and lent out at an easy price to young boyes, servant women of the better sort, and gentlemen, and vice and obscenity dreadfully propagated. Ramsay has a book in his shop wherein all the names of those that borrow his plays and books for tuppence a night or some such rate are set down, and by these wickedness of all kinds are dreadfully propagate among the youth of all sorts.

Enlightenment literature encompassed all subjects of writing, provided that they were accomplished with style, clarity, lucidity of argument, and mellifluousness. Evaluating the output in his *Picture of Edinburgh*, John Stark suggested that the principal achievement of Monro, Gregory, Cullen, and Black was the fact that these men of 'genius anad industry [had] freed the science of the medical department *from that unintelligible jargon in which it was buried for ages*' (my emphasis). In other words, they made it accessible to other intelligent men. Much the same was said of Hume, Smith, Robertson, and Blair.

Literature in the sense of artistic creation was launched on the capital with the production of *The Douglas* on 14th December, 1756, to the affright of the presbytery of Edinburgh. The author, John Home, was an old companion and fellow volunteer of Carlyle who admired his handsome demeanour, catching address, sprightliness and vivacity. He was also a minister of the Kirk.

> He was truly irresistible, and his entry to a company was like opening a window and letting the sun into a dark room.

On the opening night of his deathless drama, an apocryphal member of the *claque* in the stalls bellowed forth (surely in a Glaswegian accent)

'Whaur's ye're Wullie Shakespeare noo?' The piece caused ructions in the Kirk: ministers were suspended for going to performances, and the play attacked on

> account of its pretended irreligious and immoral tendency, alleging in support of their charge, that there were certain impious invocations or mock prayers in it; and an expression of horrid swearing. Besides, that it encouraged suicide.

Jupiter Carlyle, who had gleefully assisted with the publicity for the play and acted in a dress rehearsal, was hauled before his presbytery on the libel that by keeping company, eating, drinking and conversing familiarly with actors and actresses *without necessity*, he had disgraced his calling. He was duly vindicated by the General Assembly itself. Bruised by the attacks upon him, Home resigned his charge, and pursued the life of a literary man in London.

The following year, David Hume remarked to Sir Gilbert Elliott of Minto:

> is it not strange that, at a time when we have lost our Princes, our Parliament, our independent Government, even the Presence of our Chief Nobility, are unhappy in our accent and pronunciation, speak a very corrupt Dialect of the Tongue which we make use of; is it not strange, I say, that, in these circumstances, we shou'd really be the People most distinguish'd for Literature in Europe?

One assumes that he had more in his mind than *The Douglas*.

On 14th August, 1773, Samuel Johnson arrived at Boyd's Inn, at the head of the Canongate, and directed a cadie to inform his friend James Boswell up in James Court of the fact. Boswell sailed downhill to retrieve his mentor for tea back with his wife. Over the next four days, Johnson met many of the *illuminati* – Ferguson, Robertson, Forbes of Pitsligo, the advocate Crosbie (thought to be the original of Scott's Pleydell), Dr Blacklock and Dr Gregory. There is no record, however, of his having met Edinburgh's finest poet, Robert Fergusson, who delighted at the luscious opportunity of parodying the doctor's orotund vocabulary in several such deeply impenetrable strophes as these:

> Great Pedagogue! Whose literarian lore
> With syllable on syllable conjoined,
> To transmutate and varify, hast learned

> The whole revolving scientific names
> That in the alphabetic columns lie,
> Far from the knowledge of mortalic shapes:

Poor Fergusson, a much better poet than satirist, was creator of some of the most enduring images of the city. Born in a close, and maintaining his family as a legal copyist, no poet felt more at home in the catacombs of the Old Town. Elected by his colleagues to the Cape Club in 1772 under the title of Precenter, he fell into a decline in early 1774 and, after banging his head in a fall down a close, died raving mad in Bedlam later that year, aged only twenty-four. In a spasm of intense creativity lasting almost three years, Fergusson had written some eighty-three poems, thirty-three of them in Scots including a vivid quartet illuminating Edinburgh life: 'Caller Oysters', 'Leith Races', 'To the Tron Kirk Bell', and 'Auld Reekie'. Edinburgh buried him in the Canongate churchyard, a pauper without a headstone (for classlessness went only so far) which so infuriated Robert Burns (often a near pauper himself) that he remedied the matter on his arrival in the capital.

Robert Burns arrived in Edinburgh to seek a national publisher for his poems on 27th November, 1786. In that William Creech gave him a hundred guineas for an Edinburgh edition of his poems, he was initially successful; although had he anticipated that it would sell 3,000 copies so promptly, he might have ensured that a greater proportion of the handsome profit would go to poet and not publisher. In its classless days, Edinburgh was still well able to accommodate him. (It had become a more forlorn hope when James Hogg launched himself as the Ettrick Shepherd, in the city, some decades later.) Whereas he preferred the life of bawdy and the clubs, particularly the Crochallan Fencibles down Anchor Close and the St John's Canongate Masonic Lodge, it was in drawing rooms that he was fêted. One of the queens of Edinburgh society, Mrs Alison Cockburn, wrote to a friend:

> The town is at present agog with the ploughman poet, who receives adulation with native dignity, and is the very figure of his profession – strong and coarse – but has a most enthusiastick heart of LOVE.

He was sceptical of being toured round as 'their learned pig in the Grassmarket', and wrote with distaste to Gavin Hamilton that 'by all probability I shall soon be the tenth Worthy, and the eighth Wise Man of the World'. He had hoped that by being launched into society he might secure a patron who would alleviate the hardship of his agricultural life (for he was but a poor farmer); but it drove him to new accents and poetic emasculation with lines like 'Edina! Scotia's darling seat'.

Burns's unfulfilled passion for Agnes Maclehose, a grass widow separated from a husband in the West Indies, implies how the manners of the capital were changing: the real ploughman had to ape a fictional shepherd, as Sylvander, in making decorous and thereby uncharacteristically seemly advances to his shepherdess, Clarinda. Their relationship survived an occasion when his restraint fractured, and her departure from Edinburgh inspired him to one of his best songs:

> Ae fond kiss, and then we sever!
> Ae fareweel, Alas for ever!
> Deep in heart-wrung tears I'll pledge thee
> Warring sighs and groans I'll wage thee.

The focus of creativity began to creep from clubs down closes to genteel supper parties in New Town mansions, and this shift in social behaviour maybe spawned the literary Renaissance that so distinguished the Athens of the North. The career of Sir Walter Scott spanned both. Born son of an Edinburgh WS, Scott was furloughed to relatives near Smailholm in the Borders following an attack of polio, where he became absorbed by Scots history, legend and myth. On completion of his studies, he was apprenticed as a Writer to the Signet, but switched to advocate in 1792. The biography by John Gibson Lockhart reveals how much Scott enjoyed the Old Town milieu as a student, wearing student corduroy bags 'good enough for drinking in' when he and his cronies were off to quaff oysters in Covenant Close or to attend meetings of the Friday Club which he – elevated to the status of Colonel Grogg – had founded; with oysters in Carubber's Close afterwards.

On the rebound from a rebuffed courtship (a rebuff that must have fuelled ambition to become a person of consequence), he turned to translations and to poetry; and his essential romanticism responded to the romantic if gloomy mystery and ancient awe of the courts within the ancient Parliament House, as described by Thomas Carlyle:

> An immense hall, dimly lighted from the top of the walls, and perhaps with candles burning in it here and there; all in strange chiaroscuro and filled with what I thought (exaggeratively) a thousand or two human creatures; all astir in a boundless buzz of talk and simmering about in every direction, some solitary, some in groups. By degrees I noticed that some were in wig and black gown, some not, but in common clothes, all well dressed; that

here and there on the sides of the Hall were little thrones with enclosures, and steps leading up; red-velvet figures sitting in said thrones, and the black-gowned eagerly speaking to them – Advocates pleading to Judges, as I easily understood. How they could be heard in such a grinding din was somewhat a mystery.

Scott devoured ancient records and manuscripts – mostly, one assumes, those in the Advocates' Library which he haunted as Deputy Keeper. His output was prodigious: over sixty published works of prose, history, translation and poetry, many of them multi-volumes, and countless reviews, commentaries, rebuffs and retaliations: to the extent that malignants queried how he, as Clerk to the Court of Session, could find time to write more not only than any other author, but, as Lord Archibald Hamilton put it, 'more books than anybody could find the leisure to read'. His role as a public figure began in 1802 with the publication of the *Minstrelsy of the Scottish Border* which consists of original and recreated Border ballads with copious annotated notes and original extracts from Scots history, many published for the first time. Epic poems followed. His reason for seeking anonymity as author of *Waverley* is unclear, but implies that he regarded the writing of fiction as a greater risk, and did not wish to hazard the reputation he had earned for poetry. The scribbling of potboilers may not have been thought a becoming pastime for a Clerk to the Court of Session. *Waverley* became a literary sensation.

Soon after his marriage to his handsome, dark-haired half-French wife Charlotte Charpentier, he removed from the Old Town to the New, selecting a recently built house in Castle Street, thereafter walking to the courts each day. Once established, however, he put away his clubs, corduroys, oysters and other childish things: and replaced them by suppers. Scott records a winter's evening in 1825 thus: 'The Royal Society Club dined at 5.00 p.m. (2 soups, fish, etc and all in good order)' in the Royal Hotel, followed by port, sherry and coffee till 7.30. The principal entertainment of the evening was listening to the eighty-two-year-old Man of Feeling, the venerable Henry Mackenzie, delivering part of an essay on dreams. Supper followed in Abercromby Place with James Russell, Professor of Clinical Surgery. 'Early dinner begat suppers,' wrote Cockburn. 'But suppers are so delightful that they have survived long after dinners became late. Indeed, this has immemorially been a favourite Edinburgh repast.' He lamented their decline into 'paltry wine and water'. Supper was cheaper and shorter than dinner, less ceremonious and even more poetical: 'if there be any fun, or heart, or spirit in a man at all, it is then, if ever, that it will appear'.

Sir Henry Holland has left a delightful picture of a Scott supper:

I still hold in happy memory the little supper (a meal now lost to social life) at his house in Castle Street, of which he himself was the soul and spirit; his countenance, heavy in its ordinary aspect, kindling suddenly into life and merriment at the racy Scottish stories, which he ever had at hand to point and illustrate the matter of converse, whatever it might be . . . Frequently too at this period, I saw him when listening with enthusiastic enjoyment to 'Lochinvar' and other of his ballads, set to music and sung to him by Miss Clephane (afterwards Lady Northampton), with the fine accompaniment of her harp. This made a picture in itself. It was the poet revelling in the musical echo of his own poetry.

Where the coffee shops had stimulated the late seventeenth century, and the taverns the Enlightenment, it was bookshops that fed the Athens of the North. Bookseller and publisher moved to the centre of fashionable society between 1780 and 1830, and came to be regarded as people of equivalent attainment as the creators of the works themselves. In the ensuing century, they were to provide Edinburgh with an unequalled number of Lord Provosts: the first of whom was William Creech, of 'facetious memory' and exploitative habits, elected in 1811. Cockburn recalled Creech's shop:

the natural resort of lawyers, authors, and all sorts of literary idlers . . . All who wished to see a poet or a stranger, or to hear the public news, the last joke by Erskine, or yesterday's occurrences in the Parliament House, or to get the publications of the day, or newspapers – all congregated there, lawyers, doctors, clergymen and authors.

In *Peter's Letters to his Kinsfolk*, Lockhart offered a tour of the others, including the dusky chamber in the High Street inhabited by Archibald Constable, echoing to the 'incessant cackle of young Whigs'. The sumptuous back room of Manners and Miller across the street, however, was 'the true lounging place of the blue-stockings and literary beau-monde of the Northern Metropolis'. By the 1820s, only sixteen printers and five booksellers remained in the High Street. The New Town had early attracted William Blackwood's literary saloon – modish right up to its cupola, and the perfect setting for the literary equivalent of Regency Bucks:

an elegant oval saloon, lighted from the roof, where various groups of loungers and literary dilettanti are engaged in looking at, or criticising among themselves, publications just arrived by that day's coach from town. In such critical colloquies, the voice of the bookseller himself may ever and anon be heard mingling the broad and unadulterated notes of its Auld Reekie music; for unless occupied in the recesses of the premises with some other business, it is here that he has his usual station.

Robert Mudie was unconvinced by the 'sort of oracle' role played by Edinburgh booksellers, with the notable exception of Constable 'to whom, by the way, the literary world is as much indebted as to any man living'. Portly Archibald Constable, a jolly-looking fellow (thought Lockhart) with an admirable absence of small talk, was a singular instance of success:

> He has indeed too much sense as well as too much business for lecturing and lounging in a public shop . . . Blackwood too has a sort of den; but still, when there is nobody in to gossip, you find his hard face poking out of his shop door, just as the tongue of a church bell pokes out of the mouth of that instrument of noise and brass . . . every bookseller has . . . his evening party in which he shines. Thus Constable dines with deep-going politicians, Blackwood frequents prayer meetings.

Lockhart considered Archibald Constable 'the great bookseller of Edinburgh [and] one of the most sagacious persons that ever followed his profession', with only one, but fatal, flaw: he hated accounts (something for which he and Scott were to pay dearly from 1825). On learning of his death, Scott penned a private obituary for his diary:

> He was a prince of booksellers; his views sharp, powerful, liberal, too sanguine however, and like many bold and successful schemes, never knowing when to stand or stop . . . He was very vain for which he had some reason . . . He knew, I think, more of the business of a bookseller . . . than any man of his time.

At the turn of the century, Sydney Smith had found Edinburgh society congenial. It was 'upon the most easy and agreeable footing; the Scotch were neither rich nor ashamed of being poor, and there was not that struggle for display which so much diminishes the charm of London society.' Smith's arrival in Edinburgh had been accidental. He was tutor to the young Michael Hicks Beech, and had been prevented by the

Napoleonic Wars from accompanying his charge to the University of Weimar. Edinburgh provided a romantic alternative, with a high intellectual reputation, Attic landscape and foreign habits. When Sydney Smith came to leave Edinburgh, and the *Edinburgh Review* of which he was first editor, he transmitted his regrets back to his successor Francis Jeffrey: 'My good fortune will be great, if I should ever again fall into the society of so many liberal, correct and instructed men and live with them in such terms of friendship.' Smith had arrived tutor: he was a man of aptitude, and fortunate political and literary circumstance created the opportunity. He left a literary celebrity and wit.

The well-being and economic boom that may be inferred from the glorious structures of the Athens of the North was not universally shared; particularly not by the dispossessed from the Clearances, agricultural workers newly homeless following agricultural enclosure (financed through the Montgomery Act which allowed the costs of agricultural improvements to be charged to subsequent generations) or by political dissidents who disagreed with the views of Henry Dundas, Viscount Melville – Harry the Ninth as Cockburn called him, the absolute dictator of Scotland. All those who sought change – whether in politics, patronage, Church government, burgh government or in judicial procedures, found themselves marooned by Melville. 'It was an awful period,' wrote Smith, 'for those who ventured to maintain liberal opinions and were too honest to sell them for the ermine of the Judge or the lawn of the prelate.'

Into that repressive context falls the *Edinburgh Review*, which emerged from the debates of the Speculative Society and the Friday Club. At a time when large public meetings, political debates, unions and conventicles were forbidden, this magazine presented serious, intellectually founded anti-establishment views to the members of its forbidden audience. Given that the popularity of being a Whig was comparable, in Cockburn's phrase, to that of being a Catholic during the Titus Oates conspiracy, publishing the *Review* was like holding a Whig conventicle by post. It first appeared on 10th October, 1802 with articles by Sydney Smith, Lord Brougham, Frances Horner, and Francis Jeffrey. To Cockburn its 'effect was electrical . . . The learning of the new Journal, its talent, its spirit, its writing, its independence, were all new; and the surprise was increased by a work so full of public life springing up, suddenly, in a remote part of the Kingdom.' It offered political and artistic stimulus through learned papers on medicine, literature, poetry, and even architecture to a British-wide, and eventually a European-wide audience.

Personal considerations were given no precedence over literary judgments. In 1808, Jeffrey (advocate, editor and reviewer) wrote to Scott (advocate, poet and soon novelist) enclosing with some trepidation a preview of his review of *Marmion*: 'I have spoken of your poem exactly as I think, and though I cannot reasonably suppose you will be pleased with everything I have said, it would mortify me very severely to believe I had given you pain.' What Jeffrey published, *inter alia*, was this withering condemnation of the genre of the historical poem: 'to write a modern romance of chivalry seems to be such a phantasy as to build a modern abbey or an English pagoda'.

No wonder the magazine was a *succès fou*. The banned opposition had gained a voice: a voice that, in time, would overwhelm the establishment. 'Time and justice,' trumpeted Henry Cockburn, 'will at last triumph over even Bishops and Royal Dukes.' Over the first two decades of the nineteenth century, the *Review* championed freedom of thought and attacks upon political abuses: it legitimised dissent and encouraged the population to defy the bans upon political meetings. By 1820, illegal political gatherings were being held throughout Scotland, culminating in an enormous one in the Pantheon in Edinburgh. The establishment, as recently in Eastern Europe, was revealed to be enfeebled, able only to execute the occasional revolting weaver. Yet that they were dangerous times, is clear from Cockburn's reassurance to T F Kennedy MP that the latter's correspondence would be burnt immediately after perusal.

Once the *Review*'s political aims had been satisfied with political and burgh reform, its Whig perpetrators assumed power. On 19th November, 1830, Cockburn explained why he could not afford to accept the position of Lord Advocate: 'But for my profession, I am a beggar. The office of Lord Advocate nearly ruins the practice of any Counsel, it leads him on to great expense . . . Jeffrey is rich; and if asked, will accept . . .' Four years later, in coltish glee, Cockburn wrote to Kennedy: 'Jeffrey is a Lord of Session! An actual red gowned, proper Lord. A framer and lover of Acts of Sederunt. An admirer of the Nobile Officium. A deviser of Interlocutors. A hater of the House of Lords.' Cockburn was even more diverted at the sight of all Jeffrey's old opponents – Hope, Balgray, Glenlee and Meadowbank – fawning over him, hailing him as brother 'with ostentatious hypocrisy'.

The best tunes were not reserved solely for Whigs. In 1815, Blackwood threw down the gauntlet to the Whig *Review* by founding an explicitly Tory magazine, with contents, thought Cockburn, of 'violent personality'. Rivalry between the two magazines acted as a magnet for talent, attracting to the capital even opium eater Thomas de Quincey (whose sojourn was spent largely in the Abbey Strand debtors' sanctuary evading creditors). In 1817, *Blackwood's Magazine* published, in the disguise of an ancient Chaldean manuscript discovered in 'the great library in Paris', a savage satire on the Whigs in the language of the Old Testament. There followed enormous sales, much jocularity, anger, lawsuits and threats of horse-whipping. Blackwood had introduced a disconcerting new aggressiveness to the Athens, and the ensuing warfare had 'a painful influence upon Edinburgh society, and especially on the book trade'. The publisher Adam Black recalled Archibald Constable, on spotting Blackwood at a social occasion, saying, 'I cannot associate with that man,' and leaving immediately, followed by several others.

It was in *Blackwood's* that the *Noctes Ambrosianae* first saw dawn. *Noctes* symbolised, encapsulated and perhaps caricatured the new Edinburgh. 'Christopher North', the minor and irascible poet John Wilson (who later became Professor of Moral Philosophy with no qualifications save vehemence) told the American journalist Nathaniel Willis how the whole thing began in

> a small house; kept in an out-of-the-way corner of the town by Ambrose, who is an excellent fellow in his way, and has had a great influx of custom in consequence of his celebrity in the *Noctes*. We were there one night very late, and all had been remarkably gay and agreeable. 'What a pity,' said Lockhart, 'that some shorthand writer had not been here to take down the good things that had been said at this supper!' The next day he produced a paper called *Noctes Ambrosianae*.

Noctes purported to be literal transcriptions of nocturnal conversations chez Ambrose (variously thought to have been at Register Street and 1 Picardy Place); and implied that the deepest tenets of philosophy comprised normal conversational fare in an Edinburgh howff. The company was usually Ambrose (the publican), Lockhart (to begin with), North, Timothy Tickler and the Ettrick Shepherd, James Hogg.

Noctes conversations were printed, like those of some of the poorer contemporary journalists, as though they had been tape-recorded, viz:

> *North*: What think ye, James, of this plan of supplying Edinburgh with living fish?
> *Shepherd*: Gude or bad, it sal never hae my countenance. I couldna thole Embro' without the fishwives, and gin it succeeded, it would be the ruin o' that ancient race.
> *Tickler*: Yes, there are handsome women amongst the Neriades.

An extract like this scarcely does them justice: there is a mood to be savoured. However, literati in London regarded their popularity as yet more evidence of unjustified pretension by the Athenians, and the

Noctes were parodied by Thomas Love Peacock in *Crotchet Castle* in 1829, much of which is written in *Noctes* conversational style. From the mouth of the Rev Dr Folliott disgorges a south-easterner's resentment:

> Athenians indeed! Where is your theatre? Who among you has written a comedy? Where is your Attic salt? Which of you can tell who was Jupiter's great grandfather? . . . You call yourself Athenians while you know nothing that the Athenians thought worth knowing, and dare not show your noses before the civilised world in the practice of any one art in which they were excellent. Modern Athens sir! The assumption is a personal affront to every man who has a Sophocles in his library. I will thank you for an anchovy.

Everybody liked to patronise James Hogg. Privately nicknamed by Scott as the 'honest grunter', he was *Blackwood's* most outstanding contributor, and author of one of Scotland's most original novels, *Private Memoirs and Confessions of a Justified Sinner*, which examined dangerous perversions of Calvinist doctrine. He was lampooned by his most uncertain and less able friend, Christopher North:

> Only picture yourself a stout country lout with a bushel of hair on his shoulders that had not been raked for months, enveloped in a coarse plaid impregnated with tobacco, with a prodigious mouthful of immeasurable tusks, and a dialect that sets all conjecture at defiance.

In 1810, Hogg founded a magazine, the *Spy*, but his anchor serial, the 'Love Adventures of George Cochrane' was deemed too lubricious for the drawing-room ambience of the New Town. The project failed and after five years' indifferent sojourn in an increasingly rigid capital, he quit Edinburgh for further unsuccessful farming. Even making allowance for his acidity, there is something uncomfortably telling in Mudie's conclusion that:

> there has never been an author in the Athens who has lived even decently by literature alone – as little is there, at this moment, within the whole of her compass, a single person above starvation who has not some other occupation or emolument than that of a literary man.

There was neither aristocratic nor civic patronage for literature within

171

Edinburgh, even at this, the most literary period of the capital; and the city could simply not sustain that level of literary sales beyond thirty years. Had not the *Edinburgh Review* been patronised in London, Mudie thought, it would have been written in vain, for both Francis Jeffrey required 'his fees to bear him out', and Scott 'would long ere now have been mute or a maniac had he not possessed some property, held a public office, and been a fierce and forward party-man'.

As a consequence of the success of the *Edinburgh Review* Jeffrey became as much of a literary lion as Scott. He was 'sharp English, with few anecdotes, and no stories, delighting in the interchange of minds, bright in moral speculation, with a colloquial elegance and always beloved for . . . an affectionate and cheerful heart'. Pilgrimages were made both to his home in Moray Place and to his villa at Craigcrook Castle, sheltering in the lee of Corstorphine Hill. It entranced Cockburn:

> No unofficial house in Scotland has had a greater influence on literary or political opinion. Beautiful though the spot, as he has kept it, is, its deepest interest arises from its being the residence of such a man . . . Escape from the Court and town, to scenery, evergreens, bowls, talk, mirth, friendship and wine.

It was here that they let their hair down. A W Callcott had dined with a relaxed Jeffrey and friends when he was surprised to see Jeffrey put his wine glass into his pocket and say:

> 'We have sat long enough', threw up the window & leapt through it to the grass plot and being followed by the rest, they drank champagne in the open air, and then played at leap frog.

Political opponents were equally welcome as Scott noted:

> I do not know why it is that when I am with a party of my Opposition friends, the day is often merrier than when with our own set. Is it because they are cleverer? Jeffrey and Harry Cockburn are, to be sure, very extraordinary men, yet it is not owing to that entirely. I believe both parties meet with the feeling of something like novelty.

Jeffrey's 'Court', as Cockburn christened it, remained influential even after his retirement as editor of the *Review*. On his death, Cockburn lamented: 'Edinburgh without Jeffrey! and his Court! He was its light and its pride.'

In 1834, the American journalist Nathaniel Willis visited the two opponents: Christopher North (Tory) and Francis Jeffrey (Whig). His breakfast at North's seems to have consisted of cold food and an extempore lecture:

> The tea was made, and the breakfast smoked upon the table, but the Professor showed no signs of being aware of the fact, and talked away famously, getting up and sitting down, walking to the window and standing before the fire, and apparently carried quite away with his own too-rapid process of thought.

After an hour, North proposed eating to which Willis (most particular in recording what he managed to eat and drink) readily agreed.

> Without rising, he leaned back with his chair still towards the fire, and seizing the teapot as if it were a sledgehammer, he poured from one cup to another without interrupting the stream, over-running both cup and saucer, and partly flooding the tea tray. He then set the cream towards me with a carelessness which nearly overset it, and trying to reach an egg from the centre of the table broke two.

Willis was also invited to Moray Place to dine with Jeffrey, whose wife was American, but did not relish the occasion:

> Politics were the only subject at table. Politics is seldom witty or amusing and, though I was charmed with the good sense and occasional eloquence of Lord Jeffrey, I was glad to get upstairs after dinner to chasse-cafe and the ladies.

It was a curious inversion that the Tory talked poetry and the Whig politics.

Perhaps it was Scott's romanticism and picturesque descriptions; or it may have been the output of memorialists like Henry Cockburn, artists such as James Skene of Rubislaw, James Drummond and Walter Geikie, and researchers and historians like Daniel Wilson, and Robert and William Chambers: but Edinburgh was tempted to become dangerously absorbed with its own past. The result was to change the perception of the Old Town from a living community to a museum of bloody romance. Our benefit lies in the unusually detailed knowledge we now have about that great sixteenth- and seventeenth-century winged citadel: it would not be difficult to produce a guide book to it. But antiquarianism turned to a self-absorption leading to a narcissism that persists to this day.

Since the mid-eighteenth century, landmarks of Old Edinburgh had been under threat. An eccentric satirist called James Wilson, going under the pen name of Claudero took to (according to Daniel Wilson) humorous and somewhat coarse verse lampoons first, in defence of the Holyrood Gatehouse: an 'echo of the Royal Porch of the Palace of Holyrood House' which fell under military execution, anno 1753 which concluded:

> Regardless they the mattock ply,
> To root out Scots antiquities.

That was followed by 'the last speech and dying words of the Cross of Edinburgh which was hanged, drawn and quartered on Monday 15th March 1756 for the horrid crime of being an incumbrance to the street'; but which Claudero postulated was condemned for having been the scene of Bonnie Prince Charlie's declaration of regency. In 1764, Claudero turned to prose to save the Netherbow, in the form of 'The last speech, confession and dying words of the Nether Bow port of Edinburgh, on its demolition'. Soon thereafter, he quit for London commiserating with the capital that 'Satire from your streets is fled, poor Edinbroo!'

The removal of the Tolbooth in 1817 was closely observed by Charles Kirkpatrick Sharp (one of Edinburgh's great eccentrics whose calling card was the simple musical notation C sharp), Cockburn and Scott himself who secured the iron cage and other bits for Abbotsford.

> The iron chest was so heavy that the large body of workmen could not, with all their might, pull it out. After stripping it of its masonry, they endeavoured by strong levers to tumble it down into the street. At last, with a 'Yo! Heave ho' it fell down with a mighty crash . . . It was quite a scene. A large crowd had assembled, and amongst them was Sir Walter Scott . . . Sir Walter was still the Great Unknown, but it was pretty well known who had given such an interest to the building by his fascinating *Heart of Midlothian* . . . there was a rush of people towards the iron chest to look into the dark interior of that veritable chamber of horrors . . . as soon as the clouds of dust had been dispersed we observed, under the place where the iron box had stood, a number of skeletons of rats, as dry as mummies.

The mood of the time had turned antiquarian: in 1827, Sharp sought

Scott's aid in the rescue of the castle from a proposed barracks, and against the proposed 'improvement' of a heavy stone cornice to Holyrood House. 'I fear you will think me a worse plague than any bore that ever sprang in Europe,' he wrote, 'in a word, the dangers of our Castle spoils my sleep.' He also addressed the *Edinburgh Observer*:

> I have lived to see in the course of 40 years, the Old Town lose much of its primitive features from unavoidable decay, from the rage for *improvement* and the little less destructive elements of fire; though I have beheld Salisbury Craigs irretrievably injured and Calton Hill utterly destroyed, yet never did I expect to witness such a bold attack as this upon the rock of the castle in Edinburgh.

The barracks were nonetheless built. Removal of antiquity was most apparent with the construction of Johnston Terrace, George IV Bridge and the removal of the West Bow after the 1827 Improvement Bill. Immediately before Major Weir's house in the Bow was demolished in 1835, Victoria Street's architect, Thomas Hamilton, undertook a measured survey of what James Ballantine, in the *Gaberlunzie's Wallet*, called 'the most unique specimen of antique irregular architecture to be found in Europe'. Ballantine (a close friend of George Meikle Kemp) lamented the removal of its kenspeckle inhabitants:

> The West Bow was one of the most noisy quarters of the city; – the clinking of coppersmiths' hammers, the bawling of speech criers, ballad-singers, and venders of street merchandise, were mingled with the scraping of fiddles, the beating of drums, and the squeaking of cracked clarionets . . . Most of the shops were such as dealt in the common necessaries of life with which they were generally crammed to the door; – broadcloth, caps, kebbocks, stockings, wooden dishes, crockery and other equally useful articles . . . a sort of emporium of homely merchandise and curious nick-nacks, and the source of great amusement to the urban wanderer.

Lord Cockburn also revelled in antiquity – in the narrow stone stairs, oak tables of immovable massiveness, high-backed carved chairs with faded tapestry, the strong heavy cabinets, passages on miscalculated levels, long narrow halls, and little inaccessible odd-shaped rooms of Trinity Hospital. His was the outraged voice lifted against its demolition, along with the venerable Trinity College Kirk, for the construction of

Waverley Station. He remained unmoved by the proposal to re-erect (and complete the uncompleted bits of) the College Kirk on the brow of Calton Hill.

> An outrage by sordid traders, virtually consented to by a tasteless city, and sanctioned by an insensible Parliament. I scarcely know a more curious instance of ignorant insensibility than the apology that is made for this piece of desecration. It is said that edifice is to be replaced exactly as it is in some better situation. And is it really thought that the pyramids would remain the pyramids, or Jerusalem Jerusalem provided only their materials were replaced in London? . . . these people would remove Pompeii for a railway and tell us they had applied it to better purpose in Dundee.

It is suitably appropriate that Edinburgh's history and amenity are now guarded by the Cockburn Association, an important fixture in whose calendar is the celebration of Harry Cockburn's birthday.

Scott's later years were irretrievably marred by the bankruptcy of London publishers Hurst and Robinson, to whom Constable and Cadell (and thereby he) were joined. Faced with debts of almost £100,000, Scott rejected offers of public assistance as shameful. He determined to pay off the debt by the exertions of his right hand, an effort which culminated in the majestic, annotated forty-eight-volume edition of his novels. By the time of his death, he had paid off £40,000, and the balance was offset against future royalties.

His journal is dominated by financial anxiety: in May 1827, for example, he listened sourly to 'a fellow bawling out a ditty in the street, the burden of which is "There's nothing but poverty everywhere".' He shall not be, observed Scott, 'a penny richer for telling me what I know but too well without him'. The house in Castle Street was sold, and he stayed in variable lodgings with voracious insects, stinking gutters, and drunken chairmen when not down in the Borders in his house at Abbotsford. An unusually human side to Scott is revealed by a parting squib to his landlady when he changed lodgings:

> So goodbye Mrs Brown
> I am going out of town,
> Over dale, over down,
> Where bugs bite not,
> Where below your chairmen drink not,
> Where beside you gutters stink not,
> But all is fresh, and clean and gay . . .

His wife died soon afterwards, and Scott's health, particularly his lameness and eyesight, deteriorated. After his death, the self-taught architect George Meikle Kemp won a competition for a monument to Scott's memory: a beautifully antiquarian and picturesque monument founded upon Kemp's own conjectural restoration of Melrose Abbey. That monument, barely yards from the greatest symbols of the Athens of the North, marks the fundamental shift which had taken place from the Enlightenment and Reason, towards Romance and the Picturesque.

CHAPTER ELEVEN

DISPERSED CITY

Edinburgh had retained much of the concentrated energy and a good deal of the momentum that had characterised the Enlightenment during its reign as Athens of the North. Although the five New Towns had doubled the area of the city's regality, they were compact, compressed between the Old Town and the Water of Leith: all within easy walking distance. That was to change utterly. By 1851, almost exactly a century after the *Proposals* had suggested breaking out of a regality of only 138 acres, the city had swollen to 7,000 acres, with a population of over 170,000 people. In common with all large Victorian cities, it entered a new phase consequent upon the arrival of canal and railways: one that would inevitably lead to what Lewis Mumford christened 'megalopolis'.

As the city spread, its energies dissipated. Its functions became petrified into geographically separate locations, and the city's momentum began to slacken. Professions began to work in isolation from each other: each discipline tightened within its specialism, and lacked the lubrication of cross-fertilisation with others which had been a key to the Enlightenment. The new territories of expanded Edinburgh – Leith, Dalry, Morningside, Murrayfield, Portobello – failed to maintain the strong sense of identity that characterised the Old and New Towns; and had it not been for the omnipresent Firth of Forth, the soaring rock of Arthur's Seat or the Pentlands, there was little to distinguish this new Edinburgh from much of Victorian Scotland.

The achievements of nineteenth-century Edinburgh were worthy (so sober, indeed, that the irrepressible Harry Cockburn lamented its 'degenerate temperance') as befitted a city dominated by the middle class in the absence of the giants of the Athens of the North. Barring the retention of its professional élite and religious focus, Edinburgh was like to settle into a role not dissimilar to that of any large British city: a Bristol, rather than Athens. The nineteenth-century history of the city is one of the triumph of the professional, the doctor, surgeon, minister, lawyer or architect: and their victory over the public health problems which faced all large Victorian and Edwardian cities. Battle honours were gained for slum clearance, sanitation, drainage, public health, Ragged Schools, and city missions. It was the period of Improvement Acts, and housing for the working classes. These creditable achievements replaced the capital's earlier aspirations to world-class performance. 'We want safe men here you know, and so we generally get them,' wrote Sir Patrick Geddes scathingly to a colleague about the gutlessness of the university in its *fin de siècle* professorial appointments (not altogether without interest: the city had consistently rejected his own applications). Although good men still slipped through the inspection, 'they are pretty free of the stigmata of genius which characterised the older generation.'

The *idea* of Edinburgh, firmly anchored to the ridge of the Old Town, became the catalyst of Edinburgh's new industry: romantic tourism. Its career in tourism was launched with the twenty-one-day pantomime in August 1822 which comprised the first formal visit of a monarch since 1641. It was no state visit. The King had come to neither General Assembly nor to address parliament. Government, in the person of a snappishly irritated Robert Peel, sailed north with him. The jaunt absorbed Peel little; but, to Peel's fury, precluded him, marooned far from London, from seizing adequate benefit from the suicide of Lord Londonderry. George IV had come to Scotland, not as monarch to one of the nations which he ruled, but as a sightseer. Overweight, gouty, sixty years old and dogged by the personal ridicule directed at his private life, George was scarcely the dashing if misguided monarch Charles I had been in 1641.

The King's admiration for Sir Walter Scott had already been expressed by the award of the first baronetcy of his reign in 1820. What he sought was the Scotland of Scott's novels; what he wanted to hear was the 'purely national and characteristic music' of the country; and when he rose to toast the nation at the civic banquet held in the Parliament House of Scotland, his toast was not to Scotland, but to 'the chieftains and all the clans of Scotland, and may God bless the Land of Cakes' – which showed, whatever else, that he had at least read his Burns.

He and his acolytes had not come to meet the luminaries of the Athens of the North. They refused the invitation to attend the ceremony of the laying of the foundation stone of the National Monument on Calton Hill which, more than any other, was an event that symbolised the Athenian aspirations of the capital. The King spent barely fifteen hours in Edinburgh during those three weeks, sliced neatly into brief appearances at receptions, levees, the civic banquet, the Peers' Ball, the Caledonia Hunt Ball, processions and a performance of *Rob Roy* in the Theatre Royal. Nevertheless, almost an hour could be found for him to explore the untouched quarters of Mary, Queen of Scots within Holyrood Palace, without company. Whatever the assumptions of those who thought they were witnessing a brief resumption of a royal court at Holyrood, the King's jaunt had the same importance in his own eyes that Neueschwanstein had to the mad Ludwig of Bavaria: it was a romantic retreat from normality.

It had partly been Scott's fault, in his unofficial role of the keeper of the nation's soul, and the guardian of its secrets and traditions. Both King and Lord Provost of Edinburgh had taken his advice when, at extremely short notice, the King's intention to venture north was confirmed. Once it was known that the King would visit only Edinburgh, Scott issued the equivalent of a literary fiery Cross to the Highland lairds and clan chieftains to greet him there in full ceremonial fig. There were no comparable invitations to the cotton lords of Glasgow, the whalers of Dundee, the agricultural improvers of Aberdeenshire, or to the shipbuilders of Greenock. The extent to which the participants' grasp of their country's reality was enfeebled is indicated by one of the toasts at the civic banquet given in the presence of the King. It was to the Lord Provost's wife who, that very evening, had been elevated from Mrs to Lady Arbuthnot, upon the granting of a baronetcy to her husband. The toast was 'Lady Arbuthnot and the Flowers of Edinburgh': and the joyous acclamation revealed that those present believed the 'flowers of Edinburgh' to refer to the capital's lustrous womankind. They were ignorant of its normal use denoting the ordure upon the pavements of the Old Town.

One of those perennial London journalists who attend royal functions, Robert Mudie, published two versions of King George's jaunt. The laudatory *Historical Account of His Majesty's Visit to Scotland* was the moneyspinner, to be bought by all those wishing to see their presence at these royal occasions recorded for posterity. For his appreciative London audience, however, he castigated Edinburgh's pretensions in the vitriolic *Modern Athens*. This splendidly vituperative polemic dismissed the New Town, was incisive about the literati and nugatory about everything save the capital's romantic skyline.

Later royal visits took the form of fleeting stays by the royal family on its way north on holiday, the first of which, in 1842, pointed up the sad want of a skilled Master of Ceremonies like Sir Walter Scott. Confusion seized Queen Victoria's disembarkation at Granton Harbour. The Lord Provost Sir Simon Forrest laboured under the misapprehension that a two-hour delay would elapse between the Royal Squadron's cannonade and the Queen's landing, and remained enthroned with his council in the Council Chamber in the High Street awaiting intelligence. The Queen, however, had alighted to the very sound of the cannonade.

When she passed through the ceremonial arch at Brandon Street at which she should have been presented with the keys of the city, Provost and council were nowhere to be seen.

The Celtic Society lined the route through the capital to Dalkeith Palace with appropriate tartanry, the soldiery were in full fig, the crowds huzza'd, and an intelligent archer instructed her on what she was seeing. The procession was unsuccessfully pursued in an unseemly manner by a mortified Lord Provost and council, swarmed about by a host of inhabitants equally bypassed. Grovelling at Dalkeith Palace remedied the matter, with the result that the Queen made a formal progress from the Abbey Strand up to the castle the following day. It was a trip no monarch was to repeat; and the decently attired folk thronging the rickety buildings, crumbling gables and rotting timber superstructures concealed the Old Town's decomposition from royal view. Old Edinburgh enjoyed its last echo of glory.

When Victoria returned in 1850, there were two marked changes: she arrived by train at Meadowbank (later called the Queen's Station), and she stayed overnight in a suitably refurbished Holyrood Palace – the first monarch to do so since the seventeenth century. While Albert went on a formal progression with military escort to lay the foundation stone of the National Gallery of Scotland, in front of an audience of thousands who had been liberated to witness the occasion by the declaration of a day's holiday, Victoria took a coach drive round the park which was later to be known as the Queen's Drive.

Royal visits crowned the capital's status as a nineteenth-century tourist destination: its exotic location, romantic history, literary associations, intellectual inheritance and quaint accents proved irresistible, and the lesser royalty of Europe came to admire. For the foul inns of the Canongate, St Mary's Wynd and the Grassmarket were substituted elegant establishments located in the New Town, for which the word 'hotel' (previously restricted to its French use to describe a grand town house), was purloined. In 1834, Nathaniel Willis stayed in Douglas' Hotel, a grandly pillared pavilion designed by Robert Adam to flank one side of Sir Lawrence Dundas's mansion in St Andrew Square. What he received as a 'Scotch breakfast' at nine o'clock in the morning was

> cold grouse, salmon, cold beef, marmalade, jellies, honey, five kinds of bread, oatmeal cakes, coffee, tea and toast; and I am by no means sure that this is all. It is a fine country in which one gets so much by the simple order of 'breakfast at nine'.

Tourism was initially compressed into August when the Edinburgh natives, like the Parisians, quit the city and abandoned it to the visitor. Not only was society accustomed to return to its villa or country seat in summer: there were grouse to be shot. The city became, as Sir Thomas Dick Lauder describes, like an unruined Pompeii:

> Everyone acquainted with Edinburgh is well aware that, crowded and busy as her streets are during the winter months of the year, when the courts are sitting – when the University, the schools, the societies, the gaieties of the city, the killing ennui of the country, and the severity of the weather, conspire to draw and to drive people into it, like woodcocks into cover, it is frequently quite deserted during the best months of summer and of autumn; and that, especially towards the end of August and the beginning of September, the causeway of some of its most important squares and places – such as Charlotte Square, Moray Place and others – became beautifully verdant, save only where the persevering hackney coach crawls like a snail over a path of its own wearing, or a rapid minibus cuts through it with terrific pace, but yet with half-deadened sound, increasing danger to unfortunate pedestrians. This urban crop of grass is reaped by rows of old men, who, moving on their knees across the causeway, with a progress hardly vying with the shadows produced thereon by the sun, eradicate the plants with old forks and crooked bits of iron.

Tourism represented one of the few bright spots on the city's economic horizon in Cockburn's view. In his vigorous *Letter to the Lord Provost on the ways of spoiling the beauty of Edinburgh* in 1849, he observed that Edinburgh only had its beauty to depend upon. The picture otherwise was grim: little trade, almost no manufactures, a population precariously fed, pauperism, disease and crime all in excess. No longer did its lectures, law, or intellectual reputation give the city its particular fame: it was its physical character and scenery.

> It is our curious and matchless position – our strange irregularity of surface – its picturesque results, – our internal features and scenery, – our distant prospects . . . Extinguish these, and the rest would leave it a very inferior place. Very respectable; but not what it is.

Cockburn's plea was misconstrued as being one of preservation of the past at all costs, obstructing modern improvements, such as railways, which would enhance the economy and improve the lot of the poor. Dr

James Begg counterblasted in favour of the removal of 'the slaughter-houses and the antiquated filth of the Low Calton, the clearing Princes Street of carriers' carts.' Railway money could be used to enhance Eastern Princes Street Gardens, which – unlike Edinburgh's private gardens – could be accessible to the public. Edinburgh should be more even-handed and devote 'the funds of our monkish hospitals to the universal education of the people'; it should reform the pauper system and remove the city from bankruptcy. Loss of amenity would be a small price to pay for such advances. It was a false opposition. Amenity did not need to be lost to achieve social justice; and as Sir Patrick Geddes was to reveal in his study of the city some fifty years later, the expedient way in which Edinburgh had allowed itself to be carved up by the railway companies failed to produce the benefits for the poor in any case.

Whatever the argument, Edinburgh had established itself on the tourist trail by mid-century. In 1865, the poet Alexander Smith, Secretary of the University, yearned for the Highlands, happy to leave his city in the hands of visitors:

> Edinburgh is at this moment in the full blaze of her beauty. The public gardens are in blossom. The trees that clothe the base of the Castle Rock are clad in green: the 'ridgy back' of the Old Town jags the clear azure. Shop windows are enchantment, the flag streams from the Half-Moon Battery, church spires sparkle sun gilt, gay equipages dash past, the military band is heard from afar. The tourist is already here in wonderful tweed costume. Every week the wanderers increase – they stand on Arthur's Seat, they speculate on the birthplace of Mons Meg, they admire Roslin, they eat haggis, attempt whisky-punch and crowd to Dr Guthrie's church on Sundays – and in a short time, the city will be theirs. By August the inhabitants have fled.

After mid-century, the growth in stature of the three General Assemblies of the various Scottish Kirks which met in May provided a new focus for visitors and extended the visitor season.

The university basked in a legacy inherited from the Enlightenment; but now that it occupied its majestic quadrangle, it was less involved in town affairs than it was once wont to be. Rather, it would invite the town, from time to time, to enjoy functions in its own palatial chambers in the manner of a sniffy laird.

The wavering of its inherited medical reputation, symptomatic of what was to happen to Edinburgh as a whole in this post-Athens period, was heralded by the scandal of Burke and Hare. At the time, the university's

Medical Faculty's reputation was probably never higher: partly the consequence of the reputation of James Syme, Professor of Chemical Surgery, considered to be the best surgeon then alive. The Department of Anatomy, however, was otherwise. Professor Alexander Munro III had inherited the post from his father, who had, in turn, inherited from his: and Tertius, but an indifferent successor to his father, was reputed simply to read his grandfather's lecture notes. There was a cruel *canard* that he had been heard to begin, 'When I was studying at Leyden', which his grandfather had, and he had not. When Munro finally ceded the professorship to John Goodsir in 1846, it was the first time that Edinburgh had had a Professor of Anatomy who was not called Alexander Munro since 1726. The impressive surface of Athens had concealed nepotism and its cosy oligarchy could exclude genius. One excluded new talent was the charismatic anatomist Dr Knox, who had to survive outside the system.

Burke and Hare had both been attracted to Edinburgh by opportunities of navvying on the Union Canal: when complete, one had established himself as a shoemaker, and the other as a landlord in the West Port. Burke fed Knox's disestablished classes with at least sixteen recently terminated corpses. Careless greed lead to an incautious selection of victim, and the secret was out. Hare turned King's evidence in return for his life. Burke vehemently denied that he had done anything so low as grave robbing, but admitted some murders in a successful attempt to secure the escape of his mistress with a Not Proven verdict. The poor of the West Port were revealed as worth more as corpses for anatomists than they had been alive.

His execution was attended by enormous crowds on 28th January, 1829 at the head of Liberton's Wynd, which gave vent to great cheers when the deed was accomplished. Some 24,000 people later went to gaze at his body when it was laid out on Alexander Munro's dissecting table. The anatomy lessons then given by the Professor were said to have been the only well-attended classes he had ever held. The skin was later flayed from Burke's body to make into tobacco pouches and other curious souvenirs for the morbid.

Walter Scott, who had marked the saga with fascinated interest, wrote to his son Charles that 'I was shocked in the midst of all this by receipt of a very polite card from the Medical Society inviting me to dine with them.' The West Port quickly became a tourist attraction for ghouls, reinforcing Scott's uneasy realisation that the 'state of high civilisation to which we have arrived' had been at the expense of those who had been

brutalised and degraded, and the same nation at the same time
displays the very highest and very lowest of state in which the

human race can exist in point of intellect.

The actions of Knox had been a 'horrid example of how men may stumble and fall in the full march of intellect'.

The Medical Faculty of the university, which had at one time attracted students from throughout Europe and the Americas, lost its preeminence in British medicine once London's University College Hospital established a medical school in 1834. It was but a sad compliment to the parent that the London School was run along Scottish lines. The separation of the university from the town meant that the driving ambition of the early eighteenth-century city fathers to invest in medicine had withered by the nineteenth and, handicapped by lack of investment, Scots medicine became unable to compete with the medical advances that were being made, for example, in Germany. That is not to say that the university's reputation fell. It remained high, and doctors trained in Edinburgh were exported to all neuks of the Empire, spreading a reputation for Scottish medicine comparable to that of Scottish engineering in the developing worlds.

That Edinburgh was the location of Sir James Young Simpson's discovery of chloroform showed that the pioneering spirit had not altogether vanished: but it was a rare success. In his house in Queen Street on 4th November, 1847, Simpson enjoyed a live experiment:

> I had the chloroform for several days in the house before trying it, as after seeing it such a heavy, unvolatile-like liquid, I despaired of it, and went on dreaming about others. The first night we took it Dr Duncan, Dr Keith and I all tried it simultaneously, and were all 'under the table' in a minute or two.

The city's medical reputation left the university for the streets, and became more thirled to that of the general practitioner: those who lived in George Square, and had their consulting rooms in Charlotte Square, their carriages ready to take them out on an emergency errand at a moment's notice; or the doctors and Medical Officers of Health who led the campaign for serious improvements to the Old Town to prevent the spread of disease.

The trigger was the advent of Asiatic cholera in January 1832. It had been anticipated for over a year, when the Police Commissioners compelled the cleansing of streets and the removal of pigs from the closes. (Some ten years later, Thomas Guthrie, when one of the ministers of Greyfriars, encountered a pig in an upper storey of a tenement facing the Cowgate. Astounded that its owners had been able to get so large an animal so high, he enquired how the feat had been achieved: only to be informed that it had been born up there.) Cholera entered the wynds like a plague on 7th January and scythed remorselessly. A day of expiation and humilation was ordained for 9th February, followed by a fast and day of prayer on 22nd March. Vagrants, beggars 'and people of an unhealthy or unclean appearance' were prevented from entering the town by policemen stationed on the outskirts. Somewhere between 600 and several thousand were dead before the fury of the disease slackened in autumn. It returned both in 1848 and 1849.

Many other fevers suppurated in the Old Town: some 500 victims were in hospital in autumn 1843 when a new cemetery was established at Warriston as part of the plan to eradicate infectious disease. It was intended to be Edinburgh's Père Lachaise, comparable both to its Parisian progenitor and to that planned for the Necropolis of Glasgow.

In 1847, Dr James Stark's *Enquiry into the sanitation of Edinburgh* reassured the natives that the capital's mortality record compared favourably with other cities. He concluded that the new sewers which had been laid in the Old Town were more than adequate, and that arrangements for scavenging ordure from the closes in the Old Town were amply satisfactory. The Water of Leith was well able to wash away all sewage and effluent from the New Town. Endemic typhus indicated otherwise. Indeed, anyone with good eyesight or a reasonable sense of smell would have been able to detect trouble down the closes – 'stinks older than the Union' observed Robert Southey.

Insanitary habits in the Old Town were gravely exacerbated once the principal water supply had been diverted to the New Town: what had once been abundant became scarce. Since few tenements had running water, each drop had to be queued for and borne from the nearest well. In 1850, the city read with alarm pamphlets of the most disconcerting kind published by Dr George Bell. The denizens of the Old Town, he wrote, were as ignorant, squalid and savage as the aborigines of New South Wales. One hundred and fifty-nine closes were seriously deficient in drainage and water, and suffered all the evils resulting from overcrowding. The inhabitants were no longer the industrious poor who had first replaced the lairds and Law Lords in the Old Town: most of them seemed to be unemployed, many of them Irish or dispossessed country people. Their curse was alcohol: 'From the toothless infant to the toothless old man the population of the wynds drink whisky. The drunken drama that is enacted on a Saturday night and Sabbath morning beggars description.' Well, no it did not. Alexander Smith managed it with his usual charm:

The Cowgate holds high drunken carnivals every Saturday night; and to walk along it then, from the West Port through the noble open space of the Grassmarket . . . For nights after, your dreams will pass from brawl to brawl, shoals of hideous faces will oppress you, sodden countenances of brutal men, women with loud voices and frantic gesticulations, children who had never known innocence. It is amazing of what ugliness the human face is capable . . . many a face flits past here bearing the sign-manual of the fiend.

George Bell counted 142 dwellings housing 1,000 people in Blackfriars Wynd: most of a single chamber, at a density of rather over five per room, with no drain at all. He visited the room of a cinder woman, hardly six feet square, without a fireplace and lit only by a skylight.

We observed some garbage on a plate in a corner of her den which she had found in an ash bucket and told us it was for the cat. We believe, however, that the cat preferred the mice and the rats, and that she herself devoured the garbage.

The minister Dr Thomas Guthrie conveys a horrid picture of what greeted him upon his appointment as one of the two Greyfriars ministers in 1836. He took a house in Argyle Square, so as to be able to carry the gospel into the depths of the Cowgate. His first winter, 1837-8, was of such severity that he was besieged every day

by crowds of half-naked creatures, men, women and children, shivering with cold and hunger; and I visited many a house that winter where there were starving mothers and starving children with neither bread, bed or Bible.

Raising money from the wealthier in the congregation, he established a soup kitchen.

Those only who had been City Missionaries can understand what I had to suffer daily in the course of my parochial visitations. Typhus fever was raging like a plague; and as, taking due precautions against infection, I visited every case I was called to, nor fled from any I happened to meet, I had often to face that terrible disease, and had one, two or three lying ill of it in one room, to breathe a pestilential atmosphere . . . but it was not disease or death, it was the starvation, the drunkenness, the rags, the heartless, hopeless miserable condition of the people – the debauched and drunken mothers, the sallow, yellow emaciated children – their wants, both temporal and spiritual, which one felt themselves unable to relieve – that sometimes overwhelmed me.

Guthrie became one of the great orators of the Evangelical Party within the Church of Scotland whose determination to free it from establishment interference was to bring about the Disruption in 1843. His sermons were prepared self-consciously upon ancient models, with a keen eye for audience reaction. Lord Cockburn described the result thus:

Practical and natural; passionate with vehemence; with perfect self-possession and always generous and devoted, he is a very powerful preacher. His language and accent are very Scots, but nothing can be less vulgar; and his gesture . . . is the most graceful I have ever seen in any public speaker.

An attempt to squeeze into the standing room in his church in the Royal Mile became *de rigueur* for any self-respecting tourist.

The Disruption in the Church of Scotland, the last great political act of Edinburgh's history worthy of national status, created a new Church. Many thousands of Scots put their lives and livelihoods at risk on the point of principle of freedom of conscience: that presbyteries should be empowered to select their own minister. Where that selection concurred with the laird's preference, well and good: where it did not, they rejected the laird's power to impose an unpopular preacher. The law disagreed. After the General Assembly promulgated the 'Veto' Act in 1833, which gave presbyteries the power to reject an unpopular presentee, the Court of Session declared it illegal. Notorious disputes between vehement patron and tenacious presbytery in Auchterarder and Marnoch went to the House of Lords: but once the Lords permitted the rejected presentee at Auchterarder to sue for damages, there could be no peaceful solution.

The government thought that only a few fanatics would make a protest by walking out. There was no need for a renewed Summons of Plotcock: scores of farewell sermons were preached on Sunday, 14th May, 1843. When the Assembly met in St Andrew's Church in George Street the following Thursday, 472 ministers of the Church of Scotland – the best part of the Scottish Church including the majority of Edinburgh ministers – disestablished themselves and disendowed themselves from their livings and their incomes. Accompanied by many of their elders, they followed Thomas Chalmers, Guthrie close behind, in solemn procession from St Andrew's Church down Dundas Street to Tanfield Hall at the bottom, where they established the Free Church of Scotland. In his last sermon in Old St John's, Guthrie had stated:

> We shall give them their stipends, their manses, their glebes and their churches. These are theirs, and let them 'make a kirk or a mill' of them. But we cannot give them up the crown rights of Christ, and we cannot give them up our people's privileges.

They did not. When news of the extent of the rebellion reached Lord Jeffrey in his library in Moray Place, he sprang to his feet saying, 'I am proud of my country! In not another land in the world would such a thing have been done.'

After the Disruption, Guthrie's role changed from Cowgate minister to fund-raiser: for the Free Kirk required money for new churches and manses. Until his semi-retiral on grounds of ill-health in 1847, it occupied most of his attention. However, in 1846 he went for a stroll with a friend round Arthur's Seat and when they came to rest beside St Anthony's Well, they were accosted by 'ragged boys who pursue their calling there. Their "tinnies" were ready with a draught of the clear cold water in the hope of a half penny.' On catechising them, particularly about their education, Guthrie discovered one was an orphan and neither had attended a proper school.

> By way of experiment I said, 'Would you go to school if, beside your learning, you were to get your breakfast, dinner and supper there?' It would have done any man's heart good to have seen the flush of joy that broke in the eyes of one of them.

One of the boys offered to bring all the children in the entire tenement he lived in, but fearing that would overstretch the food, exclaimed, 'I'll come for but my dinner sir'. Guthrie became a proponent of the establishment of Ragged Schools in Edinburgh along the lines of that initiated in Aberdeen by Sheriff Watson. His 1847 *Plea for Ragged Schools*, followed by two more, received strong support from Hugh Miller, then editor of *Witness*, and Lord Provost Adam Black established a committee to carrying the matter forward. By the end of the year, three schools had been established under the auspices of the 'original Ragged Schools Association' attended by 265 children. One of the strongest advocates was the Governor of Edinburgh Prison who noted that five per cent of his prisoners in 1847 were under fourteen years old, whereas it had dropped to less than one per cent four years later. Guthrie's endeavours are commemorated in the Guthrie Schools in Liberton, by a marble statue in Princes Street – and by folk memory. Whereas the threat to a naughty laddie of the west is that of the Black Douglas, in Edinburgh the wean is given the dreadful warning: 'Wheesht, or Dr Guthrie'll come an' tak ye away to his school . . .'

The Old Town was faced with the curiosity that the new railway was inaccessible from it: they could look at it, indeed go over it but, by carriage, they could not reach it without going a long way round. In 1853 the Edinburgh Railway Station Act authorised the construction of such an access through the backs of ancient closes. It was desirable, agreed parliament, 'to preserve as far as possible the architectural style and antique character of the locality' to secure harmony in the new buildings with those of the Old Town; to ensure which they appointed the venerable senator Lord Cockburn as referee. The following year, Cockburn Street was sliced through equally venerable properties to the rear of the City Chambers.

That the new architecture should be in harmony with the old was a new preoccupation. It had emerged from the intensifying demand for things Scottish in the wake of George IV's visit in 1822. The country had been without a native architectural language with which to respond to the surge of romanticism, and even by the time Scott died, a native Scottish architecture had still not yet emerged. Kemp, the Scott Monument's designer, with his designs for the full restoration of Melrose Abbey and Glasgow Cathedral, had been expected to do the trick. This man knew his antiquities. So he was despatched round Scotland to sketch ancient buildings with a view to publication, but in 1844 tripped on his way home to Canaan one night, fell into the Union Canal, and drowned at the unfulfilled age of forty-nine.

The following year, the architects William Burn and David Bryce imported an English antiquarian, Robert William Billings, who, over the next five years, travelled the country to record Scotland's historic architecture. The results were published in the four volumes of the *Baronial and Ecclesiastical Antiquities of Scotland* in 1852. The term 'baronial architecture' as a title for this first Scottish architectural revival derived from Billings's mistaken use of the term 'baronial' (which in Scotland had more connotations with the law than laird). The fashion swept the country from one end to the other. Since Victorians considered that architecture should be appropriate for its use, rather than seeking the universal style of the Athenians, people who were perfectly content to live in the most neo-classical of terraced town houses, or to work in the most opulent and secure of Italianate banks in the New Town of Edinburgh might retreat at night or at weekends by coach or train to the lairdly folly in Aberdour, North Berwick, or even a suburb.

Baronialism penetrated central Edinburgh only in Old Town tenements. Improvements in Jeffrey Street and St Mary's Street were compelled to adopt appropriate architectural camouflage and Billings's volumes offered the perfect crib. Those studying the fine tenements designed by John Lessels, particularly in St Mary's Street, can see a reconstruction of details from Archbishop Beaton's House in the Cowgate, and many a Billings oriel window, bay, corbel or turret. Its most dramatic utilisation was for the later tenements which marched across the slopes of Marchmont scratching the sky with gables and pinnacles.

The St Mary's Street tenements had been the consequence of a new phase of city improvement. Just as it had required a tenement collapse in 1751 to spark off the *Proposals*, so also did it require another, in November 1861, to stimulate action. A tenement in Chalmer's Close collapsed 'with a hideous uproar' killing thirty-five people; and as the rescuers probed the debris, they heard the shout from a boy now immortalised in stone on the building that replaced it: 'Heave awa' lads, I'm no deid yet.' Shame led to the appointment of Dr Littlejohn as Medical Officer of Health, who published his findings in his *Report on the Sanitary Conditions of Edinburgh* in 1865.

The improvement of the Old Town became a personal crusade of the Lord Provost, William Chambers. At the urgent request of Dr Littlejohn, he ordered the flushing of closes with water and purified chloride. A walkabout accompanied by the City Architect convinced Chambers that the best way to bring light and air to the closes was by cutting through cross-streets like Jeffrey Street, by the removal of the wooden fronts of tenements which so overhung certain closes as to cut out the daylight (such as the removal of the front of the Regent Morton's house in Blackfriars Street), and by the demolition of all semi-ruinous buildings to form open courts upon the sites. Chambers also recommended the construction of a spacious new thoroughfare from South Bridge to George IV Bridge running along the northern flank of the university, extinguishing Adam Square, Brown Square, and Argyle Square. Meeting with opposition, opinion was taken from the Architectural Institute of Scotland which concluded, stern men, that the improvement did not go far enough: the proposed street should be 130 feet wide, with no buildings on the north side down to the Cowgate which should be left open as a public garden decorated with reconstruction of any of the interesting relics of Old Edinburgh which might have to be demolished for the new street. They also suggested, mercifully unsuccessfully, that the entire Old Town should be reconstructed.

The 1867 Improvement Act empowered the council to build Market

Street, Jeffrey Street, Blackfriars Street, St Mary's Street, Guthrie Street, Lady Lawson Street, and the new street between South and George IV Bridges – named Chambers Street after its promoter. Hospitals and charitable institutions were relocated and Minto House demolished. With the construction of the Royal Scottish Museum, the James Watt Institute, the Dental School, and the University's Staff Club and Adam House, the street was gradually transformed into the educational enclave it remains today. Its current dominance by cars and parking meters belies the original concept its authors had of it – a campus for learning which might go some way to replacing similar qualities that had been lost from the High Street.

The eastern side of Blackfriars Street was demolished and rebuilt set back, as is recorded on an inscription, partly by twenty-four working men who comprised the Blackfriars Building Association. They were the first dwelling houses to provide accommodation for the industrial classes on the site of those demolished by the city's authority. The impetus for such a self-help co-operative had been created a few years earlier by the establishment of the Edinburgh Co-operative Building Company by a group of stonemasons, whose first major project was the construction of the celebrated Colonies in the haugh of the odiferous Water of Leith from 1861. It was a noble, almost Enlightenment achievement. The company had 341 shareholders, the majority of whom were skilled craftsmen, particularly in the building trades (although they included a furrier, cabinetmakers, gardeners, compositors, sculptors, waiters and a commercial traveller). Most became occupiers. This visionary achievement was commemorated not just in the names – for example the terrace named after Hugh Miller – but also in the quality of the sculpture and armorial panels of which many a more expensive house was bare. The company built developments on five other sites in the capital (for example, behind Haymarket and behind London Road) and at one time was employing some 250 people.

The *illuminati* of the Enlightenment had enjoyed the absolute contrast between the concentrated humankind in the old city and the spacious peacefulness of a country villa on the other. It provided the excuse for a split personality, nowhere better indicated than in this truly Jekyll and Hyde letter from Lord Cockburn to Sir Thomas Dick Lauder: whereas His Majesty's Solicitor General was a

> decorous person – arrayed in solemn black – with a demure visage – an official ear – an evasive voice – suspicious palate – ascetic blood – and flinty heart. There is a fellow very like him who traverses the Pentlands in a dirty grey jacket, white hat with

a long pole. That's not the Sol.Gen. That's Cocky – a frivolous dog.

Creative tension between town and country underlies much of the writing of Robert Louis Stevenson, who oscillated between his family's house in Heriot Row and the ancient farmhouse at Swanston where, serviced by three maids and a gardener of Old Cameronian stock, Stevenson could ruminate upon the distance between him and his city; and upon the ancient values of Scotland. He enlarged upon such themes in *Weir of Hermiston*.

Town remained town, and country country until the development of the estate of the Grange of St Giles, around 1850. But population pressure could not be gainsaid, and the lower middle classes – those who had occupied the houses of people of quality and fashion in the Old Town back in 1792: the French teacher who occupied Lord Justice Clerk Tinwald's house, the wheelwright in the Duke of Douglas's and hosier in the Marquis of Argyle's house in Castle Hill – aspired to better than the overcrowded and disease-ridden Old Town. Unless they were specifically servicing the inhabitants of the New Town, there was no accommodation for such respectable businessmen and tradesmen in that quarter. They moved out and created a ripple effect as they went: an effect that left its impact upon Edinburgh in concentric wrinkles that hung about the face of the capital like jowls on a bulldog.

Early villas were built by the affluent as an occasional retreat from town pressures. Before long, the privacy, freedom from disease, and rural setting of villas within reasonable walking distance of the centre began to supplant the attractions of the town house. In addition to the pleasure he took in his 'very pleasant little garden enclosed with a high wall, well stocked with flowers and fruit trees', George Meikle Kemp was attracted to his villa in Canaan, Morningside by lower taxes and more accommodation for the same rent than he had had in Stockbridge. Dr Thomas Chalmers first rented a house in Morningside Place, but so relished these 'quiet country quarters' that he built a house which he called Churchill (now number 1 Churchill) after the extension church which he had caused to build there. It was on their way to this villa to plan the Disruption over breakfast that Chalmers's evangelical co-conspirators, led by Thomas Guthrie, met Solicitor General Lord Cockburn striding back from Bonaly on his way to sit in the Court of Session. Upon learning of the purpose of Guthrie's visit, Cockburn expressed regret he was not one of those invited for breakfast.

The detached villa was the model for Sir Thomas Dick Lauder's new suburb on the estate of Grange: a self-conscious, low-density suburb of streets and crescents of middle-sized detached and semi-detached stone houses. Even the limited social intercourse that might have existed between families living adjacently in Heriot Row was excluded by the magnificent stone-walled gardens and sturdy iron gates. As the original villas and estates of south Edinburgh became swamped, their owners realised their value by the sale and the feuing of their lands. Down they tumbled, one after another, leaving only East Morningside House, Bruntsfield House and White House as rare survivors. Trinity, perhaps as a consequence of its independence from Old Edinburgh and relationship with the sea captains of Newhaven, Granton, and Leith, was less spacious, less formal and infinitely more picturesque. Like Hampstead, it was an appropriately discreet haven for a Victorian mistress.

The new suburban villa breathed privacy: to the extent that the garden gates of some villas in Braids were kept permanently closed, and could only be opened by pulling a lever inside the big house. The lace curtains of Morningside, and the hypocrisy that they were supposed to conceal, became a music-hall joke. In counterpoint, as privacy became prevalent, so did Edinburgh abandon its public personae. The High Street, the only open space in the capital in which its citizens could meet, throng, discuss, debate or dissent – the *grande place* so admired by Brantôme – was punctured by the construction of the Bridges and North Bank Street, and surrendered to carriages, all impedimenta removed. Although it seemed that the city considered using the space around the Royal Scottish Academy and the National Gallery as a public forum comparable to Trafalgar Square in London, George Square in Glasgow, and the Tuileries in Paris, nothing transpired.

Received wisdom attributes Stevenson's portrait of the dual-personality Dr Jekyll and Mr Hyde to the story of Deacon Brodie, but that seems unnecessarily restrictive. Dual personality was endemic in the city, as it was throughout Scotland. From his habit of creeping in his velvet jacket away from the essence of bourgeois respectability in Heriot Row up to enjoy the underworld on Calton Hill, Leith Walk or at Tollcross, he would certainly have been alive to the contrasts of a city founded upon public probity and private vice. Stevenson, as Burns and Ramsay before him, celebrated this submerged Edinburgh in poetry:

> I love night in the city,
> The lighted streets and the swinging gait of harlots.
> I love cool pale morning,
> In the empty by-streets,
> With only here and there a female figure,
> A slavey with lifted dress and the key in her hand,

A girl or two at play in that corner of waste-land
Tumbling and showing their legs and crying out to me
Loosely.

So memorable was this to Stevenson that a lament from exile in 1881 which celebrated his city in its richness and atmosphere contained this: 'O for ten Edinburgh minutes, sixpence between us, and the ever glorious Lothian Road or dear mysterious Leith Walk.'

Respectability had not obliterated bawdy Edinburgh: merely tidied it away, made it dirty and the subject of sniggers. In 1947, Moray MacLaren recalled his great-uncle telling him of the weekly arrival of an 'extremely disreputable Highland piper', one eye disfigured, and clothes that seem to have grown from his body, in the kitchen of his house in Moray Place in the later nineteenth century. His purpose in touring the better parts of the New Town each week, and announcing his arrival by pipes, was to tempt the young lassies from below stairs to a regular after-hours bacchanalia in the upper rooms of a Rose Street bar: 'It was a rendezvous drawn from all classes who wished to fling by night defiance at their life by day.' Not necessarily a bawdy house, it was a place where the 'young rips from the town' (who might include MPs or at least their children) kicked against Victorian respectability by drinking whisky, dancing and singing the night through with maidservants.

Stevenson identified two other contrasts or polarities in his *Picturesque Notes*. From the top of South Bridge, one class could look down upon another in the Cowgate below. The other contrast was that between town and country, which he praised for offering the Edinburgh citizen the opportunity to overlook the country whilst yet in the thick of business. 'It should be a genial and ameliorating influence in his life; it should prompt good thoughts and remind him of nature's unconcern.'

The new villas of Newington and Morningside symbolised everything against which he reacted: a decomposition of urban values, an insufferable cosy respectability if not hypocrisy, and a destruction of countryside:

Day by day, one new villa, one new object of offence, is added to another; all around Newington and Morningside, the dismalest structures keep springing up like mushrooms; the pleasant hills are loaded with them, each impudently squatted in its garden, each roofed and carrying chimneys like a house . . . They are not houses; for they were not designed with a view to human habitation, and the internal arrangements are, as they tell me, fantastically unsuited to the needs of man . . . Indifferent buildings give pain to the sensitive; but these things offend the plainest taste. It is a danger which threatens the amenity of the town; and as this eruption keeps spreading on our borders, we have ever the further to walk among unpleasant sights before we gain the country air. If the population of Edinburgh were a living, autonomous body, it would arise like one man and make the night hideous with arson.

His anathemas were to no avail. Edinburgh spread inexorably as the respective tradesmen of Rose Street, Thistle Street and Cumberland Street sought to share the swelling respectability of the suburbs. Ancient villages were engulfed and suburbs became towns as their main streets were crammed with tenement flats, and the fields beyond striped with long two-storeyed red sandstone Edwardian terraces, whose plasterwork and fireplaces echoed in a miniature way some of the grandeur of the magnificent Heriot Rows whence they had been imitated.

The palaces of Victorian Edinburgh were not the warehouses, emporia or factories of Glasgow; nor even the suburban villas, for they were but small beer. The city's steady growth in wealth and worth was reflected in the two types of palace that a city dependent upon the professions would demand: great schools and charitable institutions. The next generation of monuments after Register House and the university consisted of the Merchant Maiden Hospital, John Watson's (now the Scottish National Gallery of Modern Art), the Orphan Hospital (now the Dean Education Centre), and James Gillespie's Hospital. These had been followed by the splendidly Renaissance Daniel Stewart's in 1854, and a proposal to construct yet another, in response to Sir William Fettes's mortification of a 'hospital for the maintenance, education and outfit of children whose parents had fallen into adverse circumstances'.

R H Stevenson, the city's chronicler, was dismayed at the possibility of yet another palace of that kind because of the abundance of existing ones. He recommended that parliamentary authority should be sought to divert the money to the aged and destitute instead. He had before him as cautionary example the 'princely edifice' of Donaldsons's Hospital. Designed by William Playfair as a hospital for poor children in the most destitute circumstances, following the legacy of James Donaldson, proprietor of the *Edinburgh Advertiser*, it was the architect's last major design. It is a curious hybrid. Playfair had moved from the austerity that distinguished his Royal Scottish Academy to something more picturesque. But in the absence of an accepted Scottish architecture, he chose English Tudor, in what he called the best old style of English architecture, to produce a palace in which Henry VIII could well have first eyed Anne Boleyn. Stevenson disapproved, in that it had 'more the appearance of a

Royal palace than a building for the reception of children maintained on the bounty of its founder whose parents are in the humbler walks of life'. Surplus funds created by abandoning useless outward decoration could have been deployed to the benefit of a greater number of the poor. 'Children who are maintained by charity,' he sniffed, 'are not entitled to reside in palaces.'

Donaldson's Hospital was so admired by Victoria and Albert that folk memory is certain that she suggested exchanging it for Holyrood. The architect was man of the day. Cockburn carolled:

> Think of Phiffy's [Playfair's] facility yesterday! At One o'clock, Albert laid the foundation of his Galleries and at 4 The Queen went over his hospital . . . and admiring everything. It was his great day. And delighted, modest and amiable he was – in spite of all the laughter and bad jokes & parodies that I could exhaust myself in pouring out on him . . .

In response to multiple sycophantic plaudits thereafter, Playfair growled: 'I am like to laugh at the smiles bestowed on me since the Queen and Prince spoke to me at the Hospital by people who would hardly have acknowledged me the architect before. Fools, don't they see it is the architecture that is noticed and not the man?' Royal adulation could not be gainsaid. Playfair was appointed as the architect for another such palace to celebrate Sir William Fettes's mortification in Comely Bank, but died soon thereafter, and was replaced by Scotland's greatest Victorian architect, David Bryce. Halfway up the brow of Comely Bank, Fettes College became his masterpiece, and perhaps the finest exposition of the first revival of Scottish architecture, of which Bryce was to become the acknowledged master.

Charitable schools aspired to be public schools. Whilst Fettes retained a certain number of scholarship places, it transformed itself into a school along Rugby lines, pleased at its sobriquet of the Eton of the North. [It remained curiously flattered in the 1960s when Ian Fleming despatched James Bond there after his expulsion from Eton.] The cachet lay in being a school for boarders – no matter the reputation for academic excellence of the Academy or of Heriot's. There was a paradox in the fact that Edinburgh citizens would send their own children away to school, away from the city with the greatest concentration of such schools, to England or north to Glenalmond (if not English, at least the next best thing – Episcopalian) rather than enjoying the riches at home. For Edinburgh had become well endowed with education: it was as possible to stumble across a procession of boys from Cargilfield in their Eton suits as it was, later, to

watch the girls of Esdaile, all daughters of ministers, trudging embarrass-
edly in crocodile in their hated blue pinafores along the roads of Blackford.

Enduring images of Victorian Edinburgh must begin with schools and
the myriad churches that sprouted remorselessly throughout town and
suburbs following every new sect, only rarely rising to the majesty of F T
Pilkington's Barclay Church (which conceals a Presbyterian auditorium
behind a Germanic Gothic confection of stone used like plasticine).
There were the mostly political clubs – the Liberal, the Conservative and
the New – that perched on Princes Street; the plate-glass windows of the
mercantile emporia which were always being – as they are today – rebuilt
to suit fashion; the banks – which so infuriated John Ruskin with their
solid unimaginativeness and lack of variety; the wonderfully Baroque
gateway to the Old Town when they rebuilt the *Scotsman* offices; the immense Teutonic solidity of St Mary's Cathedral; and the vivid luxuriance
of Kennington and Jenner's Christmas bazaar viewed beneath the 'superb
sub-Arctic sunsets, with the profile of the city stamped in indigo upon a
sky of luminous green' in Stevenson's words. The multicoloured windows, lights and exotic continental goodies of the mercantile palaces
along Princes Street entranced children. Stevenson immortalised even
the lamplighter who had care of the lamp outside 17 Heriot Row, into
which he moved in 1856:

> For we are very lucky, with a lamp before the door
> And Leerie stops to light it as he lights so many more;
> And O! Before you hurry by with ladder and with light,
> O Leerie, see a little child and nod to him tonight!

Popular entertainment was various. For twenty years of intermittent
glory, the Royal Patent Gymnasium on the site of Canonmills Loch provided a cheap (if unusual) opportunity for Edinburgh folk to get equal
measures of exercise and enjoyment. It was the brainchild of a philan-
thropist, John Cox, whose fortune lay in gelatine: and it seems most to
have resembled how the Victorians would have created a health or fitness
club with apparatus by Heath Robinson. The centrepiece was a circular,
rotary rowing boat in which 600 rowers could exert themselves at one
time. Beside the Patent Velocipede (bicycles on a fixed track) the Chang
(a 200-capacity seesaw) and the Compound Pendulum Swing, there were
bands, a curling pond, quoits, stilts and vaulting poles. Culture would be
enjoyed at the operetta house that had roosted in Chambers Street to the
affright of that staid educational locality. On Friday nights, it offered a
'go as you please' competition which half affronted and half seduced

Alasdair Alpin Macgregor:

> Both for performers and for audience it was a night of unmiti-
> gated riot . . . at the Operetta House the amateur performer was
> there by reason of his conceit, to be assessed by the public with-
> out either fear or favour.

Alternatively, you could visit the Myorama, filing past Mr Poole, the
proprietor, standing in full evening dress by the entrance in Castle Terrace, to watch his reconstructions of battle scenes. At Christmas, Moss's
carnival occupied 'that immense roofed space known as the Waverley
Market', to which almost every Auld Reekie youth went as part of his fes-
tive season, whereas Evans's Carnival on open ground at Tollcross
offered booths, merry-go-rounds and brilliantly illuminated caravans.
The city also boasted three circuses and two menageries, of which the
most famous was Bostock and Wombwell's annual circus in the Grassmarket, announced by the roaring of its lions and the howling of its
wolves which echoed up King's Stables Road into Lothian Road. San-
ger's circus, with its swingboats, rifle ranges, laughing mirrors and hall of
horror, could be found off Leith Walk, and Cook's circus in Grindlay
Street.

Toward the end of the century, the only regular, national events that
attracted people to Edinburgh were the General Assemblies of the Kirks,
which took place in May each year. Princes Street would be flooded with
sober men in black frock coats and tile hats, every tenth one being a
minister, and the other nine being representative elders. They mingled
with a new throng that had become accustomed to parade there each
morning. Many of the shops and hotels exploited the supreme views of
the castle and Old Town by installing tea or coffee rooms with glazed
verandahs at the first-floor level. People walking down Princes Street
felt, as nowhere else, as though they were walking in the public gaze, and
it had become a formal promenade – the capital's Rotten Row – about
11.00 each morning. Largely feminine society, properly coated, hatted
and gloved, could be observed sauntering elegantly along the gardens
side of the street, conscious of the gaze fixed upon them, and enjoying
the consequent adulation until it was their turn to go inside to enjoy
their morning refreshment. At this one time in the year, their douce
gaiety was subordinated to clerical black.

The late Victorian tourist in Edinburgh, guide book in hand, travelling by tram and perhaps visiting that new attraction, the Forth Bridge,
by one of the many tripper steamers that lay waiting at Queensferry pier
might, like as not, have been a visitor to these General Assemblies.

There was nothing else like them in Britain. 'The meetings of the three great ecclesiastical parliaments – the Established, the Free and the United Presbyterian' attracted the Rev Samuel Green up from London, who was pleasurably amazed at the importance accorded to men of the cloth, and the coverage given to religious affairs in the newspapers. In the opening processions, the levee, and the majesty of the High Commissioner, the capital enjoyed a measure of spare ceremonial from these events. In the evenings, after the Assembly Hall had disgorged its flock, delegates would congregate in the smoking rooms of hotels like the Old Waverley 'and until the small hours of morning, and amid incense burned in honour of My Lady Nicotine, and small sodas for libation, they will discuss the last cynical speech of Dr Story . . .'

Most of the clergy had arrived by rail. However attracted they were by the romance of the Old Town, the skyline, the sunsets, and the sight of the cliff walls of the High Street illuminated at night, the coming of canal and rail earlier in the century heralded Edinburgh's next phase of change. The city had taken its first steps toward megalopolis.

CHAPTER TWELVE

THE MARCH TO MEGALOPOLIS

Transport formed modern Edinburgh. The first sod of a canal to link it to the Forth and Clyde Canal was dug at the Fountainbridge in May 1818, and its thirty-one-and-a-half-mile length was complete four years later. The canal meant that the west of the city, together with Leith, developed as one of its two centres of industry. In the ten years following August 1836, Edinburgh became connected by rail to Berwick and London, Bathgate, Granton, Leith, to Carlisle and the south-west, and to Glasgow.

Rail fever so gripped the country that few dared be branded eccentric by opposing the consequences. Lord Cockburn was one – appalled at the complaisant way in which the burghers were prepared to allow the Glasgow railway to ravish Princes Street Gardens, tunnelling under the Mound to join the Leith railway beside the North Bridge:

> The whole of that beautiful ground will be given up to railways, with their yards, depots, counting houses and other abominations, at least on the one side, which will ruin the peculiarity of the valleys between the Old and the New Towns . . . the apathy of the [unexcited] public is astonishing. The majority would sacrifice the beauty of Edinburgh to its trade.

A few years later he wrote in his journal: 'The notion of these modern Huns is that everything (a very natural sentiment for them) even amenity and the disturbance of old habits, can be valued in money.' The offending railway was opened on 18th February, 1842, with a descent into Glasgow so steep, that returning trains had to be pulled up the Cowlairs incline by a rope. Celebrants, dignitaries and officials from Edinburgh returning from its maiden voyage were marooned in Queen Street for almost four hours after a miscreant (a Cockburn sympathiser?) had cut the Cowlairs rope. It was perhaps a sign of Edinburgh's hunger for tourism that its principal station was named after the fictional English manor house that happened to be the title of Scott's most famous novel: *Waverley*.

Edinburgh's rail network was virtually complete by 1850, but instead of encircling the city, competitive railway companies penetrated to its very heart, creating inconvenient segments of industrial no-man's land, with attendant barrack-like tenement houses. As Cockburn forecast, the castle was sundered from Princes Street and – worst of all – their carpet-baggers followed. The railway hotels, those ponderously vulgar mammoths plonked upon the sunny southern shelf of Princes Street, symbolised the primacy of commerce over good planning. The Caledonian deserved its *canard* that it had been conceived and reared in Glasgow, before being shunted along the railway only to burst out of the tunnel at the other end of the line. Familiarity breeds affection, and few would now endorse George Scott Moncrieff's depiction of the North British (sadly rechristened Balmoral) as a 'colossus of nastiness, a giant wart', or the Caledonian as a 'pink scab'. Yet if the yardstick were the sense of regularity and order of the original New Town, he was not far wrong.

It is sobering that a city inheriting such a resplendent example of far-sightid town planning as the New Towns could have been so overwhelmed by the desire to get rich quickly as to jettison its values. The 'outrage by sordid traders' symbolised by the replacement of Trinity College Church and Hospital by the marshalling yards of Waverley, in Sir Patrick Geddes's phrase, 'exceeded in its present disorder and waste of space, time and energy' anything that could be alleged against the decay of the mediaeval, Renaissance or eighteenth-century cities. It was, he wrote, 'half-ruinous to the beauty of Edinburgh . . . structurally bungled and economically wasteful'.

Nonetheless, you can understand the reaction of the American tourist emerging from Waverley, when he complimented his taxi driver upon the foresight of the city fathers in locating the castle so close to the railroad. Visitors relished the sensation of emerging from a tunnel, not into some sordid railway suburb or industrial backyard, but directly into the glories of Princes Street. Even the station was, so to speak, underground, thus sparing Edinburgh the intrusion of railway termini such as Charing Cross or St Pancras. The easy and convenient accessibility of the lines was also magic for train buffs. Alasdair Alpin MacGregor loved to

dawdle on the Waverley Bridge, or at the bend in the Mound, to watch the coming and the going of the LNER trains that have absorbed, and so largely displaced, our North British rolling stock . . . I can smell at this moment the train smoke that, rising in black clouds where the Haymarket tunnel terminates by St Cuthbert's kirkyard, hangs about for a few familiar seconds.

The carelessness with which the capital coped with railways, and its lack of direction once they had been encouraged, symbolised Edinburgh's uneasy relationship with modernity. It cast its greatest assets beneath the wheels of progress as a demonstration of its intention to become more than just a pretty face: it toyed with the ambition of reaching the apogee of Victorian Britain – becoming an industrial city. Vain hope. The city's industry extended only to those needed to service, feed, clothe and supply its natives; although it was a discriminatingly copious importer of drink. The Victorian industrialist was almost entirely missing: or, at the most, was one man deep. That man was the extraordinary James Gowans, knighted by the Queen when she visited the 1886 International Exhibition in the Meadows for which he had been largely responsible.

Gowans was another of those outsiders like George Drummond (Perthshire), Patrick Geddes (Perth), Burns, Carlyle, and Hume who, assimilated into Edinburgh, moulded his adopted city to his vision. Born a mason's son in Linlithgow, he was apprenticed as architect, but turned to railway engineering in 1846, constructing much of the Edinburgh-Bathgate line, and much for the Highland Railway Company. His father had become proprietor of a quarry, and Gowans duly became substantial quarrymaster, builder, architect, developer of Castle Terrace, planner of Edinburgh's tramway system, active improver in his capacity as chairman of the city's Public Health Committee, architectural innovator and Lord Dean of Guild. A *rara avis* in doucely professional Edinburgh: and, to a certainty, the man to be entrusted with the organisation of an industrial exhibition planned for 1886, to follow earlier 'international' exhibitions of fishery and forestry in the Waverley Market and in the grounds of Donaldson's Hospital.

Gowans set out to make the 1886 International Exhibition of Industry, Science and Art of a different order. Its rather ungainly Exhibition Hall in the Meadows, designed by the Glaswegian Sir John Burnet, covered seven acres, and in its five galleries national and international exhibits included Constable paintings and Turkey rugs, American watches and Clyde locomotives. A typical Gowans's innovation, it was illuminated at night by 3,200 electric lamps, and opened by Prince Albert Victor on 8th May, 1886. The affair was a great popular success and visited by nearly three million visitors. In the evenings, people would walk in from outlying suburbs and villages – from Liberton and beyond – to enjoy the balmy weather, the military bands, and some Fry's cocoa. There was enthusiasm to retain the exhibition building as a benefit to Edinburgh, but a restrictive Act of Parliament thought otherwise and the entire circus vanished without relic. The fragility of Edinburgh's industrial aspirations was confirmed by the much greater success of the copycat exhibition staged in Glasgow two years later.

The exhibition had tickled national sentiment with an 'Old Edinburgh Street' of demolished Edinburgh buildings recreated by architect Sydney Mitchell from antiquarian drawings by Daniel Wilson. The organisers hoped to achieve:

> a return to a style of building at once suited to the varied scenery and changeful skies of Scotland and the character and history of the Scottish people.

The mood of the time was turning against industrialism back to revivalism. In the dying decades of the century, a scholarly reawakening of interest in matters Celtic was encouraged by nationalist murmurings, the tales of J F Campbell and the haunting and plaintive melodies of Marjorie Kennedy Fraser. Official imprimatur was lent by the establishment of a Chair of Celtic Studies at the university whose first professor, John Stewart Blackie, had been a founder of the Scottish Home Rule Association. In its way as partial a view of old Scotland as had been George IV's pink tights and the subsequent baronial excesses, the new revival was characterised by a further retreat from the city to a mythic rural Scotland before the Fall. The pretty, rather remote village of Colinton, whose manse had been serenaded by Stevenson as though it were set in the Elysian Fields, became rail-linked and suburbanised by picturesque villas in the old Scots style for Edinburgh bourgeoisie *sympathique*.

That 'old Scots style' was the product of a new wave of 'Scottishness' founded upon the study of lairds' houses of the early seventeenth century: a way of learning architecture, as Edinburgh's leading architect Sir Robert Rowand Anderson put it, analogous to the role of anatomy in medical education. It did not produce an architecture of great terraced streets: rather picturesque, quasi-rural houses more suited to the suburbs or exotic locations by the Water of Leith. An early example was the 1883 workers' courtyard of Well Court in the Dean Village, designed by Sydney Mitchell for the philanthropic owner of the *Scotsman* Sir John Ritchie Findlay, down upon which he could gaze from his drawing room window at 3 Rothesay Terrace. Under the influence of Anderson and his pupil Robert Lorimer, Edinburgh waxed as a centre of resuscitation in the building crafts and applied arts – stonemasons, carvers, iron workers, stained-glass makers, tapestry weavers and furniture maker: all of whose skills blended gloriously in the creation of the Chapel of the Knights of the Thistle in St Giles in 1911 (for which Lorimer was knighted).

The new Scottish mood swept the country, and spread in Glasgow to applied arts in publishing, furnishings, wallcoverings and even china.

Edinburgh's not insignificant place in this wider mission was the natural consequence of its unexpected mid-century blossoming as a centre for art, under the influence of the Trustees' Academy and its most distinguished teacher, Robert Scott Lauder. His pupils, including Pettie, Orchardson, McTaggart and Herdman, had formed an Edinburgh school of painting distinguished by their vivid use of light and colour.

If there was to be an 'Edinburgh style' to match the Glaswegian, its catalyst was that polymath Professor (later Sir) Patrick Geddes: biologist, campaigner, founder of town planning and altogether a most unsettling person. Geddes was driven by two compulsions: a belief in the applicability of animal biology to human habitats, and a burning desire to assist Scotland's culture to restore itself. He had been particularly upset by Scotland's loss of the *Encyclopaedia Britannica* to America and its editorship to Cambridge. The *Britannica* had, after all, been a creature of the Edinburgh Enlightenment. Its publishers, A & C Black, had been founded in Edinburgh (indeed Black had been Lord Provost), before they were lured to London in mid-century, and had been wont to boast that they had bought control of the three elements that had made Edinburgh great: Scott's novels, the *Edinburgh Review*, and the *Britannica*. By 1910, Geddes observed with despair how Edinburgh had lost its connection with all three. It was a loss of the first magnitude.

A vehement supporter of applied arts and crafts, Geddes founded a short-lived review, *Evergreen: a Northern Seasonal* in 1895, which offered artists the chance to illustrate or be published. Illustrators, mural painters and designers such as Robert Duncan, Robert Bough, Robert Burns, William Hole and Phoebe Traquair formed part of a crusade to reintegrate art in design in a manner similar to that of the architects and their craftsmen. It was in *Evergreen* that the term 'Scots Renascence' first appeared.

Geddes was driven by the belief that cities could be studied comparably to animal or insect communities and that, like them, humans would change according to their density, and their access to light and fresh air. A pure biologist might have concluded that as a nest Edinburgh was superannuated, and should be replaced. Geddes, however, was a romantic biologist, and his national sentiment led him to seek out what was best in the capital and to build upon it. He was too practical to be seduced by a retreat into some sort of Celtic mystery, and detested the prevailing flight to the leafy suburbs. In 1884, he had helped found the Edinburgh Social Union 'to bring together all those who feel the want of sympathy and fellowship between different classes'. By 1890, the union had built or improved fourteen properties, and held working men's classes in singing, gymnastics, experimental science, and window gardening.

From the physical features of the city, he inferred a 'strange alternation and interaction of good and evil, evil and good', in stunning reinforcement of Stevenson's perception of its divided soul. The consequence of the 'disastrous increase in the social separation of classes who had been in old Edinburgh so peculiarly mingled' was that:

> the upper and middle classes have been wont to traverse old Edinburgh by viaducts high above the festering squalor below, and to live and die in practical indifference to it, and thus maintain that practical indifference to deplorable conditions which strikes every Continental visitor, even every American tourist, with an outspoken astonishment far from flattering to Edinburgh . . .

The original New Towns had turned their backs upon industry and wealth-making. Their artisan streets – Rose, Thistle and Young – contained no provision for making things: they merely serviced the houses and their inhabitants. That lack was just as damaging as the 'wretchedly unplanned industrial suburb of Dalry' which now choked the western entrance to Edinburgh. Geddes proposed a reorganisation of the railways, and an 'industrial city and garden city in one' to the east and south-east of the city close to the Midlothian coalfields, serviced by the 'Innocent Railway' at St Leonard's.

The Mercat Cross of Edinburgh was the symbol of what he christened 'civic revivance' – no less than a proposed reoccupation of the old city. Geddes took over Shorts Observatory on the corner of Ramsay Street (site of the town house of the Lairds of Cockpen, immortalised by Lady Nairne's song, one of whom had been Lord Cockburn's father) for a Camera Obscura and public exhibition. He wanted to engage popular interest in the future of his metropolis. An 'Outlook Tower and Open Spaces Committee' discovered seventy-five open spaces among the slums of the Old Town, totalling some ten acres. Ten of those were

> renewed as gardens for the people. Thus, after long ages of warlike history, our women and children are returning to their gentle tasks of old, their setting of herb and tending of flower.

Others would follow 'as circumstances and scanty funds allow'.

Geddes's inspiration was Enlightenment Edinburgh, and his vision was to convert the old city into a 'collegiate Street and city comparable in its way with the magnificent High Street of Oxford and its noble surroundings'. He sought to combine into creative activity the city's rare heritage 'of beauty, of intellectual and practical endeavour, and of moral and spiritual intensity – however temporarily forgotten or depressed'. For reasons of 'antiquarian piety and conservative artistic purpose' the old buildings of Edinburgh should be protected and re-used – but only so long as they had utility. The University of Edinburgh should follow European examples and recolonise the High Street, particularly the Lawnmarket.

Soon after his marriage in 1886, he had quit the safety of Princes Street to move into James Court, then little better than a slum. Over the next twenty years, he persuaded the university to create four university residences housing 120 students within such buildings, adding eighty-five reconditioned flats or apartments in slum areas for working families. The extension of Ramsay Lodge, Allan Ramsay's house, into the magnificently Scots flats of Ramsay Garden, by his architect S Henbest Capper, was intended for university lecturers and professors, to complement the students further down the street; they were instantly fashionable and remain so to this day.

Unfortunately, Geddes was better at inspiration than finance. It was said that he had the propensity to light a candle in your hand and then run off. A vivid, inspirational, bearded visionary, perhaps he had underestimated the importance of being earnest in the city. He left others to attempt to achieve financial viability, and the reaction of the city and its university was a normal frigid tolerance but little commitment. As his vision broadened, he became a planning missionary in Grenoble and in India. The Edinburgh initiatives faltered in his absence, and the university disengaged. Although the Outlook Tower and Camera Obscura survive to this day, one floor housing the Patrick Geddes Centre, it is but a whisper of what Geddes had imagined. His influence, nonetheless, was considerable. Not only was he the father of town planning, but the works of restoration or careful rebuilding of the Old Town that mark the 1930s can be traced back to him.

Something peculiar happened to Edinburgh between the wars. During the brief twenty-year period christened 'the long weekend' by Robert Graves, Scotland enjoyed a reanimation of nationalism accompanied by a forceful cultural revival known as the Scottish Literary Renaissance. The Renaissance literati rejected the twisted Celtification into which the idea of Scotland had slipped, their distaste well expressed by Robert Bontine Cunninghame Graham of Gartmore (the writer and traveller 'Don Roberto' who became the first President of the Scottish National Party) who, in 1930, wrote to his fellow-nationalist R E Muirhead:

> What makes me despair at times is the (I think) perverted channels into which Scottish sentiment runs. Burns Clubs, St

Andrew's Nights, whisky and talk about the Misty Hebrides.

Graham directed post-war authors to a greater realism, particularly in the somewhat grim and steamy novels of Clydeside, and Scotland began to experience a creative urge last experienced during the Athens of the North:

> The stir amongst the Scottish writers was positively exhilarating. It started with the poets, scores of them led by Hugh McDiarmid. It spread to the historians . . . it infected the controversialists, and their discourses on the general theme of 'what's wrong with Scotland' are now [1938] two-a-penny on the book-barrows.

From that, it might have seemed that Geddes's vision of the High Street was about to come alive; but the description is William Power's, writer, novelist, Scottish President of PEN and literary editor of the *Glasgow Herald*. For the first time in Scots history, the spirit had quit the capital, and cultural leadership passed into other hands. It was in the west, at Glasgow University, that Compton Mackenzie unfurled their political aspirations in his 1930 Rectorial Address:

> I believe that Scotland is about to live with a fullness of life un-dreamed of yet . . . if Nationalism be something more than a sentimental emotion, it must be able to fight for itself in the arena of mundane tendencies . . . I believe that by stepping back and living upon herself [Scotland] can leap forward to the spiritual and intellectual leadership of mankind.

It was in Glasgow that the Scottish National Party was launched, it was a Glaswegian Professor of Scots Law who became its chairman, it was in the Glasgow Art Club that Tom Johnston, James Bridie and Tom Honeyman conspired to attract back to Scotland its valuable expatriates; and it was in Glasgow, with club premises at 144 Wellington Street, that the Saltire Society was founded in April 1936 to safeguard and enrich Scottish culture. Its founder members came to include D Y Cameron, Eric Linklater, John Grierson, Walter Elliott, Kurt Hahn, Edwin Muir, Agnes Mure Mackenzie, William Power and Compton Mackenzie. It was in Glasgow rather than Edinburgh that the society held its exhibition of contemporary art, at a time when artists lamented the antagonism shown by the Edinburgh establishment to the subject. When Leith-born artist J D Fergusson returned to Scotland in 1939, he refused to return to Edinburgh (where he would have found Peploe and Cadell) on the grounds that it had become a suburb of London: he immigrated to Glasgow instead. It was at the club rooms in Wellington Street that, as one of the series of lectures on Scots culture, Robert Hurd launched (as will be seen) into his diatribe against the destruction of outer Edinburgh.

The Society sought

> a new Scotland with a vigorous intellectual life, drawing on the past for inspiration to new advances in art, learning and the graces of life. All who care for the preservation of what is best in Scotland's legacy from the past, all who want to see Scotland distinguish a distinctive culture of her own . . . are invited to become members.

From time to time, the Glaswegian nationalists dispatched scouts to the capital to enquire whether it was yet fit for leadership of their revived kingdom. It remained a sad disappointment. They found it dilapidated: a 'gaunt, bleak or shabby look where it is not absolutely frowsy', thought Power, and the Old Town a semi-abandoned slum. Alasdair Alpin MacGregor doubted that the mass of his fellow-natives much cared about it (apart, presumably, from the fanaticks of the Old Edinburgh Club):

> with the exception of the professional guides, cab men, charabanc-drivers and the street urchins who shoot out at you from dingy alleys and bawl in your ears a rigmarole about the buildings and monuments, which is really a round-about way of asking for baksheesh, the people of Edinburgh neither know nor care a great deal about Edinburgh's storied past.

The optimistic generalisation that once a parliament sat within sound of St Giles, the capital's latent genius for intellectual, creative and industrial vigour would be reanimated did not equate with the flight of artistic vitality to the west. Interwar Edinburgh failed in most of the comparisons with either the Enlightenment or Athens. Even publishing could have been more vigorous, despite the continuing success of Nelson and Oliver and Boyd, and the eruption of new imprints – the radically Scots Porpoise Press and the Moray Press with its bookshop on Princes Street. The books of the time were predominantly sourced in Glasgow. In any case, Scots authors would have starved without a substantial non-Scottish audience. 'At one time,' lamented Glaswegian James Bridie in 1938 (wallowing luxuriously in a good flyte against the capital),

> Edinburgh was a literary centre or, at least, a centre of literary

criticism the ferocity of which was feared throughout the three kingdoms . . . there is no literature in Edinburgh now. There is no art . . . the high places of the city are full of Watsonians – chubby yes; confident moderately, but princely, No.

The capital's ruling class failed miserably to resurrect the larger-than-life personality of its eighteenth-century predecessors.

Take them for all in all, the lawyers are a queasy shabby lot, nothing like the fine whales and porpoises who used to wallow in seas of port and claret in the great days of the capital. As for the clergy, they have lost their Hell and have a very nerveless hold on the Absolute. The General Assembly itself is given over to skippers and dancers and dalliers with dames.

It was the 'tearing, rumbustious wind' that intoxicated Eric Linklater's Magnus Merriman on his return to Edinburgh as he began his short career as a Nationalist candidate: its bellows and its buffets inspired him – not the disengaged, mildly amused and profoundly sedate cloak that overlay the city's character. In his 1937 autobiography, William Power – who had only recently enjoyed a brief sojourn as a Morningside resident – wrote in despair:

Read *Magnus Merriman*, *Father Malachi's Miracle* or any other book that depicts modern Edinburgh and then read *As I was going down Sackville Street* [Oliver St John Gogarty's autobiography of life in Dublin]. You will be overcome by despair about Edinburgh. Son of man, can these bones live?

Down in the Canongate, Linklater's hero Merriman had found the underbelly of the capital.

Half these ragged fellows, these slouching dole-men, these pot-bellied deformities had once stood rigid and magnificent on parade, and marched behind the pipes with kilts swinging, and eaten their food under the storm clouds of death . . . here, with foul shirts and fouler breath were Mars's heroes. Kings had fallen and nations perished, armies had withered and cities been ruined for this and this alone: that poor men in stinking pubs might have a great wealth of memory.

Industrial Edinburgh, out of sight and mind, avoided the depths of the

Depression, although conditions in Leith and Dalry were, as you might expect, close to the disaster suffered by the Clyde Valley towns. Even during the slump, people still had to read, write and enjoy a drop: and Edinburgh's role as a centre of fine printing, and thereby a principal market for one of the largest United Kingdom paper-making industries, stood it in good stead. As anybody with a decent nose on a wintry morning could discern, it was also the second largest brewing district in the kingdom, and possessed the kingdom's second-largest rubber factory.

During the thirties, Edinburgh enjoyed its first explosion of popular consumerism. It cossetted the seventy-five per cent of people still in work, but rejected the rest. Chain stores surged across the Border to displace family businesses in the first of many such invasions. Edinburgh folk were seduced by the presence of sixty-five cinemas (in some, with a truly baroque approach to sanitation, seats were paid for in jam jars), a new ice rink in Murrayfield, the Maybury Roadhouse for the essentially suave, and by the Ravelston Garden mansion flats.

The people without choice, however, were spread out in some 15,000 new houses toward Saughton, Piershill and Craigmillar, as part of the deliberate depopulation of the Old Town – a classic stage in the route to megalopolis. Where demolition in the High Street seemed inevitable, City Architect Ebenezer MacRae had the old building carefully recorded for posterity. Designed in the old Scots style, there was meant to be nothing second-class about his new housing schemes out there in the country. They formed part of MacRae's aim to recreate old Edinburgh in its rebuilding and its expansion. These stately schemes were laid out in sweeping crescents and formal avenues of three-storeyed tenement flats, inhabited originally by what was then called the 'industrious poor'. Proud of their new houses (although rather alarmed at their great size and distance from work), they were well capable of looking after themselves and of raising the finance necessary for their new churches and community halls. The literati remained unconvinced. In 1936, Robert Scott Morton wrote in *Outlook*: 'The sordid areas of Niddrie are so depressing that already social workers have been asked to relieve the conditions.' The problem was not architectural: it was that of creating an enormous single-class ghetto so distant from the city.

Tourists visiting modern Edinburgh were directed to the 1933 Portobello swimming pool, one of the largest in Europe and the first with a wave machine; by far the grandest exposition of the open-air fad that had swept the country. Designed to the Olympic specification of the time, it had seating accommodation for 6,000 spectators, lockers for 1,284 bathers, a snack bar, restaurant, lounge hall, open-air tea gardens and rest rooms. Visitors were also encouraged to visit the Forth Bridge, or the Zoo on Corstorphine Hill, established in 1909 and opened in 1913. 'A most delightful place to loaf about in,' thought J R Allen, who was impressed by its success in encouraging species to breed.

Cultural nationalists stood shoulder to shoulder, however, to repel the most remorseless southern invader since Maleus Scotorum – the bungalow: a 'term of abuse' wrote the architect Robert Hurd, 'meaning a regrettable one-storeyed dwelling, distinguished by its slender chimneys, matchstick porch and asbestos roof'. The word bungalow, according to a teacher at Boroughmuir, was 'an Indian word for a flimsy shelter. There is little else. It will blow down before Christmas.' Small consolation for the young printer's son Robert Chalmers whose family was about to quit a tenement flat to move into one. His friends were even more knowing: 'Their ceilings are so low that all you can have for tea is kippers.'

The private speculative bungalow sucked the lower middle classes from their tenements with offers of privacy, a small garden, a garage or driveway for their new £90 Morris, free removal and no legal fees. The market was insatiable. Sir James Miller, later Lord Provost of the city, once related that when he advertised his first twelve houses in Blackhall in 1927, as yet unfinished, all were sold within the day. Few families had to pay more than one-sixth of their income for a mortgage. Bungalows were finely tuned to their market, class-consciousness implicit in every brick. A knowing Edinburgh native could gauge the cost of his neighbour's bungalow to the nearest £10 by studying its external appearance: those faced with brown (Dorset Pea) harling at the bottom of the pile, and those in brick at the top. Advertisements facing each other on the same day in 1938 in the *SMT* (later *Scotland's*) *Magazine* offered for virtually the same price of around £589 a four-apartment bungalow and a Buick Regal Coupé. The Buick was a mass-produced quality car not dissimilar to an Audi 100 in comparative terms.

The resultant bungalurbia affrighted the Saltire Society which had become the cultural arm of the nationalist revival. Robert Hurd addressed the Saltire Club on the threat to Edinburgh's character: 'Many acres of land on the south side of Queensferry Road are controlled by the City authorities, and yet it is one of the grimmest areas of bungalow development in the east of Scotland . . . That district today is one huge wasted opportunity.' It was as though Edinburgh itself had not noticed. Others weighed in: Edinburgh, thought Power, had surrendered to the speculative builder and Agnes Mure MacKenzie trusted that there was 'a special hell for the inventor of asbestos roofing' with which bungalows were capped. Their vehemence stopped just short of Robert Louis Stevenson's incitement to arson (see p 195).

Princes Street held little joy for the new puritans. Where Stevenson had enthused gaily over the 'mile of commercial palaces', they lamented over a deplorable hotchpotch of vulgarity. Such opinions were portentous. If the guardians of the nation's soul could see no value in Victorian Princes Street, was it surprising that there were soon moves to rebuild it entirely in a more gracious, complete and regular manner? It was even held to represent the worst of Edinburgh bourgeois life. In *Scottish Journey* Edwin Muir noted how promenaders were unknowingly blended with whores who seeped up from Leith Street, and was astounded at the public drunkenness. It was in savage contrast to the smug assurance of the tea rooms which, by that time, virtually lined the street at first-floor level from end to end. Afternoon tea was a quintessentially Scots affair between the wars which all visitors had to experience; but Muir disliked the ersatz nature of the Edinburgh variety – particularly those which had replaced the live orchestras of more traditional establishments with an early intrusion of radio muzak:

> The tea room is an institution of Edinburgh, a convention through which the middle classes and the upper middle classes express themselves . . . The effect that these places is designed to produce is one of luxury, and the more select of them strive for an impression of gently muffled silence . . . Into this silence the discreet sounds of the radio may be safely decanted . . . The luxury is intended to build up a deception, to lead the hypnotically blissful tea drinker to the mistaken conclusion that here is something as good as the richest and most leisured can enjoy.

All was not well, however, in the wider city. A public exhibition organised in the RSA by students and the Edinburgh Architectural Association in 1937 reiterated Geddes's indictment of the city's failure to plan. It warned of the dangers likely to be caused by increasing traffic and an unco-ordinated road pattern. It proposed that the city should rescue its magnificent sea front from industrial squalor and neglect by constructing a civic promenade from Cramond to Musselburgh. The city, however, was not yet ready to listen to planning: particularly from students.

The future of the High Street, however, had become brighter with the forced exodus of its people. The Marquess of Bute, toying with the idea of paying for external repair to most of the ancient buildings in the Royal Mile, commissioned Robert Hurd to begin with the retrieval of Acheson House in the Canongate, then an over-occupied slum housing thirteen families. Hurd undertook its full-scale restoration. The result so impressed Bute that he was persuaded to concentrate his funds on thorough rather than superficial restoration of other buildings, beginning with Andrew Lamb's house. A campaign to prevent the demolition of the splendid early seventeenth-century Tailor's Hall in the Cowgate became a *cause célèbre* as architects, the Saltire Society and the Cockburn Association sought to place an injunction on the city council to inhibit its action. Sentence was deferred, and the battle thought to be won; but in the immediate post-war period, those stately structures softly and silently vanished away when nobody was looking.

The retrieval by Edinburgh of its role as capital of Scotland may have been spurred by a dragon under the hill: when the *genius loci* set out to protect the Scottish Acropolis of Calton Hill against desecration. The origins of the affair lay in the revival of the office of Secretary for Scotland back in 1885 as a placebo to 'redress the wounded dignities of the Scottish people – or a section of them – who think that enough is not made of Scotland'. In 1928, the government dusted off a proposal to centralise all his departmental offices then scattered throughout Edinburgh into a single megastructure on the site of the prison on the flank of Calton Hill: a mass of civil service offices on an unfortunately prominent site, to a design snatched by the Office of Works in London on the grounds that it had 'more experience as regards the housing of large masses of officials than any private architect can possibly have'. In 1927, however, Parliament had talked out the Government for Scotland Bill: and the following year the National Party of Scotland emerged led by Cunninghame Graham and Muirhead. Wrong time, wrong place, wrong attitude. The natives were getting restless.

The issue welded together disparate people who would never have supported the Scottish Renaissance, nationalism, or even the revivication of Edinburgh. A Scottish National Committee, led by the Moderator of the General Assembly of the Church of Scotland, with the Dukes of Atholl and Montrose, Lord Elphinstone, the Marquess of Aberdeen, and half the Scottish nobility and gentry, with industrial magnates, institutions, associations, Provosts and writers in tow, raised the fiery cross. Driven by invisible forces, the natives of Edinburgh disdained to accept the desecration of Calton Hill by bureaucratic offices. At the very least, they demanded what John Buchan called an 'outward and visible sign of Scottish nationhood'. A bruising battle between an increasingly sullen government and an ardently vehement populace followed.

When, with regal modesty, Queen Mary weighed in on 20th July, 1930, to express the earnest hope that nothing unsightly would be built on the flank of Calton Hill that might spoil the outlook from her palace of Holyrood, the government knew it was beat. In response to the royal expectation of 'something noble and worthy of this site', it appointed as architect Thomas Tait in 1933. The outcome was that the original plan for plain offices became metamorphosed (to the great hurt to the public purse) into the seat of the Secretary of State for Scotland and his administration, with a dignity and quality (and at an expense) never originally envisaged.

It was also very Edinburgh: modern, but not sufficiently so to affright the bourgeoisie which remained profoundly doubtful about the applicability of the modern world to the capital. They had been aghast in 1930 when John Summerson in the *Scotsman* had declared his enthusiasm for rebuilding Princes Street from end to end in steel and glass; and even more so in 1938 to see R Furneaux Jordan's perspective of regular glazed blocks like square diamonds facing widened roads, with a pavement at first-floor level. The natives had largely succeeded in keeping the fashionable 'steamboat architecture' at bay, and the new seat of the Secretary of State for Scotland and his departments, St Andrew's House, symbolised the extent of their compromise. It was opened in mid-September 1939.

Carp as they might, the literati and the nationalists could scarcely jettison Edinburgh, and so they attempted to goad it back to life by excoriating its establishment timidity and retrospection. There was a pioneering attempt to colonise bars in Rose Street (so much more successful after the war), recalled by Hector MacIver:

> How the walls of the Abbot(sford) or the Café Royal or Milne's Bar echoed to the talk at this time as Chris [Hugh MacDiarmid] and Sydney [Goodsir Smith] and I set the world to rights. Clouds of blue smoke, gallons of beer and whisky – witty talk – heart to heart – narrowness and prejudice flown out of the Abbot door.

In 1934 the city hosted the PEN conference, attracting some 400 delegates to a banquet in the Music Hall. Power, enjoying his brief exile in Morningside from 1932, recalled many evenings of 'symposia, song, harp-playing, piping and dancing' in Arthur Lodge. There were, he thought, 'an abnormally large number of cultured people in Edinburgh. But they are lost among social cliques.' Against A G MacDonell's perception of the city as 'the greatest dead thing in the world' (many other of the literati had been considerably less complimentary) Power set the Scottish Arts Club, cosily ensconced in Rutland Square. It was the citadel, he wrote, 'from which a good deal of what is now Boeotian territory might be won back for Athens'.

To enter the smoke room at eight or nine in the evening is to come among a band of brothers . . . All the others, artists and laymen, would contribute their share of reminiscence, anecdote or opinion. Good nature and equality reigned; nobody scored points or insinuated his own importance.

Just before the Second World War, Power returned to prepare a vision of the future of Edinburgh which he called the 'high-set Jerusalem of the Caledonian tribes'. He found it subsisting entirely on visitors, 'fresh air, sermons, history, literature, a little oatmeal, and a great deal of whisky'. He recommended a ban on future ribbon development, the prohibition of building on agricultural land, a tree-lined green belt encircling Leith from the Links to Granton, industrial workers relocated to new schemes in East Leith, the 'deslumming' of the Old Town and its displaced population housed out towards Liberton, or in satellite townships at Dalmahoy and Gorebridge, and the stone-cleaning of the fog-stained New Town.

He proposed the transformation of the Royal Mile into a living museum, its historic buildings restored for people such as literary, scholastic and artistic workers capable of being seduced by the attractions of living in such picturesquely historic surroundings. The Canongate was to become Edinburgh's *rive gauche* – a 'literary and artistic faubourg': Edinburgh's Chelsea. When that happened, the Old Town of Edinburgh would be restored to its rightful place in the life of the capital of Scotland. It was a dream of an updated Enlightenment Edinburgh cleansed of the masses.

A brief ray of glory glanced upon the capital during Tom Johnston's reign as Churchill's Secretary of State for Scotland during the war. He established a Scottish Council of State, consisting of all surviving Secretaries of State for Scotland, whose actions gave the country a sense of purpose. In October 1941, Johnston organised a debate on Scottish issues for Scots MPs in the ancient Parliament House, and it was at an emotional dinner in the North British Hotel that the country first learned of the USA's intention to support Britain against Germany. As Johnston wrote in his autobiography, Scots tails were up: 'there was a new spirit of hope in our national life. You could sense it everywhere, not least in our Civil Service . . . We met England now without any inferiority complex. We were a nation once again.'

CHAPTER THIRTEEN

EDINBURGH LOST AND FOUND

By comparison with other cities, Edinburgh escaped lightly in the Blitz, but it was not quite so fortunate in the blizzard of improvement that followed. The capital had a bedraggled aspect after the war; it was delapidated and increasingly strangled with traffic. Returning ex-servicemen, some forced to squat to get accommodation, were dissatisfied with what they found and impatient with its manifest inconveniences. Radical change was the mood of the time. A plan for the future embracing all south-east Scotland prepared by Sir Frank Mears (Geddes's son-in-law) and issued from the emotive address of the Outlook Tower, was welcomed; although, apart from proposing a city bypass (which, to the veriest whisker, is what was completed forty-two years later) and suggesting a green belt to protect the city's rural aspect, it impinged little. The same, however, could not be said of the *Civic Survey and Plan* published by Professor Patrick Abercrombie the following year which, however humane and beautifully produced, was to change Edinburgh more, even, than James Craig's plan of almost 300 years earlier.

Abercrombie's survey data provided the first reasonably accurate picture of the swollen city that Edinburgh had become ever to have been prepared. Whereas Geddes, however, had had a vision for Edinburgh as capital of Scotland, Abercrombie had only rational proposals. His plan failed to recognise the role of Scotland's capital: he had no vision of the *idea* of Edinburgh other than just another large city, with unusual obstinacies of terrain.

Abercrombie revealed how clearance had drained the old centre of over a quarter of its population since 1924. He planned to accelerate that process by a formal division of the city into zones. Substandard and overcrowded tenements concentrated in districts such as Gorgie, Dalry, Leith, Portobello, Pilrig and the Pleasance were to be cleared and new communities grafted on to Drylaw, Muirhouse, Gilmerton, Oxgangs and Wester Hailes. If they were to be a success, they would naturally require all the appurtenances of new townships – shopping centre, library, community club with its hall, craft and lecture rooms, clinic, cinema, dance hall and swimming pool reasonably near at hand.

The university was offered a large 'cultural precinct' between Chambers Street, Lauriston Place and the Meadows. Faced with ex-pansion in student numbers, scattered accommodation throughout the city and overcrowded and inefficient buildings, it commissioned a de-velopment plan from Basil Spence who responded with a platoon of high-rise towers along the Meadows, guarding a 'city within a city' focused upon George Square. It was a withdrawal from city life and the Old Town into a semi-private, semi-suburban cultural enclave, within which the authorities would be free to start with a virtual *tabula rasa*. It was the antithesis of what Geddes had had in mind when he proposed the reintegration of the university with the fabric of the Royal Mile.

George Square became Edinburgh's necessary sacrifice to modernity; for upon its ruins, much of the rest was saved. In defending the square in *Architectural Prospect* in 1959, Eleanor Robertson wrote: 'The great fasci-nation of the George Square and Buccleuch Place enclave is that it seizes and fixes in stone a point of transition. The idea of the Old Town had been abandoned, but not quite, the idea of the New, as we know it, not yet conceived, though its conception has become inevitable.' Abercrom-bie, by contrast, had concluded that 'the architecture of the buildings in George Square by no means deserve pride of place in Edinburgh's heri-tage. Why therefore allow them to stand in the way of a great project?' As the following quotation from *Prospect* shows, unmatchable heavy-weights concurred:

> *Professor (Sir Robert) Matthew*: Why preserve George Square?
> *Professor (Sir Basil) Spence*: I will preserve the essence of George Square.
> *Both*: No architect of standing defends George Square.

So its fate was sealed. The battle generated a huge public outcry, revived the quiescent Cockburn Association and created the Scottish Georgian Society. The martyrdom of the square may well have saved the New Town.

Abercrombie had reacted to the evident success of the second Edin-burgh Festival in 1948 by suggesting the creation of a 'Festival Centre' – either in the Grassmarket or, by preference, at each end of Princes Street. St James' Square should make way for a civic theatre and concert hall. Edinburgh accepted that the square was dispensable, but replaced it instead with the fearsome but fashionable incubus of offices, hotel and shopping that comprise the dispiriting stained grey concrete St James' Centre. It irretrievably diminished most views in Edinburgh. Its design would have been considerably more tyrannical had not Scottish Office apparatchiks trimmed its substantial bulk.

Traffic was to be the mainspring of modernity in Edinburgh, although even Abercrombie could not have forecast the colossal growth in car ownership, nor the death and premature removal of trams and railways. He proposed an inner Leith bypass just north of Pilrig, and a new road underneath Regent Bridge, spanning over Waverley and tunnelled through the Old Town ridge to debouch in the decaying districts of the south side. That proposal blighted, in various guises and alignments, everything within its path for the next thirty years, coming close to exterminating the Pleasance, Nicolson Street and Causewayside.

The plan itself, furthermore, was the generator of much of the additional traffic and relentless pressure to widen roads to accommodate it. The populace, its activities now zoned into different districts, was compelled to shift from isolated suburbs to the centre, and from zone to zone, for its daily tasks. Such intermingling of people and disciplines that had survived the dismemberment of Enlightenment Edinburgh into the New Town, and then the dispersed city, could not withstand the zoning; and that invisible quality of Edinburgh, a place where activity was generated by people interacting with other people, was shredded.

Like the Renaissance literati, Abercrombie concluded that Princes Street could do with some smartening up. With the exception of the clubs, he thought its entire length was ripe for reconstruction, and suggested the grandeur of a single design which, 'while avoiding the monotony of the Rue de Rivoli of Paris, may oppose a great façade of ordered variety to the infinite historic picturesqueness of the Old Town across the valley'. Infinitely seductive drawings charmed their way to success. No intellectual of note could be found to defend the brash Victorian joys of the street. A Princes Street Panel was soon encouraging the replacement of that 'sea of nullities' to a common straitjacket in emulation of the ordered legacy of the New Town. A neo-classical design of huge, plain city blocks with continuous first-floor pavement linked by bridges across to Princes Street Gardens (releasing more space for cars below) was introduced, but never fully achieved. As in Charlotte Square, execution was left to individual developers; unlike Charlotte Square, the concept was only rudimentary and great latitude was permitted in execution. To achieve Abercrombie's aims, greater rigour would have been required. The city therefore sacrificed joyful vulgarity for a Calvinist hotchpotch.

According to the 1949 plan, Edinburgh was destined to develop as a city with a dead administrative centre of offices, governed by the spatial needs of traffic transporting people from here to there. The recipe was that for megalopolis: the fact that megalopolis did not quite materialise may be attributed partly to Edinburgh's obdurate nature. The rock, the ridge of the Old Town inhibited the clean sweep planned and achieved in other cities. Contrary to the norm, a sufficient residential population remained both in the Canongate and in the New Town just long enough to ensure opposition and survival. The forces of 'improvement' may have won the battle for George Square in the late 1950s, but they were held to a standstill at a public enquiry in 1967, when the inner ring road was routed.

The population was exported, as forecast, to the periphery, and the braes of southern Edinburgh swarmed with expatriate flats in towers and in terraces, overwhelming and swamping ancient demesnes like the Inch and the Drum, and characterful communities such as Liberton, Gilmerton, Slateford and Juniper Green; and then – to the sorrow of the Esks – most communities south to Penicuik. The social buildings and facilities that Abercrombie had considered essential were not built; these enormous dormitories became ghettos – remote from but yet dependent upon the centre.

In common with all large provincial cities, Edinburgh enjoyed mutilation during the redevelopment boom of the 1960s as it strove to keep up with fashion, and slake the thirst of the commercial predators who preferred not to complicate real-estate with sentiment. High-rise office blocks, whose evident prefabrication could be compared to stacked caravans on stilts, erupted by Torphichen Street and infected the inner area and the south side. The line was held, after 1967, by guerrilla action which sometimes extended to petitions in London. It was not that there was a new vision of the city. Far from it. But in its absence, it was easier to be certain of what was to be rejected rather than what was to be welcomed.

Once the Cowgate was virtually derelict and ready for stretching into an internal bypass, and the Pleasance, much of Nicolson Street, Tollcross, George Square, Torphichen Street and Bristo Street almost a memory, the mood began to change. If Edinburgh was to survive as recognisably Edinburgh, its citizens would have to shed their comfortable suburban disengagement to challenge the city's febrile pursuit of fashion inspired by envy of other cities. As did Cockburn, they would have to rise to oppose further outrages by traders no less sordid in the 1960s than they had been in the 1840s.

Things were little better down by the waterside. By the late eighteenth century, Leith had settled down to being Edinburgh's principal industrial quarter; and by the late nineteenth, replaced much of its history by warehouses, mills, and workers' tenements. The railway took out more, and after the war the residual stuffing of old Leith was surgically excised when they created the pedestrianised Kirkgate shopping centre and the cliffs of multi-storeyed flats. At the time of Abercrombie's plan, Leith had become the primary generator of Edinburgh's commerce, and nobody could have foretold the demise of ships and their replacement by aeroplanes and long-distance lorries. The port slumped, and by the early 1980s the entire community seemed doomed. Most Leithers were exported to Wester Hailes in the clearances; and immediately they got accustomed to damp-free and warm houses, they put their names on the housing list to transfer back to the Shore again. Leith came to resemble a graveyard of human endeavour. Gaunt shells that had sheltered its industries stood like solitary and blackened teeth in a rotting mouth. Litter-strewn cobbled tracks remained mute evidence of streets once dense with folk. Concerned about hazard from the ammonia works, genial planners secretly plotted towards the extinction of all houses in Leith altogether. How those sixteenth-century Edinburgh burghers would have crowed: Leith was finally going to be tamed.

Inertia followed boom in the city centre. Vast swathes of derelict, windswept and litterbound inner railway land, redundant as the railway system was carefully dismembered, symbolised a city living in remembrance of things past. In that vacuum, for a short time in the 1970s, promise of reanimation came from politics. The growth of Scottish nationalism (itself founded upon the swelling abundance of the oil which the nationalists claimed as Scottish), offered the capital the first whiff of serious political opportunity for over 200 years. The government in London was impelled to dangle the tantalising prospect of significant devolution to Scotland, administered from Edinburgh. Discussion papers were circulated, policy documents issued, and the *Scotsman* correspondence columns redounded to debate. In its desire to demonstrate commitment, the government possessed itself of the former Royal High School on Calton Hill (the school being moved to modern, leafy but scarcely comparable premises in Davidson's Mains) to convert it to the debating chamber or parliament for the new Assembly. As a parliament building, it would have been without compare in Europe.

Quiescent Scottish organisations, for whom the accusation of 'nationalist' had been resented little less than an accusation of halitosis, were compelled to address how they would respond to the introduction of devolved government, and the problems of another tier of government, new taxes, and the extent to which the proposed devolution was token or real. The debate was fervent, exhilarating, and taking place upon an international stage as journalists from throughout the world converged on Edinburgh to study the surge in nationalism.

It was to be decided by referendum. Business interests propounded that the parlous Scots economy could not withstand the shock and that incoming investment would be deterred by the threat of additional taxes. Money has always been a seductive argument in Edinburgh. It was a close-run thing. Devolution attracted a substantial majority of those caring to vote but failed to achieve the percentage necessary to give the proposal life. The Royal High School was mothballed, let out to the occasional conference and evening party, and the location for the ghostly Scottish Grand Committee when MPs decided to save on travel fares to London. Yet again, if Edinburgh's fortunes were to revive, it would not be on the back of politics. Culture was another matter.

After the Second World War Edinburgh had set out to retrieve its role as the centre of literary Scotland. The Saltire Society had already returned to perch in Gladstone's Land by courtesy of the National Trust for Scotland. Sydney Goodsir Smith, Hugh MacDiarmid, and Norman MacCaig pursued the ambience of the Enlightenment in the more *outré* bars in the back streets of the New Town and quaffed oysters at the Café Royal. The raffish reputation of Rose Street undoubtedly added to the poetic glamour.

Poets, neighbouring BBC producers, literati and lawyers haunted Edwardian howffs like the Abbotsford and Milne's Bar, for it was there that they attempted to recreate the ambience of eighteenth-century Edinburgh. In 1963, an American, Lewis Simpson, encountered MacDiarmid in Milne's Bar in Hanover Street. Talk waxed hot:

> 'Sexual promiscuity,' said MacDiarmid, 'I'm all for it, but I've never encountered it myself.' A little later, he told me looking round the pub: 'I've been a caterpillar crawling on the edge, but this is the heart of the cabbage.'

Yet Enlightenment Edinburgh could not be retrieved solely on the back of a few poets behind frosted glass and their fervour could be embarrassing – as Moray MacLaren, a dedicated Edinburgh man, found when he submitted a friend to the effulgent extravagance of experimental poetry at 'an advanced literary gathering' in the Grange in 1948. It was almost as painful as the propensity to feverish provincialism, glasses of sherry and slices of douce dry cake to the sounds of a harpist.

Compton Mackenzie, praising the Edinburgh International Festival in 1955, suggested that the capital was only saved from terminal provincialism by its arrival:

> Toward the end of the Victorian era, Edinburgh was receding into provincial status. How has it come about that today Edin-

burgh is more conscious of being a capital city than at any time since the Union with England? . . . Surely we must all admit that what has revealed to the rest of the world Edinburgh's right to claim once more her position amongst the capital cities of Europe, is the Festival.

If Mackenzie was correct that only the Festival came between Edinburgh and nothingness, then its rescue from the brink was a damned close-run thing. It was only by happenchance that the Festival came to the capital at all. Its first administrator, Rudolf Bing, recalled his desire to stage a cultural antidote to the depressions of the post-war years – the rationing, licensing of building materials, the European refugee problem, and homeless ex-servicemen squatting in empty properties. He was then administrator of the Glyndebourne Festival and proposed an international music extravaganza:

Where could such a festival be held? Near London, I thought, it would have to be: Cambridge or Oxford with their architectural beauty . . . but I could not get anybody interested. Then Edinburgh came to mind . . .

Edinburgh was fertile ground. It had been host to a number of week-long musical festivals in the early nineteenth century, organised for charitable fund-raising. Choral in character, the first had taken place in October 1815, with a programme of Handel, Pergolesi, Mozart and Beethoven. Its success was such that a choir was formed with the intention to add a music hall to the Assembly Rooms. Some 8,000 people, one of 'the largest assemblages of beauty and fashion ever seen in the city', were attracted to the successor in 1819. Further Music Festivals were held in 1825 and 1841, but thereafter dwindled to concerts given by individual performers – such as by Chopin in 1848. The steam had run out of the festivals, the last of which made a loss.

The presence of international troops in Edinburgh during the Second World War ruptured the stuffy complacency that had driven much of the Scottish literary Renaissance to Glasgow before it. Czechs, Poles and Americans (Chiang Yee – the Silent Traveller then subjecting the capital to a delicate oriental microscope – was diverted by squads of GIs chewing gum uncomprehendingly as they scampered after a fast-walking geriatric guide with a megaphone down the Royal Mile) stimulated the British Council representative, Harvey Wood, to arrange readings, discussions, and lunch-time concerts. The possibility of enlarging those to a festival was first mooted in 1944. The specification which Woods and

Bing drew up for the ideal Festival City seemed to have been written specifically with Edinburgh in mind:

> A town of reasonable size, capable of absorbing and entertaining anything between 50,000 and 150,000 visitors over a period of three weeks to one month. It should, like Salzburg, have considerable scenic and picturesque appeal, and it should be set in a country likely to be attractive to tourists and foreign visitors. It should have a sufficient number of theatres, concert halls and open spaces for the adequate staging of a programme of an ambitious and varied nature.

There was no intention of trying to recreate the milieu of the Enlightenment. Rather, Edinburgh's role was to act as a stage-set, a superb backcloth for artistic achievement. The organisers sought the highest standards in art and music – contact with which, Woods believed, would benefit the native arts of Scotland immeasurably. He cast a pragmatic eye over what might accrue to the local economy:

> If, as now seems certain, the Festival succeeds, Edinburgh will not only have scored an artistic triumph but laid the foundations of what may well become a major industry, a new and exciting source of income. At a time when we need as never before to attract visitors and foreign capital to this country, it would be senseless to disguise this aspect of the Festival as it is childish to attack it.

From such modest aspirations there emerged, over the next forty years, four annual, simultaneous Festivals in Edinburgh, the original being supplemented by the Fringe, the Jazz and the Film Festivals, attracting (according to the *Scotsman*) over one million visitors to the capital during August 1990 and an income of some £50 millions. The Lord Provost in 1947, Sir John Falconer, had trusted that his city would

> surrender herself to the visitors and hope that they will find in all the performances a sense of peace and inspiration with which to refresh their souls and re-affirm their belief in things other than material. We wish to provide the world with a centre where, year after year, all that is best in music, drama and the visual arts can be seen and heard in ideal surroundings.

It did. For the next thirty years, you came to Edinburgh for the finest in

224

music from the greatest world performers at the pinnacle of their career. Their presence cast a glow upon the city.

The Festival's 1959 director, Robert Ponsonby, felt sufficiently secure in its success to broaden its range to include musical satirists like Anna Russell, and the *Beyond the Fringe* team the following year. The satire boom of the sixties, which fed and flourished in the Fringe, had its origins in the Festival; a Festival whose spirit of institutional irreverence peaked with the Hoffnung Memorial Concert addressed by a naval pipe band, and a quartet of industrial hoovers, which led an insouciant throng noisily out into the midnight Edinburgh streets after the start of the Sabbath. Beyond the confines of the rigidly organised Festival, a spirit – untrammelled by the magnificence of its programme – broke loose and peeked round corners into the unplanned hours and discreet locations. In 1961, the poet Robert Garioch wrote to a friend:

> I like being in Edinburgh, and I like meeting the literary boys, who are to be found in a strictly limited set of howffs. Not much visiting at houses seems to go on, instead one mills about in a crowd, getting a word in here or there . . . There was a poetry reading ploy, with which these people were connected, in a deep dark cellar in North St Andrew's Street, and I went to read 'Embro to the ploy' beneath a wee light to a lot of shadowy figures who laughed loudly at the funny bits, and it was good fun . . .

A characteristic of some early Festivals was the extent to which they embraced an even more dispersed Edinburgh by staging concerts in Leith and Portobello Town Halls, and in cinemas in Tynecastle and Pilton. In 1959 Yehudi Menuhin and his fellow trio members were astounded by the thronged streets which welcomed them as they entered the Embassy cinema in Pilton to perform. Menuhin and his colleagues had 'thought it would be nice to get acquainted with the people who really belong to Edinburgh and have no opportunity to get to the concerts'. Yet when the council proposed a revival of that notion in the 1980s it was met with howls of anguish on the grounds that the *zeitgeist* of the Festival would somehow be diluted.

The late Sir Tyrone Guthrie, Irish theatre-director great-grandson of Dr Thomas (whose statue still dominates Princes Street) described his search for an ideal space in which to stage *The Thrie Estaitis* in 1948:

> We visited big halls and wee halls. Halls ancient and modern, halls secular and halls holy, halls upstairs and halls in cellars,

dance-halls, skating rinks, lecture halls and beer halls . . . darkness was falling . . . I was beginning to be acutely conscious that I had led them all a wild goose chase. Then spake [Robert] Kemp in the tone of one who hates to admit something unpleasant: 'There is the Assembly Hall' . . . the moment I got inside, I knew we were home.

It was a breathtaking proposition. The Assembly Hall was the four-sided chamber that acted as the supreme court of the Church of Scotland, the shrine of Presbyterianism. Robert Kemp, a son of the manse, would have been aware of its aura, and must have wondered how the Church would react to the staging of a play – indeed a religious satire – written for a Catholic court. Repudiating its reputation for being a Calvinist killjoy, the Church willingly acceded, and the Assembly Hall became the totem performing space of all subsequent Edinburgh Festivals.

The others so assiduously ferreted out by Guthrie became the stage of the Fringe. The second Festival in 1948 had listed 'other attractions' worth visiting around the fringe, and within a decade those 'other attractions' had grown to such an extent that they had transformed what had begun as a fringe to the Festival into as great an attraction as the Festival itself. All those church halls and Free Churches washed up in the suburbs following the city's gladiatorial religious crusades of the nineteenth century provided unequalled performing space. By 1986, the Fringe was selling upwards of half a million tickets for some 9,000 separate performances in 150 different locations, with an average attendance of fifty-five. The theatre in the round created by Guthrie in the Assembly Hall, and recreated in miniature at the Traverse, removed all distance between performer and audience; and with the advent of participation theatre, the Fringe put any timid onlooker who had sat incautiously in a front row or near an aisle at risk of some species of public humiliation. It became the leitmotif of the Fringe.

The Festival Fringe is one of the most enduring legacies of the sixties, perpetuating those days of Scott Mackenzie, flower power, Richard Demarco's gallery with its incomprehensible modern importations from Hungary in an invisible basement in Melville Street, and, of course, the Traverse, blossoming in the tight, narrow, louche atmosphere of Kelly's Paradise, staging in its close little auditorium 'off off' Broadway productions such as *Futz* (an almost inoffensive play about a man who fell in love with a pig), seemingly designed deliberately to drive Edinburgh councillors into frenzy. All available walls were plastered with vivid posters, and whisky measures at the Fringe Club were lavish. Cafés with pulse salads and advanced quiches were run by winsome and delightful lady graduates with cut-glass accents whose daddies had set them up in the Grassmarket. The Fringe was restoring to the city streets that elusive eighteenth-century atmosphere, and for three weeks each summer the city metamorphosed into a vast campus of bright, intelligent, experimental young people, fortunate enough to be compressed within a spot of incomparable beauty.

There was (as there remains) a strong preference for a Fringe performing location within the bounds of the Old Town. The further away, the more it meant reliance on transport: whereas true Fringe devotees preferred the convenient joy of tripping from show to show on foot, mingling with the vast swarms who colonised streets and pavements into the darkest hours. Certainty of an audience out in the tundra of Viewforth was rare; and it was behind the gaunt and forbidding exterior of some echoing church hall in these remote spots that newcomers, the poor or the unfashionable, had to make their reputation. With a minimum of prop and costume, their task was to repel Calvinist spectres and to conjure up a world of fantasy that would blind their audience to the discomfort and distractions of scattered benches beneath an enormous timber roof of precarious stability, indifferent blackout, and (not infrequently) light penetration through slipping slates. Such was their skill that they often succeeded.

Edinburgh during the Festival could become a three-week obsession. Blue skies, roseate sunsets over the castle, balmy air, and the sound of streetwise jazz or distant pipes would create an unreal, almost fairytale atmosphere which released the capital's latent Europeanism. Visitors from Glasgow, Perth or Dundee (hastening along those pre-motorway dangerous three-lane roads) would speed to a concert in Leith Town Hall at eleven o'clock in the morning; followed by an exhibition over lunch, and a 2.00 p.m. performance. A further exhibition at 4.00 might lead to a Fringe event at 5.00; a bite in the Luckpenny or Henderson's at 6.00 (with a quick glance at the art on the walls) in time for a major performance at 7.30; a quick drive south to soak up the chill atmosphere of floodlit Roslin chapel with its thick smell of candlewax and musty antiquity and then back to the Footlights review at 10.45; before joining the crowd thronging up the High Street to the Traverse for a late late and risqué . . . (how much is going to be lost with the translation of the Traverse into the bowels of the new Financial Centre in Castle Street? Its spirit at the very least). A pre-dawn drive home, a few hours' sleep, and back in time for the following morning's concert.

Fringe drama, exhibitions and spontaneous performance contrasted well with the Festival's diet of serious music (a creative tension much diminished with the Festival's slackening grasp of music and its growing taste for spectacle). The essence of the Fringe is the absence of selection. Provided a performing space can be found, anybody can try their luck in Edinburgh during August: it is indeed a 'place for the crazies'. In this wholesale and indiscriminate acceptance of initiative, more of Enlightenment Edinburgh is summoned back to life. Curiously, the establishment remains aloof. The capital, now with two universities, can seem in August to be bereft of both. The clubs of neither Festival nor Fringe echo their eighteenth-century forebears as generators of creative dialogue; they are, instead, well-watered rest rooms for relaxation between performances.

The Festival was the cause of the rediscovery of Edinburgh. John Paterson's stunning 1968 exhibition '200 Summers in a City' (a fine summer too) celebrated the bicentenary of the New Town and unveiled its condition. Thereafter, the Edinburgh Architectural Association despatched a team of 120 volunteers to survey the New Town buildings: and just as had been the case in 1751, the results revealed dangerously widespread dilapidation, slums often sheltering behind palatial façades. A later social survey revealed an unexpectedly high presence of single parents, drugs, and poverty. The outcome was presented at an international conference of 1,100 people held in the Music Hall in George Street in 1970, and the consequence was the creation of the Edinburgh New Town Conservation Committee. Over the ensuing decades, that committee directed substantial government funds into repairs and renewal; in so doing, it earned Edinburgh a European reputation for excellence in architectural conservation. Slums were repulsed.

Although economics forced the subdivision of houses into flats, residence in the New Town had become fashionable once again by 1975. To a number of genial but elderly myopics, it had never been otherwise. Swarms of earnest international visitors came to admire the New Town and, in particular, its achievement in retaining attractive market-led accommodation close to a city centre. Talk of motorway roundabouts in Queen Street, and car parks in the gardens was heard no more. The upper-level walkway staggering along a partially rebuilt Princes Street had a seizure and died at a West End bank. Just in time, central Edinburgh had perceived the threats facing its survival as a civilised place in which to live. The notion of megalopolis was checked.

That major battle won, minor affrays were ceded without a struggle. The New Town was remorselessly eroded by the consequences of coping with the growth of traffic. Spacious and gracious cobbled vistas were modernised and colonised by parking meters and silent lumps of tin; pedestrians were crushed behind metal barriers of stupefying ugliness as pavements were narrowed, corners cut and speed of traffic enhanced. Inelegant street signs, gawky street directions, graceless street lights, and squalid plastic mini-roundabouts were imposed upon one of the most outstanding townscapes of the world. The natives seemed incapable of compelling more appropriate impedimenta upon the traffic engineers.

As Edinburgh rose imperceptibly to the top rank of European financial centres, its priorities were reflected by its preference to construct the Royal Commonwealth (swimming) Pool and the Meadowbank (sports) Stadium, rather than an opera house or a conference centre. The 'sordid traders' on the council had an imperfect vision of the facilities to which a European capital – or even regional capital such as Rennes for Brittany, Barcelona for Catalonia, or Munich for Bavaria – like Edinburgh should aspire. Its fogginess was revealed by the saga of the opera house.

Mr Poole's louche cinema in Castle Terrace had been demolished. Two competing designs for a national opera house for Scotland in its place failed to win necessary financial backing, and the project was abandoned whilst Glasgow proceeded with its glorious conversion of the Theatre Royal. Volunteers then breathed life back into the opera house with a vision of a miraculous landmark on the Leith shores symbolising Edinburgh's culture in the manner of Sydney. Now, over twenty years after the first inspiration, an opera house seems probable: a music hall decorously converted back from bingo for the purpose. Given such a history of dithering, it was fortunate that the government was prepared to fund the creation of the National Gallery of Modern Art in the redundant John Watson's School, and that volunteers could achieve the graceful conversion of a former church into the Queen's Hall.

As in the 1930s, it seemed possible that the cultural leaderhsip of Scotland could pass to the west – a sensation strengthened by the marketing success of the Glasgow Garden Festival in 1988, the latter's elevation to European City of Culture in 1990, and the continuing success of Mayfest. Sensing a malaise but unable to identify the cause, Edinburgh's council purchased the PR consultant behind the success of the 'Glasgow's Miles Better' campaign in order to reawaken a native sense of pride. Offered no sense of purpose from his clients greater than a riposte to its western clone, the consultant emerged with the immortal nonentity 'Edinburgh: count me in'. Slogans had replaced vision.

In the meantime, the Old Town imploded. Its population dropped by over two-thirds between 1950 and 1975, and the 3,000 natives who clung vestigially to their unnaturally dilapidated rookeries were too few to provide a market for their own shops. Of 292 houses in the Cowgate in 1920, only eight remained in 1980. The occasionally occupied tenement eyrie high up within a derelict close was notably short of basic amenities. As buildings fell or remained derelict, commerce was dulled. The office boom that megalopolis would have predicated for the High Street failed to materialise: the terrain was too difficult. Traditional occupations fled: of eighty-three manufacturing and warehousing businesses that roosted in three Old Town streets in 1900, only four persisted to 1980 – a loss scarcely compensated by the marginal but ominous increase in wine bars and tourist shops. Yet those 3,000 leathery inheritors of old Edinburgh proved unusually tough; the *idea* of the High Street, dormant since Geddes, awoke.

In the best Geddes tradition of survey, analysis, plan, a team of young enthusiasts surveyed close by close, tenement by tenement, monument by monument in 1984. Surprisingly few ancient buildings were revealed, but the ancient atmosphere was anchored by the adherence to the original shape of the remaining eighty-four closes. An Old Town Committee for Conservation and Renewal emerged the following year which differed from its New Town counterpart in its intention to stimulate total (rather than just physical) regeneration. Within even only a few years, the change has been remarkable. Gaps along the Cowgate, Alesius's street of palaces, reprieved from its fate as an inner city bypass, have been filled with houses, student flats, and a new Sheriff Court. Dereliction in the High Street has been replaced by houses and flats, rather than the offices prophesied by the 1949 plan. Many of the older buildings have now been rehabilitated, and wine bars sprout down closes that once housed whores and howffs.

Is it too sanitised? Drunks and beggars, by curious inversion, are to be found in the New Town: in the Old, if you wish, you may join ghoulish guides on crepuscular crawls through tenebrous closes and macabre corners to greet rats and ghosts with girlish shrieks.

CHAPTER FOURTEEN

ENVOI

This book has focused upon the *idea* – the mystical notion – of Edinburgh, the capital of Scotland symbolised by its characterisation as the Winged Citadel. It is a story of remarkable resilience: how and why the city became capital in the first place, and how it managed to retain that status with the intellectual achievement of the Enlightenment even once the country lost its parliament.

The physical nature of Edinburgh materially influenced the lives of its inhabitants: not merely as an ungiving rock in face of invading army and traffic engineer alike but – in its earlier years – as a forcing-house of human endeavour, particularly in the eighteenth century. During that period, its essential civility lay not in its romance (Scott had not yet kissed it awake), nor in its social provision (did not Fergusson die a pauper in Bedlam?) and particularly not in its sanitation: but rather in the curious combination of the city's shape – like a stone college; the city's density – which compelled physical or intellectual collision between person and person; and of its encouragement of aptitude. It was a capital freed from the overburden of aristocracy and politics.

The foe of such a city was dispersal and dissipation. Dispersal to the New Town led to further expansion as the population doubled and then redoubled, and as the city spread, its energies became diluted and its activities disassociated. Its increasing size rendered it lethargic, incapable of stimulating its former levels of thought and creativity. The vigour of Athenian literature and the literary legacy of Sir Walter Scott and his colleagues were corrupted into a folk memory, into a sub-Scottish kailyard of ersatz Celtification, in which the nation's character was summarised on shortbread tins or Edinburgh rock. Placid enjoyment of an earlier generation's achievements replaced initiative.

Later radicals plundered history seeking a model for a purer and more vital Edinburgh. They tended to bypass both its period as the Athens of the North, and the plangent but short-lived Renaissance decades. They returned, instead, again and again, to the High Street of the eighteenth century whose masters developed their philosophy and humanity from

231

the exigencies and experience of living amidst an unimaginable throng within an inconvenient and often primitive stone eyrie. Patrick Geddes had the clearest vision of how to make the High Street relevant to the swollen land mass that had become the capital: the integration of town and gown, with a focus upon the intellect within the context of a Scottish cultural revival.

Romantic nationalists, however, pinned their entire hopes for the awakening of the capital upon a resurrected parliament. Yet, as was reiterated during the 1970s devolution debate, there was no assurance that the Scottish culture embraced by nationalism would necessarily eschew kailyard. Much of the evidence was to the contrary. There was an undertone of anti-intellectual bias, antagonism to the Scottish Arts Council, and the implication that a popular nationalism would run on the cultural basis of a never-ending Hogmanay special.

When the Secretary of State for Scotland quit his ghastly offices surmounting the St James' Centre and returned to a revivified St Andrew's House on the edge of Calton Hill, he may have added lustre to his office, but little further power; and political power remains the lure. Like the Thirties Renaissance literati, Neal Ascherson accords the capital an inadequate destiny without politicians:

> It seems to me that Edinburgh has never quite discovered an alternative raison d'être in all the 283 years since the last session of the Scottish Parliament . . . the most European of urban destinies is to be the capital of a nation regaining the use of its limbs.

Yet Edinburgh's greatness had not depended solely upon its being a seat of monarch or parliament. Only once the King had left for London did the capital boom; and it was only once parliament had followed that the capital reached its pinnacle: no parliament, little patronage, little fawning and begging: but the exercise of men of ability. The renewed siren song, a midsummer night's dream of some form of devolved government exercised from Edinburgh is proving so seductive that it illuminates only too clearly the persistent primacy of politics over culture. Enlightenment literati were of sterner stuff. Provincialism was only an attitude of mind: intellectual rigour was universal. Indeed, the presence of a parliament, concluded Faujas de St Fond, would have militated *against* Edinburgh's achievements.

If the promise of political return were used yet again as an excuse for failure to release Edinburgh's inherent potential, it would be a lost opportunity. For the portents of self-regeneration are more optimistic than they have been during the century. This great city has potential as powerful (if yet dormant) as that revealed in the eighteenth century. How to tap it is the problem.

A notable feature of earlier chronicles of Edinburgh has been their portrait of Edinburgh in their time. It seems less simple now. Contemporary Edinburgh, as it enters the last decade of the millennium, would appear – to some extent – tame in comparison to the plague of prostitution witnessed by Creech or the roaring boys and drunks of Stark. It has no stinking Tolbooth and few Regency beaux. The lager louts who howl the back streets of the New Town in the wee hours with their hurley, having exploited to the full the relaxation in licensing laws; or the sad drug addicts on desolate doorsteps, and dejected homeless in the Grassmarket, are to be seen in every large city: Edinburgh's distinction is that they are perhaps more discreet than elsewhere.

There is a certain self-indulgence in the air. The good life has provided Edinburgh with well-favoured restaurants, wine bars, clubs, leisure centres and sports clubs. It has the largest dry ski slope in Europe clutched to the slopes of the Pentlands at Hillend, within a stone's throw of the Stevenson retreat at Swanston. Yet the sybaritic self-indulgence of being dragged effortlessly up the side of those gracious hills once bestrode by Cockburn in his white smock, to slide down again on regional council subsidy seems strangely antithetical to all one's sensations of Edinburgh. That black spur poking obdurately against the blue Forth beyond is an uncomfortable reminder of how much fortitude and labour was formerly required for success.

Once one of the finest views in Europe, the prospect from the Pentlands is no longer as pristine as it was when Grecian Williams came to paint comparisons between Edinburgh and Athens. It has been modified by curious slabs and towers, and a rash of suburban roofs. But there is nowhere better to savour the extremes of weather enjoyed by the capital of Scotland: balmy days of bluest horizon like the Gulf of Corinth, autumn gales of golden leaf-whipping sharpness and the faint smell of woodsmoke, or deeply and silently impenetrable haars. Beneath them all there is an underlying severity. The place is peculiarly unsuited to an age of global warming. Palm trees would be no improvement to the prospect.

Between the ski slope and the distant castle crag, and indifferently related to both, lie many of Edinburgh's large housing areas. Distance from the centre and a consequent remoteness have created a cycle of dependency in the peripheral housing estates; inevitably it is there that the capital's disproportionately severe drugs and AIDS problems are concentrated. The city's response began as one of incomprehension, as though such problems were only coincidentally related to the capital: a comfortable reaction strikingly similar to its forebears' curious if sympathetically disengaged reaction to the depredations of Burke and Hare. The people's dispersal has diluted their power and their rage: only rarely has there been a glimpse of the Edinburgh mob – in the copycat riot in Pilton, for example, which followed those in Toxteth: feeble in comparison with its former fury when it infested the High Street catacombs.

Optimism is implied by increasing devolution of civic power to local organisations whose purpose is to foster a certain self-sufficiency. The pioneer, whose success undoubtedly proved their value to the city fathers, was the Edinburgh New Town Conservation Committee, established after the 1970 conference. It has been followed by a Leith Project, the Old Town Committee for Conservation and Renewal, and an Enterprise Trust in Wester Hailes. More are likely in the future. After all, to accept that large cities consist of myriad smaller districts with surplus initiative waiting to be tapped, is one way of taming megalopolis.

Leith manifests welcome signs of revivification. Property values warm to water and sea fronts. Tentative restoration and conversion of warehouses into flats and restaurants has been assisted by stone-cleaning and finance from the Scottish Development Agency. Professional firms have begun to cluster round, excellent back-room restaurants are opening, and gaping eyesores on the Shore are being filled up with flats, as Leith nudges toward becoming Edinburgh's Docklands. There is much yet to do: the upper banks of the Water of Leith require rebuilding, the seventeenth-century North Leith Church rescue, and Bernard Street relief from the heavy traffic that thunders through it. The process of recovery is insufficiently deep to ensure permanence; but signs are so propitious that Leith could become what William Power had planned for the Canongate: a *rive gauche* (or, in Leith's case, a *rive droite*). Closer links with the continent after 1992 could lead to a revival of the docks, and a return of the port's ancient purpose.

The Labour council, which swept to power in 1984 after decades of inaction tempered only by the temptation to sell to the highest bidder, inherited inertia, and substituted frenzy. Office redevelopments in Tollcross, Castle Terrace, Haymarket, Caledonian Goods Yard, Fountainbridge and Morrison Street seem likely to cause an unforecasted lurch in the city's economic balance from the New Town to the south-west side of the city. They extend, in aggregate, to a territory larger than the original New Town. A sensible Edinburgh approach to change of that scale might have been to dust off Lord Provost Drummond's far-sighted method of holding a competition for a master plan which builders would have to follow. Instead, the council rouped, as it were, large swathes of real-estate in a series of 'developer competitions'. The widespread intellectual debate and philosophy that had surrounded the creation of the first New Town was replaced during the eighties by secret confabulation between council committees (hoping to squeeze marginal benefit) and remote and anonymous financiers.

The market proved less capable than Drummond's shoulders at ensuring civilised levels of development adequate for the capital. Within the terms of the roup, financial criteria were set by the developers; the spaciousness compelled upon the New Town by the original plan was not reflected in a contemporary graciousness. Economics implied overdevelopment and bulky buildings without the safeguard of minimum standards and guaranteed quality which the feu conditions had imposed upon the New Town. All the while, the rest of Edinburgh looked on, its conscience pricked only by the followers of Harry Cockburn. Those organisations that had played such a prominent part in Enlightenment Edinburgh – the university, the institutions, the clubs and the professional bodies – remained disengaged and the city duly got what it deserved.

The distinction of George Street is that it now mingles its elegant shops – its outfitters and alcoholic emporia, jewellers and bookshops – with art galleries and auction houses, and the remainder of the first New Town has metamorphosed into the financial heart of Scotland. South Bridge has declined into amusement arcades, and Princes Street (most of its original stores gone) into the litter-strewn, short-let shopping parade that used to be South Bridge. Quality shops that might once have aspired to Princes Street have begun to move out to South Clerk Street, Stockbridge, Bruntsfield and Morningside. Peripheral shopping centres flourish to the (sometimes terminal) pain of smaller businesses. Already under pressure from the burgeoning suburban supermarkets and superstores, the city-centre economy is likely to be further drained by the temptations of the American-style drive-in plaza by Craighall.

Edinburgh's tenements underwent a programme of improvement, conversion and restoration during the 1980s. It revealed the latent popularity of tenement living amongst urban Scots, in contrast to the prevailing belief that the summit of every Scot's ambition was a brick suburban box with cat and milk bottle on the doorstep. Stone-cleaning, road closures and paving, the planting of trees and the revival of back courts returned a sense of self-respect to tenemental areas. Leith Walk, indeed, is being transformed from a wide, dour grey canyon into something almost Parisian by the planting of an avenue of trees down its centre. The inherent qualities of many of the old tenements facing it, with their high and ornate ceilings, reproach the squat brick stacks of their modern equivalent that sprout like clumps of prematurely aged toadstools throughout the inner suburbs.

Edinburgh has been much blessed by what Lewis Mumford, thirty years ago, described as 'uniform, unidentifiable houses lined up inflexibly at uniform distances on uniform roads in a treeless communal waste inhabited by people of the same class, the same income, the same age group, witnessing the same television performances, eating the same tasteless prefabricated foods from the same freezers, conforming in every outward and inward respect to a common mould'. They have gobbled up the farmland and colonised the fringe. Planners now forecast that if people continue to move from the centre to live at that density, the bounds of Edinburgh, unable to contain its population, will sunder and spill its surplus across the Green Belt to wreak further havoc on innocent communities like Penicuik and Linlithgow that have done nothing to deserve it.

There is a new air of confidence within the Old Town: population has doubled in the last ten years and, with some 7,500 residents, has returned to the level of 1960. The increase has been in smaller flats for younger people and students, leaving a serious shortage of family flats. Eighteen closes have been repaired, and into them have moved a number of small but important organisations: the Saltire Society down Fountain Close, the Cockburn Association in Trunk's Close, the Old Town Committee in Advocates Close and the Scottish Poetry Library in Tweeddale Court. The Fringe enjoys a vividly humorous office facing the High Street and, high above, windows are cleaned and newly adorned with curtains. Food shops have begun to reappear and second-hand bookshops are re-emerging in the West Port.

The principal danger faced by the Old Town has been a surrender to tourism and to tat, and the more the residents who live in it to balance the distortions of visitors, the less abject that surrender will be. Conversely, visits to the Old Town have become much more satisfying since a living community and culture has begun to thrive. The threat is symbolised by two developments: the threatened closure of the city's three principal modern art galleries – all within the Old Town bounds; and by the enthusiastic reception awarded the spuriously ancient Scandic Crown Hotel, which has erupted between Niddry's and the Friars' Wynds, and abutting the great (but dilapidated) early sixteenth-century house of the dangerous Earl of Morton.

There has been more debate over the Scandic Hotel than over any other building since the St James' Centre: the latter because of its ungainly and ill-placed modernity, and the Scandic because it seems to be the architectural equivalent of Harry Lauder or Edinburgh Castle on biscuit tins: a pantomime retreat from reality. Yet its scale is right, and it performs a signal service in closing one of the worst ruptures in the High

Street walls. It is symbolic, however, of Edinburgh's uncertain cultural stance. It is praised for being a sensitive and appropriate building in that locality. Of a certainty, if that is all that can be said for the hotel, it is evidence that the city has lost all sense of a thriving and appropriate contemporary culture visible, say, in Vienna, Oslo or Copenhagen.

The recovery is still fragile. The number of residents in the Old Town will have to double again to ensure its permanence. Men of aptitude of the many varied disciplines and activities in Edinburgh should once again meet others on a regular basis for the purposes of communicating outside their discipline in intellectual exchange. Whereas in Enlightenment Edinburgh it happened naturally, as the consequence of everyone being trapped within the stone cloister of the High Street, it now requires to be stimulated almost artificially if people are to be tempted furth of their elegant fortresses. Lawyers must once again converse with doctors, doctors with philosophers, philosophers with architects, architects with politicians, politicians with wigmakers, booksellers and shopkeepers, shopkeepers with writers and writers with ministers. We are in an era where it seems to be easier to create what they call 'intelligent buildings' than it is an 'intelligent society'.

'People in cities lose the habit of intimacy the further they live apart,' wrote the fourth-century Antioch orator Libianus: 'the habit of friendship is matured by constant intercourse.' The essence of civilised city life, the habit of intimacy, could be reintroduced to old Edinburgh (without its eighteenth-century olfactory disadvantages) by closing the ruptures in the walls of the High Street and rebuilding upon derelict or ignored backlands to increase the number of people who live within its bounds. Closes such as the Advocates and the Fishmarket could be rebuilt upward, reusing the airspace of this soaring city, whilst retaining, as need be, contemporary uses upon the ground. To such spots need to return people without young children or a burning need to garden, the dispersed and aloof academics from Newington, Currie and Riccarton, bankers back from the Grange and professionals from Trinity, Cramond, and Blackford, to swell a vastly increased throng of people resident at the heart of the city. Willy-nilly, that would force the contact and exchange which was once the key to its creativity.

Reversing the habits of the last 200 years is unlikely to be easy. Freed from the constraints of unchosen proximity, Edinburgh developed the isolated cliques noted by William Power and John Allan during the 1930s. Pronouncements by the Chamber of Commerce remind one of those smaller merchants who used to secrete their 'movabill geir' in Baillie MacMorran's house when disturbance threatened. It is still the kind of city where the only people to talk to you at bus stops are expatriate

Glaswegians. Spontaneous hospitality is not a native Edinburgh characteristic.

The financial establishment has now overtaken law, government and
the Church as the city's prime mover. For one of the largest financial
centres in Europe, there is an observable dearth in the New Town of the
symbols of conspicuous consumption - none of the boastful BMWs or
Rolls so ostentatiously obvious in London or Zurich. Perhaps it should
cause little surprise. After all, is it not the decorum with which they fulfil
their duties that sets Edinburgh folk apart? Since quitting the Old Town,
appearances have mattered horribly. It might be expected of the capital
of a country that perfected a habit of public probity and private vice that
ostentation would be absent from its streets. The large vehicle and converted castle are not the spoor so much of the Edinburgh native as of new
money: the arriviste who prefers lunch at Prestonfield rather than in the
New Club in Princes Street.

Sheltering behind the camouflage of their stockholders, policyholders
and unit holders, Edinburgh's furtive financiers rarely permit Scots sentiment or preference to affect financial judgment. They enjoy the palpably
preferable lifestyle of Edinburgh to that of London, yet often remain un-
committed to the city, save the occasional sponsorship of a frivolity in
the Fringe. How many of our contemporary financiers would, as did Sir
William Dick of Braid, exchange their fortunes for the 'sillie honour' of a
Lord Provostship? They are worthy successors to the merchants who invariably preferred to promote their own 'particular'. It has led to a curious
legacy: it was incomers – from George Drummond to Adam Smith,
Thomas Guthrie to Patrick Geddes – who provided much of the innovation, inspiration, drive and impetus for Edinburgh's development;
and it largely remains so today. Even the fanaticks of the Cockburn Association, to whom we have devolved responsibility for protecting the
quality of the city, are disproportionately in number *gastarbeiter*.

Many of the incomparable, incidental, unplanned joys of greater Edinburgh are, as John Ruskin warned, more the gifts of God than the
creation of man: whose duty is to waste them as sparingly as possible. A
white winter's view, eastwards past the romantic turrets of the Royal Infirmary to snowclad cliffs of the Salisbury Crags against a gunmetal sky,
offers an experience given by few cities in the world. It is a prospect that
came dangerously close to being obscured by tall constructions. Those
overwhelmed but ancient villages with their narrow roads, high stone
walls with overhanging trees, church spires, gravestones and sound of
Sunday bells that so recall the Edinburgh of Stevenson barely repel the
pressure for road widening and colonisation by brick boxes. The footpath
through tunnel and gorge along the Water of Leith, or that up the River

Almond, which can offer wonderful contrasts of urban and rural at the same time, are swamped by litter and canine defecation. No one dares holler, 'Haud your paw!' There is a feeling of dilapidation as much in the leafy walks as along Princes Street.

A sense of ebbing civic dignity is particularly evident at the new ceremonial entrance for most visitors to Edinburgh. Those who arrive by air first experience the city along its western approaches. They are presented with a superabundance of supermarkets, bypasses and bungalows, tawdry industrial estates, filling stations, brick rejects from Welwyn Garden City, glass slabs and spotty construction. Their first view, from East Craigs across to the Pentlands, embracing the homes of the majority of Edinburgh citizens and crowned by the lights of the Hillend ski slope, is not a distinguished one. Undifferentiated grey roofscapes cover almost half a million people, square miles of amorphous hobbitland punctured only by high-rise towers. Castle and crag – the saving graces of the capital of Scotland – are round the bend to the east.

It was a subtle idea to embody tawdriness in the outer stages of entry into Edinburgh so that a visitor's reaction when the castle heaves in sight would be enhanced. Of a certainty, however, it was unwise for the city fathers to have overestimated the sensibilities and perceptiveness of their tourists. However erroneously, they miss the point, and conclude that the city has but a nerveless grip on how to welcome strangers to a great capital.

Ancient villages, kirks, greens, burns, dells, walled lanes, golf courses, hospitals, exciting corners, bypassed crannies and other unexpected remnants of rural Midlothian that had been absorbed into Edinburgh are also being gathered up for sale. The green wedges that so lightened the thickening mass of city construction, acting as its lungs and its incidental greensward – Corstorphine Hill, the bleak braes and splendid aspect of Brunstane, the rural glen of Glenlockhart, graves in Morningside, Swanston and swathes of southern and eastern Edinburgh – are to be sacrificed in the belief that the population cannot restrain its fervour to quit apartment dwelling in the city centre to inhabit a marketing man's dream in a distant outpost.

Edinburgh cannot avoid being a modern city: but as such, it is becoming an indifferent one. Many great European cities have an antique vision of themselves every bit as refined as that of Edinburgh: but it is not as static. Modernity is not something that they relegate to their equivalent of Pilton. If commercial Edinburgh's insatiable hunger to expand westwards in South Gyle and Maybury, southwards at the Bush estate, and towards Livingston cannot be contained – and if the farmland beside the motorway at Maybury and sheep-filled braes overlooking Cramond and Silverknowes are replaced by wriggly tin and glass factories, it will be at grievous cost to the city's identity. The desires of its inhabitants for roads, parking, supermarkets, offices, hypermarkets and palpably plastic neo-Tudor suburbs seem out of control. The divided soul of the city, in the absence of a commonly accepted vision for its future, is unable to counter the pressure. Edinburgh tends to leave the initiative to others, although it has a tendency to greet their proposals with a slow and sullen acquiescence. The council's preoccupations over recent decades have resembled more those of a local council than the governing body of the capital of Scotland. They do things better in Paris.

The introduction of the Festival of Science and the Edinburgh Vision organisation indicate that the city has perceived a problem. The extent to which it will develop the grandeur of concept required for a European capital remains to be revealed.

August remains the wild card. The genie that is unleashed becomes more reckless each summer, summoning excited crowds of all nationalities to the cavern of the High Street well into the tiny hours of the morning, encouraging them to repossess the crown of the causeway from the wheeled vehicles (upon which it was so carelessly bestowed 200 years ago), rejecting the artificial barriers between street and pavement, and shaking off the douceness that so nearly smothers the capital. All it requires are the smells of some overnight bakery and the availability of freshly baked hot bread or croissants for the city to seem as though it has floated across the channel and alighted upon the continent. As the dream of great genius, Edinburgh is never more ethereal than during the Festival. Lord Harewood wrote of his sojourn as Festival Director:

> Every time I drove from the airport to start one of the dozens of visits I made to the city for meetings, my first glimpse of the castle, whatever the weather, whatever my mood, never failed to produce that lifting of the spirit which is commonly associated with love.

It has seemed, at times, that there rests concealed beneath Edinburgh's crag an unusually active *genius loci* guiding the city in its obdurate resistance to certain types of change and its encouragement of others. It is the spirit of the Summons of Plotcock, the Beggars' Summons, the Stony Sabbath, the Porteous affair, the Enlightenment clubs, the Athens of the North, the saga of Calton Hill and the fury of the Fringe. It has endured sackings and three Civil Wars; it has faced threats of obliteration and abandonment, and it has surmounted them all. Yet, created from unforgiving stone by harsh politics in a harsh climate, it now faces its greatest danger – the deconsecration of its character as it succumbs heedlessly to the pursuit of a private, isolated, suburban mythical comfort in a warming climate.

On his way to the Court of Session in 1825, Walter Scott paused to obtain a 'dog cheap' rendition of 'Pibroch of Donhuil Dhu' from a piper for a shilling. In 1987, on his pilgrimage to find Scotland amidst the stores of Princes Street, Kenneth Roy paused outside an empty shop to be colourfully entertained by a young piper with spiked green hair playing a lament for the Massacre of Glencoe, closely observed by a girl with red and black spiked hair as she cuddled a man with spiked orange hair. No cost to Roy is recorded.

Edinburgh remains one of the most vivid stages in Europe upon which crazies, financiers and romantics can act their part. It grips people, and they cannot shake loose. As Robert Louis Stevenson wrote from Boulogne in 1872: 'After all, new countries, sun, music and all the rest can never take down our gusty, rainy, smoky, grim old city out of the first place that it has been making for itself in the bottom of my soul . . . My heart is buried there – say, in Advocates Close!'

The Bible says that a city built on a hill cannot be hid. On the contrary, as the grey mist swirls in from the Forth reducing visibility to the nearside of the close mouth and swaddling the buildings in a thick, eerie silence, an Edinburgh haar acts like a magic cloak more than adequate to hide it. Almost invariably, the *genius loci* arranges for such a haar on the last weekend in the Festival. The Old Town remains palpably present beneath. As you move through half-seen vennels and acknowledge half-heard echoes of distant noise, it is then, in its invisibility, that the personality of the Winged Citadel never seems so powerful.

BIBLIOGRAPHY

A Hundred Years in Princes Street, Jenners, 1938. *Summer in Scotland*, John R Allan; Methuen 1938. *The Gaberlunzie's Wallet*, James Ballantine, John Menzies, 1843. *Scotland, a Literary Guide*, Alan Bold; Routledge, 1989. *The Perambulator in Edinburgh*, James Bone, Cope 1926; *Building for Books*, Iain Gordon Brown; Aberdeen UP, 1989. *Festival in the North*, George Bruce; Robert Hale, 1975. *Some Practical Good*, George Bruce; The Cockburn Association, 1975. *The Journal of a Tour through North Britain*, Alexander Carlyle; Aberdeen UP nd. *Traditions of Edinburgh*, Richard Chambers; W & C Tait, 1825. *Walks in Edinburgh*, Robert Chambers; A & G Brown. *Reekiana or Minor Antiquities of Edinburgh*, Robert Chambers; William and Robert Chambers, 1833. *Tour in Scotland*, William Cobbett; Aberdeen University Press, 1984. *Memorials of His Time*, Lord Cockburn; T N Foulis, 1910. *Eccentricities of Edinburgh*, George Coleman; John Ballantyne, c.1820. *Looking Back*, Stanley Cursitor, 1974. *Journey through the Whole Island of Great Britain*, Daniel Defoe; Folio Society, 1983. *Diurnal of Occurrents*; Bannatyne Club, 1833. *Scotland: James V – James VII*, Gordon Donaldson; Mercat Press, 1987. *Journal of Sir Walter Scott*, Douglas & Foulis, Edinburgh, 1927. *The Book of Old Edinburgh*, J C Dunlop & A H Dunlop; T & A Constable, 1886. *The History of Scotland*, Robert Lindsay of Pitscottie; Charles Elliott, Edinburgh, 1778. *Edinburgh – a literary anthology*, ed. O D Edwards and G Richardson; Canongate, 1983. *Edinburgh Papers*, Robert Chambers; James Stillie, 1856. *Edinburgh – 1329-1929*; Oliver & Boyd, 1929. *The History of Edinburgh*, William Maitland Edinburgh, 1753. *Scotland: 1689 – Present*, William Ferguson; Mercat Press, 1987. *Diary of Sir Archibald Johnston etc*; Edinburgh University Press, 1896. *Scots Poems*, Robert Fergusson; Saltire Society, 1974. *Scots Classics Reprint: a farmer's ingle and other poems* by Robert Fergusson; John Menzies, 1898. *Autobiography*, Dr Alexander Carlyle T & N Foulis, 1910. *The Building of the Old College*, Andrew G Fraser; Edinburgh University Press, 1989. *The Histoire of the Lyfe of James Melville*, ed. J G Fyfe; Oliver & Boyd and Saltire Society, 1948. *The Fringes of Edinburgh*, John Geddie; W & R Chambers, c.1900. *Scotland in Eclipse*, Andrew Dewar Gibb; Humphrey Toulmin, 1930. *Peter's Letters to his Kinfolk*, John Gibson; Scottish Academic Press, 1977. *Edinburgh in the 19th century* ed. W M Gilbert; J & R Allan, 1901. *A Directory of Edinburgh in 1752*, J Gilhoolie; Edinburgh University Press, 1988. *Makar's Walk*, Duncan Glen; the Scottish Poetry Library, 1990. *Edinburgh in the Days of our Grandfathers*, Sir James Gowans; John Nimmo, 1886. *Memoirs of a Highland Lady*, Elizabeth Grant of Rothiemurchus; Canongate Classics, 1989. *Old & New Edinburgh*, James Grant; Cassell Petter Galpin, 1882. *Berwick and the Lothian Coasts*, Ian C Hannah; T Fischer Unwin, 1913. *Scottish Chapbook Literature*, William Harvey; Burt Franklin, 1971. *Early Travellers in Scotland*, ed. P Hume Brown; James Thin, 1973. *Autobiography of Thomas Guthrie DD*, William Isbister, 1873. *Scottish Lifestyle 300 years Ago*, H & J Kelsall; John Donald, 1986. *The Album of Scottish Families 1694-96*, ed. H & K Kelsall; Aberdeen UP, 1900. *The History of the Reformation*, John Knox, ed. Ralph Walker; Saltire Classic, 1957. *Georgian Edinburgh*, Ian G. Lindsay; Oliver & Boyd, 1949. *Life of Sir Walter Scott*, J G Lockhart; Adam & Charles Black, 1896. *The Early Modern Town in Scotland*, ed. Michael Lynch; Croom Helm, 1987. *Edinburgh &*

The Reformation, Michael Lynch; John Donald, 1981. *The Turbulent Years*, Alasdair Alpin MacGregor; Methuen, 1945. *Festival City*, Mackay & Morris; C J Cousland, 1949. *Scottish Pageant, Volumes 1-4*, Angus Muir Mackenzie; Oliver and Boyd for the Saltire Society, 1950. *Historic Morningside*, William Mair; John Menzies, 1947. *Mary of Guise*, Rosalind K Marshall; Collins, 1977. *In Praise of Edinburgh*, Rosalind Masson; Constable. *Edinburgh: an Illustrated Architectural Guide*, Charles McKean with David Walker; RIAS, 1982. *Stern and Wild*, Moray McLaren, Chapman & Hall, 1948; *Scotland Described*, J Moir; Edinburgh, 1806. *A Short Account of Scotland*, Revd. Thomas Morar; Thomas Newburgh, 1702. *Memoirs of the Affairs of Scotland*, David Moyses; Bannatyne Club, 1830. *The Modern Athens*, Robert Mudie; Knight & Lacey, 1825. *Scottish Journey*, Edwin Muir; Flamingo, 1980. *The Beauties of Scotland*, Sarah Murray, ed. W F Laughlan; Byways, 1982. *The New Edinburgh Review No.8*, Sheriff L R Orr; Hodder, 1923. *Sir Walter's Postbag*, selected by Wilfred Partington; John Murray, 1932. *Crochet Castle*, Thomas Love Peacock; Macmillan, 1895. *The King's Jaunt*, John Prebble; Fontana, 1988. *The Face of Edinburgh*, William Power; John Smith 1939. *Once Upon a Haugh*, Juliet Rees, 1991; *Letters on the Affairs of Scotland to T F Kennedy MP*, William Ridgeway, 1874. *The Early views and maps of Edinburgh*; the Royal Scottish Geographic Society, 1919. *Precipitous City*, Trevor Royle; Mainstream, 1980. *Lectures on Architecture & Painting*, John Ruskin; George Allan, 1907. *Mary Stuart's People*, Margaret Sanderson; James Thin, 1987. *Lorimer & The Edinburgh Craft Designers*, Peter Savage; Paul Harris, 1980. *A Sense of Place*, ed. Graeme Cruikshank, 1988; *Thomas Guthrie*, Oliphant Smeaton; Oliphant Anderson & Ferrier, 1900. *A Summer in Skye*, Alexander Smith; Byways, 1983. *The History of the Troubles & Memorable Transactions in Scotland*, John Spalding; new edition John Rettie, 1830. *Picture of Edinburgh*, J Stark; Archibald Constable 1806. *The Chronicles of Edinburgh*, R H Stevenson; William White & Company, 1850. *Edinburgh: Picturesque Notes*, Robert Louis Stevenson; Seeley & Company, 1900. *Memoir of Frances, Lady Douglas*, Lady Louisa Stewart; Scottish Academic Press, 1985. *Scot Easy*, Wilfred Taylor, Reinhardt, 1955; *Scotland in Quest of her Youth*, ed. David Thomson; Oliver & Boyd, 1932. *Abbotsford Series of the Scottish Poets* ed. George Eyre Todd; William Hodge & Company, 1896. *The Book of Edinburgh Anecdote*, Frances Watt; T N Foulis, 1913. *Pencillings by the Way*, N P Willis; Henry Bohn, 1845. *An Illustrated Guide to the Canongate Kirk*, Robert Selby Wright; Oliver & Boyd, 1965. *The Silent Traveller in Edinburgh*, Chiang Yee; Methuen, 1948. *The Making of Classical Edinburgh*, A J Youngson; Edinburgh University Press, 1970.

ACKNOWLEDGMENTS

Many people have assisted this book directly or indirectly, often unknowingly. To Ian Gow, David Walker, Douglas Grant and Deborah Howard I owe a great debt for their encouragement of my speculation. Invaluable resource material was provided by the Libraries of the Royal Incorporation of Architects in Scotland and the Edinburgh Architectural Association, and by the countless antiquarian booksellers which are reviving in Edinburgh. The above Libraries, together with the National Gallery of Scotland, the *Scotsman* (particularly Bill Brady), the National Library of Scotland (particularly Iain Gordon Brown), and Edinburgh Central Library have provided illustrations. My great debt to printed sources is implied in the Bibliography. Walter Makey provided invaluable advice. Dorothy Smith was incomparable in the translation of volumes of ideas into readable text. Duncan McAra fought a magnificently helpful rear-guard action in defence of his native city. Morag Lyall was a gentler copy editor than I thought I was entitled to. Euan Cameron was unfailingly supportive and encouraging. Most of all, however, my family has tholed much: they recognise the cat with greater facility. Without their patience, there would have been no book.

INDEX

Queensberry, Marquis of 105, 106

Raeburn, Henry 136, 147
Ragged Schools 189-90
railways 200, 201-3
Ramsay, Allan 126-7, 129, 130, 133, 134, 161, 194
Ramsay, Sir Andrew 93
Ramsay Garden (Lodge) 126-7, 207
Randolph Thomas 2, 57, 58
Reformation 18, 42-4, 45-6, 47-8
Regent Bridge 150, 153
Register House 142
Reid, Robert 77, 145, 149, 150
Riccio, David 50-1
Richard II, King 2
Riddle's Close (Court) 21, 65, 130
Robertson, Eleanor 218
Robertson, William 129, 135, 144, 161, 162
Rocheford, Jorevin de 75, 76, 94
Romantic tourism 179-80, 190
Rose Street 142, 155, 195, 206, 215, 222
Rough Wooing 14, 17, 40-1, 116
Royal Botanic Garden 125n, 129
Royal College of Physicians 99, 124, 125n, 129, 150
Royal High School 149, 150, 153, 221, 222
Royal Infirmary 23, 125n, 129
Royal Institution 149, 150, 153
Royal Scottish Academy 150, 153, 194
Ruddiman, Thomas 125, 126, 130, 131n
Ruskin, John 9, 154-5, 198, 229
Ruthven, Sir Patrick 84, 85
Ruthven, Patrick, 3rd Lord 44, 50

Sabbatarianism 45, 115
St Andrew's Church 142, 143, 188
St Andrew's House 214-15, 232
St Andrew's Square 142, 143
St Fond, Faujas de 131-2, 232
St George's Church 150
St Giles' Cathedral 16, 23, 44, 45, 66, 72, 204
St James' Centre 218-19, 232
St Mary's Street/Wynd 14, 59, 121, 140, 190-1
St Mary's in the Fields (Kirk o' Field) 22-3
Salisbury Crags 4, 5, 175, 229
Salt Tron 16, 47
Saltire Society 208-9, 212, 214, 222, 236
Saughton 81n, 211
Scandic Crown Hotel 60, 236-7
Sciennes 69, 81n
'Scots Renascence' 204-5
Scott, Lady (Charlotte) 156, 157, 165, 177
Scott Monument 177
Scott, Sir Walter 77, 111, 123, 130, 143, 145, 146, 154, 155,

156, 162, 164-6, 167, 168-9, 172, 173, 174, 176-7, 179, 180, 184, 205, 241
Scott, Sir Walter of Buccleuch 41
Scott-Moncrieff, George 202
Scottish Home Rule Association 204
Scottish National Gallery of Modern Art 196
Scottish National Party 207, 208, 214, 221
Scottish Office 214-15
Seizers 115
Seton, George, 5th Lord 26, 44
1715 Rising 109-10
Sharp, Charles Kirkpatrick 174-5
Sharp, James, Archbishop 95, 97
Sibbald, Sir Robert 99, 100, 129
Sibbald, William 149
Signet Library 145
Skene, James of Rubislaw 4, 173
Slezer, Capt John 2, 99
Smellie, William 136
Smith, Adam 129, 130, 134, 161, 229
Smith, Alexander 1, 4, 158, 183, 186, 187
Smith, Sydney 2, 159, 167-8
Smith, Sydney Goodsir 215, 222
Smollett, Tobias 122, 134
Society of Antiquaries 124, 125n
South Bridge 144, 235
Spalding, John 9, 71n, 72, 74, 81, 82, 85
Spence, Lucky 133
Spence, Sir Basil 218
Spottiswoode, John, Archbishop 68, 82
Stair, James Dalrymple, Lord 126, 129
Stark, John 145, 147-8, 161
Stark, William 145, 146-7
Stevenson, R H 196
Stevenson, R L 8, 9, 156, 159, 193, 194-5, 198, 212, 213, 241
Stewart, Archibald 112, 113
Stewart kings 16, 24, 31, 37, 113
Stewart, Lord James, Earl of Moray 47, 48, 49, 50, 51, 54, 55-6, 57
Stirling 11, 13, 36, 38, 39
'Stony Sabbath' 66, 74, 81, 110-11, 240
suburbia 193-4, 195-6
Summons of Plotcock 32, 74, 110, 240
sumptuary acts 41, 97
Swan, John 58
Swanston 193, 239

Tailors' Hall 81, 213
Tanfield Hall 188
taverns 117, 222, 166
Taylor (Darnley's valet) 51-2
Taylor, John 16, 17, 75
Test of Loyalty 91
Theatre Royal 142-3, 179

Thief Row 22, 52
Thistle Court 143
Thistle Street 142, 155, 196, 206
Tolbooth 17, 29, 46, 71, 123, 174
Tollcross 194, 199, 220, 234
Topham, Capt Edward 4, 6, 143
tourism 181-3, 184, 199, 201, 211, 236; Romantic 179-80, 190
Townis College 23, 68, 77; see also University
trade 78-80, 121
Trades Maiden Hospital 23, 119, 125n
Traquair, John Stewart, Earl 73, 74
Traquair, Phoebe 205
Traverse Theatre 226, 227
Treaty of Edinburgh (1560) 44
Trinity College 12-13, 23, 28
Trinity College Kirk 175-6, 202
Trinity Hospital 79, 99-100, 119, 175, 202
Tron Kirk, 19, 75, 76, 144, 145-6
Tudor, Margaret 20, 25, 31, 160

Uddart, Nicholas 16, 22, 60
University 77, 122, 130, 179, 183; city as 130-1; cultural precinct 218; Medical Faculty 183-51; rebuilding 144-5, 146; residences 207; Staff Club 192

'Veto' Act (1833) 188
Victoria, Queen 149, 180-1, 196-7, 203
Victoria Street 150, 175
villas, environing 81n

Water Gate 86, 89
Water of Leith 140, 155, 186, 204, 229, 234
Waterloo Place 150
Watson, Sheriff 189
Watson's Hospital 119, 125n, 150, 196, 229
Waverley Bridge 202
Waverley Market 199, 203
Waverley Station 28, 175-6, 201-2
Weir, Major 98, 175
Weldon, Sir Anthony 68, 69
Well Court 204
Wesley, John 137
West Bow 76, 175
West Port 28, 70, 79, 184, 236
Wester Hailes 217, 221, 234
White House 81n, 194
William III, King 101-2, 103
Williams, Hugh 'Grecian' 148-9
Willis, Nathaniel 157, 170, 173, 181
Wilson, Daniel 143, 173, 174, 204
Wilson, John 170
Winged Camp 1, 2, 241
Wood, Harvey 223-4

Yee, Chiang 5, 223
Young Street 156, 206

Zoo 211-12